Premiere® Elements 8 FOR DUMMIES®

by Keith Underdahl

WILEY

Wiley Publishing, Inc.

Premiere® Elements 8 For Dummies®

Published by
Wiley Publishing, Inc.
111 River Street
Hoboken, NJ 07030-5774
www.wiley.com

About the Author

Keith Underdahl is a professional video producer residing in Oregon. He works for high-tech firms shooting and editing industrial video and produces live Webcast video training sessions for international audiences. At various points in his career, Keith has also served as a program manager, graphic designer, software developer, Web designer, teacher, motorcycle road tester, soccer official, aircraft mechanic, sailor, burger flipper, and lawn mower. Keith Underdahl has written numerous books, including *Microsoft Windows Movie Maker For Dummies, Macworld Final Cut Pro 2 Bible* (coauthor), *Digital Video For Dummies* (3rd and 4th Editions), *Adobe Premiere Pro For Dummies, 50 Fast Windows XP Techniques, Wi-Fi Home Networking — Just the Steps For Dummies,* and *Mac OS X Leopard — Just the Steps For Dummies.*

Author's Acknowledgments

So many people helped me complete this project that I hardly know where to begin. First and foremost I wish to thank my family for allowing me to work two full-time jobs as I completed this updated edition *Premiere Elements 8 For Dummies.* My wife, Christa, has been my entire support staff, head cheerleader, creative advisor, and inspiration throughout my entire writing career. She was the one who urged me to start writing for a small motorcycle magazine in 1995, and that endeavor has led to so many great adventures and challenges in the years since. I owe everything to Christa.

My undying gratitude also goes out to my two very favorite movie subjects, Soren and Cole Underdahl. Not only do my boys take direction well, but they are also incredibly intelligent and look great on camera! I also received help both on-screen and behind the scenes from Ryan Holbrook, as well as James Singleton and his band, *Komakazies.*

I wish I could take full credit for the quality and content of *Premiere Elements 8 For Dummies,* but many other kind folks contributed to this work to make it what it is. I'd like to thank Amy Fandrei for giving me the opportunity to give *Premiere Elements 8 For Dummies* a much needed update, my project editor Rebecca Huehls, my technical editor Dennis Cohen, my copy editor Debbye Butler, and the many other folks at Wiley who toiled to make this one of the best references on Adobe Premiere Elements to be found.

I had help from some industry people, including Andy Marken and many fine folks at Adobe who invited me to help develop this excellent video-editing tool. I've been on the user side of Adobe software for a long time, and I am honored to contribute to their testing and development programs as well.

Publisher's Acknowledgments

We're proud of this book; please send us your comments at http://dummies.custhelp.com. For other comments, please contact our Customer Care Department within the U.S. at 877-762-2974, outside the U.S. at 317-572-3993, or fax 317-572-4002.

Some of the people who helped bring this book to market include the following:

Acquisitions and Editorial

Project Editor: Rebecca Huehls

Acquisitions Editor: Amy Fandrei

Copy Editor: Debbye Butler

Technical Editor: Dennis Cohen

Editorial Managers: Leah Cameron, Jodi Jensen

Editorial Assistant: Amanda Graham

Sr. Editorial Assistant: Cherie Case

Cartoons: Rich Tennant (www.the5thwave.com)

Composition Services

Project Coordinator: Patrick Redmond

Layout and Graphics: Joyce Haughey, Ronald Terry, Christine Williams

Proofreaders: Jessica Kramer, Bonnie Mikkelson

Indexer: Broccoli Information Management

Publishing and Editorial for Technology Dummies

   Richard Swadley, Vice President and Executive Group Publisher

   Andy Cummings, Vice President and Publisher

   Mary Bednarek, Executive Acquisitions Director

   Mary C. Corder, Editorial Director

Publishing for Consumer Dummies

   Diane Graves Steele, Vice President and Publisher

Composition Services

   Debbie Stailey, Director of Composition Services

Contents at a Glance

Table of Contents

Introduction

Back in the Dark Ages — a mere decade or two ago — most video editing was conducted in specialized TV and movie production facilities with equipment that cost millions of dollars. Then in 1993, Adobe released a program called Premiere. Adobe Premiere introduced the ability to edit video on conventional desktop computers, a revolutionary idea at the time. This dropped the cost of video-editing systems from millions of dollars down to mere thousands.

Years went by, and new technologies entered the picture. Prices continued to plummet, and more and more video professionals switched to editing on desktop computers. This switch created a growing market of users — and new competition for software manufacturers to produce programs like Adobe Premiere, Apple Final Cut Pro, Avid Xpress, and Pinnacle Edition, all of which cater to professional-consumer (or *prosumer*) users.

Meanwhile, consumer video hobbyists started editing their own movies too, using low-cost (or even *no*-cost) programs like Apple iMovie, Pinnacle Studio, and Windows Movie Maker. These programs, combined with high-quality, affordable digital camcorders, turned the rarified moviemaking profession into a hobby enjoyed by millions of people.

Adobe kept updating Premiere over the years, and when the name changed to Adobe Premiere Pro in 2003, it was only a matter of time before they also released a more affordable non-Pro version. Adobe Premiere Elements was that version. Premiere was a pioneer in desktop video editing, and Adobe's many years of experience showed in the high quality of Premiere Elements. The latest versions of Premiere Elements support modern high-definition camcorders, including those that use tapes, hard drives, DVDs, or flash memory for video storage.

Now that there are two versions of Adobe Premiere — Pro and Elements — you must decide which version is for you. When I spoke with one of Adobe's marketing people during the development of the first version of Premiere Elements, he suggested that the difference boils down to this: If you are getting paid to edit video, you should use Premiere Pro. If you're editing video for fun, use Premiere Elements.

This viewpoint seems simplistic to me for two reasons. First, even a video hobbyist can appreciate some of the extra features in Premiere Pro. But second, and more important, Adobe Premiere Elements is so powerful that you probably can use it to make movies that others would buy. In fact, I have actually used Premiere Elements for paid, professional video-editing projects.

Ultimately, the choice of whether to buy Adobe Premiere Pro or Premiere Elements boils down to price. Adobe offers Premiere Elements at a remarkably low retail price of under $100 in the United States, and Premiere Pro costs about $700 more. Although Premiere Pro does offer some extra features, it is not seven times better than Premiere Elements.

Adobe Premiere Elements allows you to get serious about your video-editing hobby without having to spend serious money. When it comes to video-editing programs, Premiere Elements truly gives you more for less.

Why This Book?

Despite the low price, Adobe Premiere Elements is an advanced program. *Premiere Elements 8 For Dummies* is an advanced reference to this program, but like Premiere Elements itself, this book doesn't come with an advanced price tag. I realize that you want to get right to work with Premiere Elements, so I wrote this book to provide easy-to-follow instructions, as well as real-world tips and tricks to help you work smarter and better.

Needless to say, you're no "dummy" — otherwise, you wouldn't be reading this book and trying to figure out how to use Adobe Premiere Elements correctly. Video editing is fun, and my hope is that you'll find this book fun to use as well. I include instructions on performing the most important video-editing tasks — along with lots of graphics so that you can better visualize what I'm talking about. You'll also find tips and ideas that you just won't find in the dry, cryptic help files that Adobe delivers with the program.

Premiere Elements 8 For Dummies doesn't just help you use the Premiere Elements program. If you're new to moviemaking, you'll find that this book helps you choose a good camcorder, shoot better video, publish movies online, and speak the industry techno babble like a Hollywood pro.

Foolish Assumptions

I hope you don't mind, but I made a few basic assumptions about you while writing this book. First, I assume that you have an intermediate knowledge of computers and the Windows operating system, and that you are ready, willing, and able to take on the challenge of movie editing.

Because you're an intermediate user, I assume that you know how to locate and move files around on hard drives, open and close programs, and perform other such tasks. I also assume that you have Windows XP or later, because that's a system requirement for the Adobe Premiere Elements software.

Early versions of Adobe Premiere were developed mainly for Apple Macintosh PCs, and the latest versions of Premiere Pro are available for Windows or Mac. Unfortunately, Premiere Elements is still a Windows-only program as of this writing.

Another basic assumption I've made is that you might not be an experienced video editor (not yet, anyway). I explain the fundamentals of video editing in ways that help you immediately get to work on your movie projects. Most of the coverage in this book assumes that you're producing movies as a hobby or a student. You may even be testing the waters of professional video editing by doing wedding videos and such, but you can't yet afford a professional-grade program like Premiere Pro. Your video projects might include vacation travelogues, birthday parties, or even amateur fictional movie productions.

Conventions Used in This Book

Premiere Elements 8 For Dummies helps you get started with Premiere Elements quickly and efficiently. The book serves as a reference to this program, and because Premiere Elements is a computer program, you'll find this book a bit different from other kinds of texts you have read. The following are some unusual conventions that you encounter in this book:

- Filenames or lines of computer code will look like THIS or this. This style of print usually indicates something you should type in exactly as you see it in the book.

    The display format for the *timecode* (the unit for measuring time in video) is hours;minutes;seconds;frames. The timecode 01;33;20;03 represents 1 hour, 33 minutes, 20 seconds, and 4 frames (the frame count begins with 0).

- Internet addresses will look something like this: www.dummies.com. Notice that I've left the http:// part off the address because you almost never have to type that into your Web browser.

- You will often be instructed to access commands from the menu bar in Premiere Elements and other programs. The menu bar is that strip that lives along the top of the Premiere Elements program window and usually includes menus called File, Edit, Project, Clip, Timeline, Marker, Title, Window, and Help. If (for example) I tell you to access the Save command in the File menu, I use arrows that look like this: Choose File⇨Save.

- You'll use your mouse a lot. Sometimes you have to click something to select it. This means that you should click *once* with the left mouse button after you put the mouse pointer over whatever it is you're supposed to click. I specify when you have to double-click or right-click (that is, click once with the right mouse button).

✔ Another mouse-related task you often have to perform is the classic click-and-drag. For example, I often ask you to click-and-drag a video clip from one window to another. To click-and-drag an item, hover the mouse pointer over the item and then hold down the left mouse button. While holding down the button, move the mouse pointer to a new location. Release the mouse button to drop the item on the new location.

How This Book Is Organized

I took all the chapters of *Premiere Elements 8 For Dummies* and put them in a bucket. I stirred that bucket with a stick and then poured the chapters out on the floor. This was how I decided which order to place things in, and I think that it has yielded a book which is pretty well organized. The chapters of *Premiere Elements 8 For Dummies* are divided into five major parts, plus an appendix. The parts are described in the next sections.

Part I: Laying the Groundwork

Adobe Premiere Elements is an advanced program, and if you're new to video editing, many parts of this program may seem unfamiliar. Part I helps you get started with your moviemaking adventure by introducing you to Adobe Premiere Elements. You begin by touring the Premiere Elements program and getting familiar with its tools and basic features. If you've never edited a movie before, Chapter 1 gets you started right away on your first movie project — you can complete it from start to finish in the first chapter.

Because Premiere Elements is just one of many tools that you use to make movies, I spend time helping you prepare your production studio. I also show you how to prepare Premiere Elements for use with a variety of media formats. Chapter 3 introduces you to the fundamentals of video technology, which you'll need to be familiar with as you create your movies. Chapter 4 shows you how to start new movie projects in Premiere Elements. The last chapter in Part I shows you how to capture video from a digital camcorder onto your computer, and I show you how to import and manage other kinds of media as well.

Part II: Editing Video and Sound

After you're comfortable with Adobe Premiere Elements, you are ready to get right to work. Chapters 6 and 7 take you through the most common and important video-editing tasks, and in Chapter 8, I show you how to work with audio and add just the right soundtrack to your movies.

Part III: Special Touches and Advanced Techniques

Adobe Premiere Elements is far more advanced than any other program in its price range. The chapters in Part III show you how to use the more advanced features that come with the software. I show you how to add graceful transitions between clips, improve colors and lighting in video images, create compositing effects with blue screens, create and customize special effects, and add titles in your movies.

Part IV: Finishing and Sharing Your Movies

Moviemaking is a highly expressive art form. The chapters in Part IV show you how to share your artistic expression. First, I show you how to put the finishing touches on your movie projects and make sure that they're ready to share with others. Next, I show you how to share your movies on YouTube and the Internet, and I show how to burn your movies to DVD or Blu-Ray disc.

Part V: The Part of Tens

I wouldn't be able to call this a *For Dummies* book without a "Part of Tens" (really, it's in my contract). Actually, the Part of Tens always serves an important purpose. In *Premiere Elements 8 For Dummies,* this part gives me a chance to show you ten advanced video-editing techniques that you can use in Premiere Elements, ten moviemaking tips and secrets used by the pros, and ten gadgets and programs that will help you make better movies.

Appendix

Video editing is a technical subject with a language all its own, so at the end of Part V, I've provided a glossary to help you quickly decrypt the alphabet soup of video-editing terms and acronyms.

Icons Used in This Book

You'll see some icons in the margins of this book. The text next to these icons includes information and tips that deserve special attention and some of them may warn you of potential hazards and pitfalls you may encounter. Icons you'll find in this book are easy to spot:

 Although every word of *Premiere Elements 8 For Dummies* is important, I sometimes feel the need to emphasize certain points. I use Remember to occasionally provide this emphasis.

 Tips are usually brief instructions or ideas that aren't always documented but can greatly improve your movies and make your life easier. Tips are among the most valuable tidbits in this book.

 Heed warnings carefully. Some warn of situations that can merely inconvenience you; others tell you when a wrong move could cause expensive and painful damage to your equipment and/or person.

 Computer books are often stuffed with yards of techno babble, and if it's sprinkled everywhere, it can make the whole book a drag, and just plain difficult to read. As much as possible, I've tried to pull the deeply technical stuff out into these icons. This way, the information is easy to find if you need it, and just as easy to skip if you already have a headache.

Where to Go from Here

If you've always wanted to be in pictures, this is your time. Video editing is *the* hot topic in computer technology today, and you're at the forefront of this multimedia revolution. If you still need to set up your movie studio or need equipment, I suggest that you start off with Chapter 2. If you aren't quite ready to start editing yet, you may want to spend some time in Chapter 3, which offers an introduction to moviemaking. Otherwise, you should go ahead and familiarize yourself with Adobe Premiere Elements, beginning with Chapter 1.

Part I
Laying the Groundwork

In this part . . .

Digital video and editing programs have been around for a few years now, and the high-def camcorders, powerful PCs, and great programs like Adobe Premiere Elements have never been more affordable.

This part of *Premiere Elements 8 For Dummies* begins your moviemaking adventure by exploring Adobe Premiere Elements and finding out just what this program can do. It also looks at what's needed for your personal video production studio and helps you configure Premiere Elements do help you with your moviemaking magic.

Chapter 1

Feeling at Home with Premiere Elements

In This Chapter

▶ Introducing Adobe Premiere Elements

▶ Taking the grand tour

▶ Making your first movie

*H*ome movies have been around for more than half a century. But until recently there wasn't much you could do with home movies except pop a tape in your VCR (or feed film into your projector) and watch raw, unedited footage. Movie editing was reserved for elite professionals with access to expensive studio hardware. But a revolution has taken place in recent years, a revolution that is putting the moviemaking arts within reach of almost anyone. The revolution has occurred in three phases:

1. Mega-powerful computers with huge hard drives have become both available and downright affordable. This has changed the rules of video editing, because almost any modern PC can edit video.

2. Affordable digital camcorders came onto the market, making it easy for anyone to collect high-quality video. New high definition (HD) camcorders deliver video quality that even the pros could only dream about just a few years ago.

3. High-end video-editing programs like Adobe Premiere Pro and Apple Final Cut Pro brought pro-caliber video editing to desktop computers, and simpler programs like Apple iMovie and Windows Movie Maker made editing software affordable.

I hesitate to call Adobe Premiere Elements the next step in the video-editing revolution, but it's definitely a step forward. Premiere Elements delivers about 90 percent of the power of high-end programs like Adobe Premiere Pro for a retail price of less than $100. Since its first release in 2004, Premiere Elements has been the value leader in video editing.

This chapter introduces you to Adobe Premiere Elements by showing you what this program is designed to do and what it has to offer. You get a tour of Premiere Elements to help you find your way around this feature-packed program; I even guide you through your first movie project!

What Is Adobe Premiere Elements?

You already know that Adobe Premiere Elements is a video-editing program. But what does that mean? It means that using Adobe Premiere Elements, you can quickly take video from your digital camcorder, delete and rearrange scenes, add special effects and credits, and then export your movie to a DVD or the Internet.

You can find lots of video-editing programs on the market, even at the $100 price point of Adobe Premiere Elements. But several important features set Premiere Elements apart from the others:

- ✔ Easily import video from almost any digital camcorder, including the latest high-def cameras.

- ✔ Automatically enhance the picture and sound quality of your movies, or fine-tune the quality by using pro-style editing tools.

- ✔ Analyze video to detect and identify shaky or blurry images. Smart Tagging offers face detection, motion tracking, and other content recognition.

- ✔ Use up to 99 separate video tracks for advanced edits and compositing. Find out about compositing video tracks in Chapter 11.

- ✔ Add and edit up to 99 audio tracks to your program. Use SmartMix to automatically adjust the volume of soundtrack music to better complement narration and other audio tracks.

- ✔ Create advanced, professional-style titles and add still graphics to your movie projects. Then you can animate these titles and graphics.

- ✔ Apply effects and transitions, which can be used in any video track.

- ✔ Add royalty-free background music by using SmartSound.

- ✔ Preview edits immediately, in real time, without having to render effects first. (Rendering is a time-consuming finalization process.)

- ✔ Upload movies directly to YouTube, or export them in Web-friendly formats like Flash, QuickTime, and Windows Media.

- ✔ Create interactive DVD menus and burn your movies to DVD or Blu-Ray.

- ✔ Integrate Premiere Elements with Adobe Photoshop Elements to quickly burn your still-image collections onto slideshow DVDs.

Even these hefty capabilities are only a smattering of what you can do with Premiere Elements. It's one of the most versatile programs you'll ever use.

Where's the Mac?

As this book goes to press, Premiere Elements is compatible only with computers running Windows XP or later. If you have a Macintosh, you might consider running Premiere Elements on your Mac by setting up your Mac to dual-boot in either Windows or the Mac OS. Boot up your Mac using Windows, and then install and use Premiere Elements just like you would on any compatible Windows PC. Apple's Boot Camp helps you configure your Mac for dual-booting. For help, *Switching to a Mac For Dummies,* 2nd Edition, by Arnold Reinhold, guides new Mac users with Windows-only programs in the art of running those programs on a newer Mac.

In any case, Premiere Elements will absolutely not run on an older Mac with a PowerPC processor. Premiere Elements must be run on a processor that supports the SSE2 instruction set. The Intel processors in current Macs support SSE2, but older PowerPC processors do not.

Taking the Grand Tour

Adobe developed Premiere Elements on the foundations of Premiere Pro, and one of their primary design goals was to make Premiere Elements much easier to use, especially if you don't have any experience with video-editing programs. Still, even though the user interface has been simplified, I wouldn't call Premiere Elements a "dumbed-down" version of Premiere Pro. Little has been left out — you are probably going to have more options than you need. And the quality of the tools is great; the basic aspects of a high-quality video-editing program are all there. In short, I think that video newbies and veterans alike will feel right at home with Premiere Elements.

Launching Premiere Elements for the first time

When you first launch Premiere Elements, you see the welcome screen shown in Figure 1-1. To launch Premiere Elements and get started, follow these steps:

1. **Click the Start button to open the Start menu, and choose All Programs➪Adobe Premiere Elements.**

   Most of the welcome screen is dedicated to advertising Photoshop.com membership (Photoshop.com is an online photo and video hosting site offered by Adobe; visit Chapter 15 for more about this service).

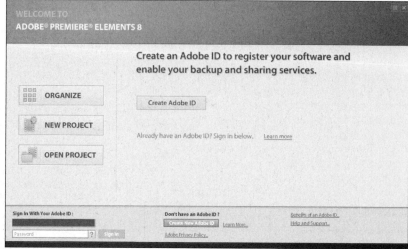

Figure 1-1:
Premiere
Elements 8
welcomes
you with this
screen.

2. **If you have a membership, use the log-on box in the lower-left corner of the screen to sign in to Photoshop.com. Otherwise, just ignore the log-on box for now.**

   On the left side of the welcome screen are three important buttons:

   • **Organize:** Click this to launch a handy tool for organizing your media. I describe the Elements Organizer in Chapter 5.

   • **Open Project:** Click here to open a previously created project.

   • **New Project:** You've probably already figured out that this is where you click to start a new project.

3. **Go ahead and click New Project to start a new project and continue your tour of Premiere Elements. Enter a project name in the dialog box shown in Figure 1-2; any name will work for now. Click OK to open the Premiere Elements workspace.**

Figure 1-2:
Give your
new project
a name.

Although the *exact* appearance varies, you see at least the three fundamental panes that make up the Premiere Elements interface — the Task pane, the Timeline/Sceneline, and the Monitor, as shown in Figure 1-3. These panes are explained in greater detail in the following sections.

Monitor   Task pane

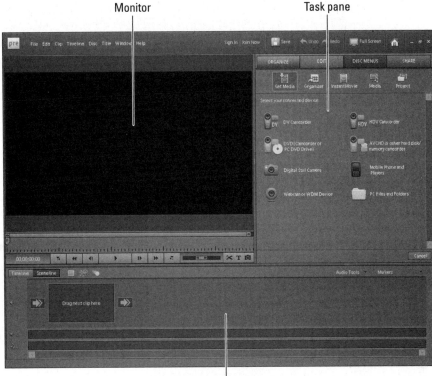

Figure 1-3:
The
Premiere
Elements
interface
consists
of several
important
panes.

Timeline/Sceneline

The exact appearance of your workspace depends upon the current screen
resolution setting on your computer, but the basic appearance should resem-
ble Figure 1-3.

Getting to know the Task pane

The upper-right section of the Premiere Elements screen is called the Task
pane. It's called the *Task* pane because you'll use this area for almost every
moviemaking task in Premiere Elements. Tasks are organized into tabs along
the top of the Task pane. When you click a tab, a row of buttons appears
showing subtasks (see Figure 1-4). Click one of these buttons to view a list of
related tasks. The tabs on the Task pane are:

✔ **Organize:** This tab is a good place to start. Here you can get media from
   your camcorder, import files on your hard drive, organize media files,
   and review files that are used in your current project.

✔ **Edit:** When it's time to perform video edits, this tab is where you find tools to add transitions, titles, special effects, themes, and more.

✔ **Disc Menus:** If you plan to share your movies on disc, navigation menus should be an important part of your project. This tab is where you design and modify disc menus.

✔ **Share:** If you want to share your movies on YouTube, DVD, Blu-Ray, iPod, videotape, or various other digital formats, use this tab. Premiere Elements supports almost any means of sharing video except carrier pigeon and telepathy.

Tabs

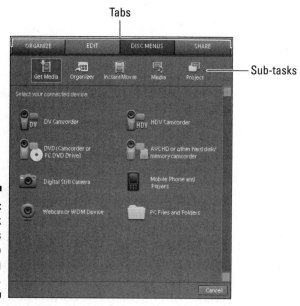

Sub-tasks

Figure 1-4:
The Task
pane is
home to
most editing
tools.

Trying out Sceneline and Timeline

The heart and soul of Premiere Elements is the strip along the bottom half of the screen. This area is called the Sceneline or Timeline, depending on your view mode. Use the buttons in the upper-left corner of the window to switch between the Sceneline and Timeline. Each one is useful for different tasks:

✔ **Sceneline:** This mode offers a simplified view of your project and is a good place to start working. Simply drag and drop clips from Organizer into Sceneline to put scenes in the order you want them. You can also quickly add transitions and soundtrack music in Sceneline. I show you how to use Sceneline later in this chapter.

✔ **Timeline:** When you're ready to spend a little more time fine-tuning your project, switch over to Timeline. Timeline allows you to add titles, trim unwanted portions of clips, add special effects, and make other advanced adjustments. Most of the tasks in this book use Timeline rather than Sceneline.

Timeline is shown in Figure 1-5. I can't completely explain Timeline here. That could fill a chapter all by itself. (In fact, it does — Chapter 7.) However, I do want you to know that by using Timeline, you can

✔ Figure out where you are in the project by using the Timeline ruler.

✔ Use the Current Time Indicator (CTI) to set the current playback and editing location in Timeline.

✔ Control aspects of a clip directly. For example, you can change the timing of video effects or adjust audio levels. (Chapter 8 shows you how to work with audio; flip to Chapter 12 for more on working with effects.)

✔ Use the Zoom control to zoom your view of Timeline in and out.

✔ Move clips by simply dragging and dropping them to new locations in Timeline. If your clip calls for effects and transitions, you can add them by dragging them to Timeline as well.

Zoom control   CTI   Timeline ruler

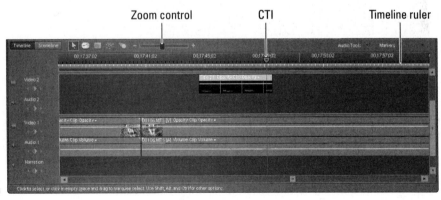

Figure 1-5:
Timeline is where your clips come together to make a movie.

Monitoring the Monitor

Imagine trying to edit video without being able to look at it. Would it be possible? Perhaps. Beethoven did compose his epic "Ninth Symphony" while completely deaf. But most of us aren't Beethovens and we need to directly experience our work. Thankfully, Premiere Elements makes sure that you can always see exactly what your movie looks like as you work on it. Monitor is where you

✔ Play through clips after you add them to Sceneline or Timeline. As you play each clip, you decide which portions to keep in the movie by setting *In points* and *Out points*. When you set In and Out points, only the portions of the clip between those two points remain in your movie.

✔ Play through your edits to view transitions and effects in real time.

As shown in Figure 1-6, Monitor has standard playback controls like Play, Rewind, and Fast Forward. It also has specialized playback controls, which I show you how to use in Chapter 6.

Figure 1-6:
Preview and edit your project in Monitor.

Timecode   Playback controls   Shuttle   Editing buttons

Commanding the interface

Adobe Premiere Elements is fairly advanced and has some unique interface features that can confuse even experienced computer users at first. Here are some helpful tips for using Premiere Elements more effectively:

✔ **Find your missing Taskbar:** If you have set up Windows to auto-hide the Taskbar (the bar at the bottom of the screen with the Start button and clock), you'll find that it doesn't want to reappear when you're working in Premiere Elements. If you run into this problem, reveal the Taskbar either by pressing the Windows key on your keyboard (this opens the Start menu), or press Alt+Tab to switch to another program.

✔ **Resize windows:** As shown in Figure 1-3, the Premiere Elements program screen is divided into three main parts: the Monitor, the Task pane, and the Sceneline/Timeline. To resize any of these parts, simply click-and-drag the border between the parts. For example, if you need to see more of the Timeline, click-and-drag its top border up to expand the Timeline and shrink the Task pane and Monitor.

Choose Window⇨Restore Workspace to quickly reset all the borders back to their default positions.

✔ **Use the Window menu:** If you ever have a hard time finding a certain program window ("How do I open the Narration tool again?"), open the Window menu on the Premiere Elements menu bar. The Window menu gives you quick access to all windows and tools in Premiere Elements.

Making Your First Movie

Sometimes the best way to get to know a program is to just dig in and get your hands dirty with it, actually putting its features to use as the designers intended. If you have a digital camcorder handy with video already recorded, and you have installed Adobe Premiere Elements on your computer, you're ready to start making movies.

If you've never used Premiere Elements or even edited a movie on your computer, the following sections should serve as a good introduction.

Starting your first project

Your first step in making a movie is perhaps the most obvious one. Launch Premiere Elements, and when the welcome screen appears (refer to Figure 1-1) click New Project. Enter a name for your project in the New Project dialog box — any old name will do, as long as it's something you will remember later — and click OK. Premiere Elements creates your project and opens to the basic Premiere Elements screen. Wasn't that easy?

Premiere Elements works with both standard and high-definition digital camcorders. When you create a new project, you should choose project settings that match the format used by your camcorder. See Chapter 4 for more on changing project settings.

Capturing video

After you've created a new project in Premiere Elements, you need some source footage to work with. For now I assume that you have a digital camcorder and you've already recorded video that you want to edit. The process of getting video from the camcorder into your computer is called *capturing*. To capture video, follow these steps:

1. **Connect your digital camcorder to your computer.**

You should use either a FireWire (IEEE-1394) or USB 2.0 port. If you're not sure which one to use, see Chapter 2 as well as your camcorder's documentation. Premiere Elements can capture video from almost any digital camcorder or camera.

2. **Turn the camcorder on to Play mode.**

If Windows automatically opens a window stating that a digital video device was detected, click Cancel to close the window.

3. **Click the Organize tab in Premiere Elements, and then click Get Media.**

A list of device types appears.

4. **Click the button that most closely matches your camera.**

If you have a hard drive–based high-definition camcorder, for example, click the AVCHD option. (See Chapter 2 for more on different types of camcorders.) The window you see next will vary depending on the type of device you have. If you have a DV or HDV tape-based camcorder, you'll see a Capture window that looks a lot like the Premiere Elements Monitor window. If you have a DVD, hard drive, or memory card-based camcorder, you see a Media Downloader window like the one shown in Figure 1-7.

For the sake of simplicity, I'm going to assume for now that you are capturing from a DVD, hard drive, or memory card-based camcorder. See Chapter 5 for complete instructions on capturing video from tape-based camcorders and other devices.

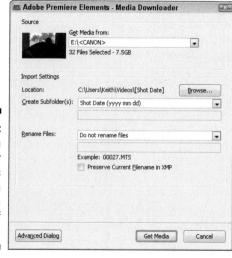

Figure 1-7:
The Media Downloader captures video from certain types of camcorders.

5. **Select your camera in the Get Media From menu.**

   If your camera doesn't appear in the Get Media From menu, make sure that the camera's power is turned on and that you clicked the correct type of device in Step 4. After powering the camera on, choose Refresh List.

6. **Accept the default location and file naming options for now, and click Get Media.**

   A dialog box appears, showing you the copying status for the video files. If you want to fiddle with the filenames or saving location, pay a visit to Chapter 5.

You now see a collection of video clips in the Organizer window, as shown in Figure 1-8. These are the video clips that you captured from the camera, and they are ready to be used in a movie project.

Figure 1-8:
Captured video clips show up in the Media window.

Assembling the movie

After you've captured some video, turning your footage into a movie is easy. (Of course, I'm skipping the fancy stuff that you can do, using later chapters in this book.) Follow these steps:

1. **On the Organize tab, click the Project button.**

   Your video clips are listed on the right side of the Premiere Elements screen. If Premiere Elements imported all your video as one gigantic video clip, picking and choosing scenes won't be easy. Use Premiere's Scene Detect feature, which I describe in Chapter 5.

2. **To preview a clip, double-click it.**

   The clip opens in a Preview window. Click Play to start playing the clip, and click the Close (X) button to close the Preview window when you're done.

3. **Click Sceneline to reveal the Sceneline, as shown in Figure 1-9.**

4. **Click-and-drag some clips and drop them on the Sceneline, as shown in Figure 1-9.**

   The order in which clips are placed in the Sceneline is the order in which they will play in your finished movie. You can insert clips between clips that are already in the Sceneline. To remove a clip, click it once to select it and press Delete on your keyboard.

5. **Click Play in the Monitor window to preview the movie you have put together in the Sceneline.**

Figure 1-9:
Drop clips in the Sceneline to assemble your movie.

Applying an InstantMovie theme

Premiere Elements makes the processes of adding and customizing transitions, titles, music, and special effects to your movies easy. Sometimes you're in a hurry and don't have time for even the most basic edits. You could just output your raw clips as-is, but the movie will lack panache. How do you make a stylish movie without spending a lot of time and energy on editing?

InstantMovie to the rescue! Premiere Elements includes a cool feature called InstantMovie that automatically applies some predefined transitions, titles, background music, and other effects that enhance and stylize your movie. To apply an InstantMovie theme, follow these steps:

1. **Click the Edit tab, and then click the Themes button.**

2. **Scroll through the list of themes, shown in Figure 1-10, and click a theme to play a small preview of it.**

   If you don't see any themes in the list, they might not be installed on your computer. If you have a Premiere Elements installation disc, use the setup program on that disc to install themes. If you purchased a download version of Premiere Elements, visit www.adobe.com and click the "Your Account" link near the top of the screen to log on and download Premiere Elements Content files.

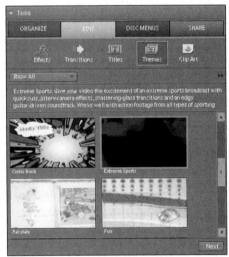

Figure 1-10:
Click a
theme to
preview it.

3. **Click a theme to select it, and then click Next in the lower-right corner of the Organizer.**

4. **Enter Opening and Closing titles, as shown in Figure 1-11.**

   The opening title appears at the beginning of the movie and should be a short, general title. The closing title usually contains ending credits.

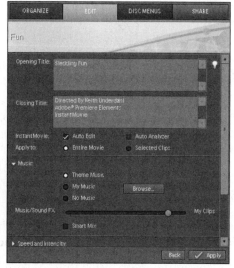

Figure 1-11: Customize Instant-Movie settings.

5. **Click the arrow next to Music, and choose what kind of background music you want:**

   • **Theme Music:** This option automatically generates some royalty-free background music with the SmartSound tool.

   • **My Music:** Select this option and click Browse if you have a specific song that you want to use.

   • **No Music:** If you don't want any background music, choose this option.

6. **Adjust the slider to decide whether the music or the regular clip audio should be louder.**

   Moving the slider closer to My Clips (shown in Figure 1-11) makes the background music softer so that viewers can hear the movie clip's audio better.

7. **Click the arrow next to Duration and decide whether the movie should be adjusted to match your music, to last a certain duration, or to simply use all video clips.**

8. **Click the arrow next to Theme Content and decide which parts of the theme you want to use.**

   For example, if you applied your own special effects to clips and you don't want the theme's effects to replace your own, remove the check mark next to Replace Existing Effects.

9. **When you're done making adjustments, click Apply.**

   You may be asked to confirm a couple of the changes that InstantMovie will make. Accept those changes and let InstantMovie work its magic.

When it's done, click Play in the Monitor window to see your finished InstantMovie.

Uploading your movie to YouTube

After you've put together a basic movie in Sceneline and made some edits (or applied an InstantMovie theme), Premiere Elements helps you quickly upload your finished movie to YouTube. YouTube is the Internet's most popular video-sharing site, and Adobe has partnered with YouTube to make sharing your movies simple. Best of all, you don't have to worry about converting your movie to any special format because Premiere Elements and YouTube take care of that conversion for you. To upload your movie, follow these steps:

1. **Click the Share tab, and then click Online under the sharing options.**

2. **In the screen that appears, shown in Figure 1-12, choose YouTube.**

   Note the size and duration of your movie listed next to File Size/ Duration. The maximum size and time limit allowed by YouTube is listed underneath. If your movie exceeds these maximums, you'll either need to shorten it or upload it in chunks. See Chapter 15 for steps to output only certain portions of your finished movie.

3. **Click Next.**

4. **In the next screen that appears, enter your YouTube user name and password to log on to YouTube.**

   If you don't have a YouTube account, click the Sign Up Now link and follow the instructions on YouTube's Web site to create an account.

5. **Enter a Title and Description for your movie.**

   The title and description are mandatory when uploading to YouTube. The Tags and Category fields are also mandatory, but you can just accept the default choices there for now.

6. **Click Next.**

7. **Choose whether you want to publicly share your movie, and then click Share.**

Your movie is automatically rendered and uploaded to YouTube. Needless to say, you need an active Internet connection to complete the upload, and the upload time varies depending on your movie size and Internet connection speed. When the upload is finished, a message appears saying, "Share Complete!" On the screen, click the link to view your movie on YouTube, as shown in Figure 1-13. You can also click a link to e-mail your movie's link to friends and family.

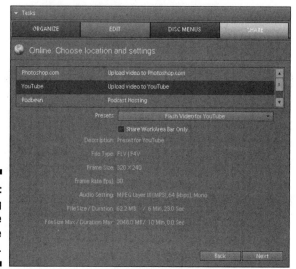

Figure 1-12:
Exporting
your movie
to YouTube
is easy.

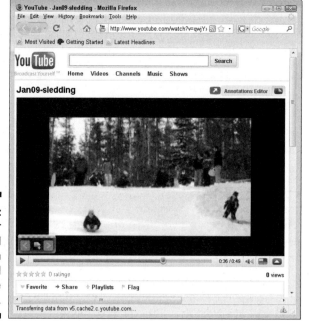

Figure 1-13:
Your
uploaded
movie can
be viewed
by anyone
on YouTube.

Chapter 2

Equipping Yourself for Moviemaking

*I*f you want to make great movies today, there are two things you absolutely need: A camcorder and a computer. A good camcorder helps you shoot high-quality video footage, and a computer helps you turn that footage into a movie worth watching. And when you're done making your movie, you'll also need your computer to share the movie on DVD or the Internet.

When I wrote the first edition of this book a few years ago, making camcorder recommendations was easy: My best recommendation was a digital camcorder using MiniDV tapes. The hard part came when it was time to recommend a computer, because back then a lot of PCs still couldn't handle video editing.

Today the situation is reversed. Video-friendly PCs are cheap and widely available, but selecting the right camcorder can be a confusing task. Do you need standard- or high-def video resolution? Should you choose a camera that records to tape, DVD, flash memory, or a hard drive? What are all these crazy technical terms like AVCHD and IEEE-1394, and why should you care?

This chapter guides you through the daunting process of selecting a good camcorder. I also help you pick a good computer for video work (some choices are still better than others), and I show you some other useful things like USB hard drives and Blu-Ray disc burners.

Choosing a Computer for Video Editing

Your computer probably spends most of its time sending e-mail, playing music, storing photos, and browsing the Internet. If your computer seems bored by this stuff, maybe it needs a more challenging assignment. Enter video editing! Nothing exercises your PC's processor, memory, and hard drive quite as intensively as video editing. The next couple of sections walk you through what you *must* have and what would be *nice* to have if your budget allows.

Stuff you need

If you've already purchased Adobe Premiere Elements, you can check the side of the box for the minimum system requirements. Rather than reprint the *minimum* system requirements for running Premiere Elements, I'm going to list the features that you truly want in a video-editing PC. At the very least you want a computer with:

- **Windows XP, Vista, or 7:** Sorry Mac users, but Premiere Elements is Windows-only.

- **3 GHz+ processor:** You can get away with a 1.7 GHz or faster processor if you work only with standard-def video, but for working with high-definition video and Blu-Ray, you need a 3 GHz or better processor.

  Processor speeds much above 4 GHz are less practical for personal computers because they consume a lot of electric power and produce too much heat. Multi-core processors, which combine two or more processor cores on a single CPU (central processing unit), offer significant performance gains at lower GHz speeds so your computer can process video efficiently without turning into a thermonuclear space heater.

- **3GB+ RAM:** Lots of random access memory (RAM) is important, so get as much as you can afford. Windows XP users can probably get away with only 2GB of RAM because XP won't hog up your graphics card the way Vista and 7 do; but no less than 2GB if you plan to work with high-def video.

- **300GB+ hard drive:** Nothing gobbles hard drive space like digital video. As with RAM, get the biggest hard drive you can afford.

- **FireWire (IEEE-1394) and USB 2.0 ports:** Get a computer with both FireWire and USB 2.0 ports to ensure fast, easy video transfer from your camcorder to the hard drive.

Can I use a laptop?

Yes, you can edit video with a laptop, but I don't recommend it.

You can buy some pretty-high-performance laptops these days, and there's no denying the convenience of a powerful PC that fits in your backpack. Some high-end laptops are even touted as being multimedia powerhouses, with video-friendly features like FireWire ports and big hard drives.

But if you're looking for the best possible video-editing computer for your money, a laptop usually isn't the top choice. Most portable computers have shortcomings, which make them less than ideal for video work. These shortcomings include smaller display screens, integrated video memory, and processors that are optimized for long battery life and heat dissipation rather than performance. Most laptops also have slower 5400 RPM hard drives (most desktops have 7200 RPM drives) that can lead to performance problems when you try to capture or edit video. Generally speaking, desktops are both more affordable and better suited for video editing.

✔ **A good video card with dedicated video RAM:** Many computers share some system RAM with the video card (also called *graphics card* or *display adapter*). If possible, choose a computer that has a good quality video card with at least 256MB of dedicated video RAM. The video card should also have a DVI port for better-quality connections to LCD monitors and HDTVs.

✔ **19-inch (or bigger) LCD monitor:** The Premiere Elements program window needs a lot of screen space. If your monitor is too small, you'll have to squint to see the postage stamp–sized video picture.

✔ **A DVD burner:** If you want to share your movies on DVD, you'll need a DVD burner. Most new computers come with DVD burners, but always double-check those specs just to be sure.

Stuff you'd like

In the preceding section, I outline the features that your video-editing computer really needs to perform the most basic video tasks. If your computer has all the features mentioned in the preceding section, you'll be able to use Adobe Premiere Elements just fine.

But what's the fun in getting by with just the bare minimums? If you're serious about editing video, you'll want some serious tools for the job. The ideal video-editing computer has

✔ **A Blu-Ray burner:** Want to share your videos in HD? The easiest way is to burn your movies onto high-definition Blu-Ray discs, and for that you need a Blu-Ray burner. Some new PCs come with Blu-Ray burners, or you can buy an aftermarket burner for under $300. Premiere Elements supports Blu-Ray burning; visit Chapter 16 to find out how.

✔ **A dual-DVI 3D video card:** Premiere Elements works best with a video card that has at least 512MB of dedicated video RAM, as well as support for Direct 3D and OpenGL 2.0 technologies. Choose a card that has multiple DVI outputs so that you can hook up multiple monitors.

Some video cards come with a *breakout box* that includes analog video outputs. These analog outputs may include S-Video, component, or composite video connections. An analog video breakout box is really handy for video editing because you can easily connect a TV monitor to your computer. TV monitors give you a more color-accurate preview of how your video will look on a TV.

✔ **Dual monitors:** If you have a video card with dual-DVI outputs, it makes sense to connect a separate monitor to each of those outputs. Placed side by side, these dual monitors behave like one giant desktop that basically doubles your digital workspace. The Premiere Elements program window needs a lot of screen space and really benefits from dual-monitor configurations.

✔ **A second hard drive dedicated to video:** If your computer has only one hard drive, that drive needs to do a lot of multi-tasking as it runs the Windows operating system and Premiere Elements, while at the same time trying to feed up large audio and video files for editing. If you can move your video to a separate (but still internal) hard drive, the performance and reliability of Premiere Elements will be greatly improved. For tips on media for storing video longer term, see "Storage options" later in this chapter.

If you want the ultimate hard-drive performance, choose a system with multiple hard drives and RAID 0 support. RAID stands for *Redundant Array of Inexpensive Disks,* and basically makes two or more hard drives behave as one. A RAID 0 configuration (sometimes called a *striped disk array*) is recommended by Adobe when working with high-def video.

✔ **A dedicated, offline computer:** The pros edit video on dedicated workstation computers with no extra software, no anti-virus software, and no connection to the Internet. Anti-virus software is crucial for any Web-connected PC; unfortunately, security software and other utilities use up a lot of memory and processing power that could be dedicated to video editing. If you can afford it, keep one computer for Web browsing, e-mail, and other fun stuff, and dedicate another, better computer exclusively to video editing in Adobe Premiere Elements.

Comparing Video Cameras

Affordable digital camcorders first started to appear around the turn of the millennium. Although the consumer digital video market has had about a decade to mature, the product choices you face are as diverse and confusing as ever. First you have to choose between standard or high definition, and if you go with high-def, you have to consider the various HD image formats (720p, 1080i, and 1080p) and file formats (HDV, AVCHD, Blu-Ray, and others). Then you have to decide whether you want a camera that records your video onto tape, DVD, flash memory, or a hard drive. All these choices are enough to make your head spin! This section is your guide to the most important choices you need to make when you select a new camcorder. For an overview of video basics, such as how video cameras work or worldwide video broadcast standards, check out Chapter 4.

 Always check the price and availability of blank media before you buy any camcorder. If blanks are unavailable or too expensive, your camcorder could become virtually useless in a few years.

Surveying camera features

No single piece of gear is more precious to a budding videographer than a good video camera. Most modern video cameras are actually *camcorders* because they serve as both a camera and a recorder. Early video cameras used to connect to separate VCR units that were hung by a strap from the videographer's shoulder. Bulky.

Whether you choose a standard- or high-def digital camcorder (I recommend high-def; see the next section "Defining high-def video" to see why), you should consider the following basic features on any camcorder:

- **Image sensor:** The part of the camera that actually picks up light and turns it into a video image is the image sensor. Modern camcorders use either a *charged-coupled device* (CCD) or a *complementary metal-oxide semiconductor* (CMOS) sensor instead. Both CCDs and CMOS chips offer similar quality and performance, so don't worry about which one your camcorder has. Some more expensive cameras have three CCD or CMOS chips, one each for recording red, green, and blue light waves. So-called three-chip cameras cost upwards of $1,000 and record richer, more natural colors. Three-chip cameras are nice to have but not absolutely necessary for the amateur videographer.

 As you shop for a camcorder, you may notice some three-chip, standard-def camcorders that cost the same (or even less) than some single-chip HD camcorders. A high-def camera is the better choice because it offers more obvious quality gains and is less likely to be obsolete next year.

✔ **Audio:** For better sound quality, the camcorder should have some provisions for connecting an external microphone. Most camcorders have a standard mini-jack connector for an external mic, and some high-end camcorders have a 3-pin XLR connector. XLR connectors — also sometimes called *balanced* audio connectors — are used by many high-quality microphones and PA (public address) systems. Alternatively, the camcorder's manufacturer may offer custom microphones that use an accessory shoe on the camera.

✔ **Batteries:** Make sure that spare batteries are readily available at a reasonable price. Buy plenty of extra batteries when you buy your camcorder. If you'll be doing long "on location" shoots, also consider a battery charger that plugs into a car's accessory power socket.

✔ **Digital Video connections:** Most digital camcorders use either a FireWire or USB 2.0 port for capturing video from the camcorder onto your computer. FireWire is also called IEEE-1394 or i.Link by some camera manufacturers. Premiere Elements supports both FireWire and USB 2.0 capture, but make sure that your computer and camcorder have matching ports.

✔ **Manual controls:** Auto focus and automatic exposure controls are great, but as you get more serious about shooting video, you may want more control over these features. The easiest manual focus and exposure controls are ones that are manipulated by a ring around the lens body. Tiny little knobs or slider switches on the side of the camera are more difficult to use.

✔ **Storage media:** If the camera uses removable storage media such as MiniDV tapes, SD cards, or DVDs, make sure that extra media is affordable and widely available.

✔ **Filter threads:** In Chapter 18, I recommend that you use lens filters to protect your camcorder's lens and improve your video images. But you can't easily use filters if your camcorder doesn't have filter threads in a standard size such as 37mm or 52mm. Some of the cheapest camcorders cut costs by eliminating filter threads in front of the lens.

✔ **Zoom:** You might see "400× ZOOM" splashed across the side of the camera. Such huge numbers usually express *digital* zoom, which is (in my opinion) virtually useless. Check the fine print next to the digital zoom figure and you should see a figure for *optical* zoom. Optical zoom is something you can actually use, and most mass-market digital camcorders offer around 10× to 25× optical zoom.

Defining high-def video

If you're getting a camcorder, buy a high-definition camera if you can afford it. As the name implies, high-def cameras record more detailed images than standard-def cameras. Standard-definition cameras and TVs are quickly becoming obsolete. Buying a new standard-def camcorder makes sense only if your budget is tight and you plan only to share low-res videos on YouTube or other online places. Remember, you can always "downsample" HD video to standard definition, but you can't turn standard-def video into HD.

Now that you've decided to buy an HD camera, your choices are as clear as… mud. High-def camcorders come with several different formats and options to consider. Table 2-1 lists the common HD video resolution formats (see Chapter 4 for a more detailed explanation of resolution, frame rates, and scanning format).

Table 2-1	HD Video Resolution Formats		
Format	*Resolution (pixels)*	*Typical Frame Rate*	*Scanning Format*
720p	1280 x 720	50 or 60 fps (frames per second)	Progressive
1080i	1440 x 1080 or 1920 x 1080	25 or 30 fps	Interlaced
1080p	1440 x 1080 or 1920 x 1080	25 or 30 fps	Progressive

Most HD camcorders allow you to choose between 720p and 1080i or 1080p recording. Although it's tempting to always choose the higher 1080 resolutions, if you're recording a subject with a lot of fast-moving action — your kids' soccer game, for example — the faster frame rate of 720p will capture the action with less blur.

In addition to resolutions and frame rates, HD camcorders also record in a variety of file formats. The most common formats are

- **AVCHD (Advanced Video Codec High Definition):** This format is used on HD camcorders that record video to DVD, flash memory, or internal hard drives.

- **HDV (High Definition Video):** This format is used on HD camcorders that record video to MiniDV tapes.

Both formats offer high recording quality, although HDV cameras are slightly better due to a higher level of compression than used on most AVCHD cameras. And as of version 7 of Adobe Premiere Elements, both AVCHD and HDV formats are fully supported.

Some HD camcorders offer a 24p "cinema" mode that records video at 24 fps (actually 23.976 fps in many cases) with progressive scanning. This frame rate is meant to mimic the motion characteristics of cinematic film, which shares the 24 fps frame rate. Adobe Premiere Elements can capture 24p video, but it's converted to 30 fps during import. This means that cinema mode is of little use to you when using Premiere Elements. If you want to make cinema-style movies, step up to Adobe Premiere Pro, which fully supports 24p.

Considering tape-based camcorders

Until recently, most digital camcorders used the MiniDV tape format. MiniDV was (and is) a good choice because the tapes are affordable, reliable, long lasting, and widely supported by video-editing programs. HDV camcorders record high-def video onto MiniDV tapes, so it remains a current and viable technology. HDV cameras also usually offer slightly superior video quality compared to AVCHD cams, due to lower image compression. But many people don't like having to rewind tapes, and tape-based camcorders tend to be a little bigger and bulkier.

Other digital tape formats have come and gone. MicroMV was a short-lived proprietary tape format offered by Sony. Sony also championed the Digital8 format, which recorded digital video onto Hi-8 tapes. MicroMV camcorders are not compatible with Adobe Premiere Elements, but Digital8 cameras are compatible.

As of this writing, most tape-based consumer camcorders use MiniDV tapes. Tape-based HDV camcorders record high-definition video onto the same MiniDV tapes used by standard-def digital camcorders. These HDV camcorders are a good choice, but they are no longer the *only* choice for serious videographers.

Some professional-grade camcorders use proprietary tape formats such as Panasonic's DVCPRO HD and Sony's XDCAM. HDV is supported by Adobe Premiere Elements, but DVCPRO HD and XDCAM aren't.

Reviewing disc-based camcorders

Some camcorders record video into standard or mini (3-inch diameter) recordable DVDs. On the surface this seems like a good idea because everyone has a DVD player, right?

Unfortunately, this is a case where reality doesn't necessarily match up with perception. Before you can play a DVD recorded by your camcorder in a regular DVD player, you have to finalize the disc in the camcorder. Finalization is a long and sometimes confusing process, and after a disc is finalized, you can never record more video onto it. Furthermore, 3-inch mini DVDs can only be used in your computer if you have a tray-loading DVD drive; mini DVDs aren't compatible with slot-loading drives. I've helped enough people through the frustration of trying to use DVD-based camcorders that I can safely say convenience is not an advantage of this format.

That's not to say that DVD-based camcorders don't have advantages. Blank recordable DVDs are cheap, and newer versions of Premiere Elements support most disc-based camcorders. Table 2-2 describes the features of the three most common types of disc-based camcorders currently available.

Table 2-2	Disc-Based Camcorders	
Camcorder Type	*Video Format*	*Premiere Elements Support*
Standard-def DVD	MPEG-4	Import and export
High-def DVD	AVCHD	Import only
Blu-Ray DVD	Blu-Ray HD	Export only

Most high-def camcorders that record to DVDs use the AVCHD format. This format is supported by Adobe Premiere Elements, but it isn't supported by most DVD players. Even if you finalize a disc in your AVCHD camcorder, it probably won't play in standard-definition or Blu-Ray DVD players. Some Blu-Ray camcorders are available, but Premiere Elements can't import video directly from these cameras.

Selecting hard drive and flash memory camcorders

Many new camcorders eschew video tapes and discs in favor of other storage methods. Digital video is really just data, so camcorder makers are increasingly turning to storage media traditionally associated with computers and other digital devices like MP3 players and still-photo cameras. Table 2-3 lists some of these formats, along with their pros and cons.

Many AVCHD cameras tout "Full HD" capability and a maximum resolution of 1920 x 1080. In theory this resolution seems superior to HDV's maximum resolution of 1440 x 1080, but in practice AVCHD cameras use aggressive image compression that yields marginally inferior image quality compared to HDV.

Table 2-3	Hard Drive and Memory Card Formats	
Format	**Pros**	**Cons**
Internal hard drive	High storage capacity	Non-removable, sensitive to shock
Internal flash memory	Reliable, easy to use	Non-removable, limited capacity
Flash memory cards	Reliable, replaceable, tiny cards easy to store	Tiny cards easy to lose and expensive

Some camcorders offer a combination of internal memory and removable flash memory cards. These are good options, and I recommend flash memory-based camcorders that use the AVCHD file format.

Selecting Gear for Video Capture, Storage, and Sharing

So you have a fantabulous new computer that is ready to edit video at blazing speeds. And you have a brand-spanking-new high-def camcorder ready to shoot amazing footage. Don't worry: You aren't done spending money just yet. You still have a lot of cool — and really important — gear left to buy. The next few sections introduce you to items that make video editing a little easier.

If you're serious about videography — or even if you just want to make your life easier and improve the quality of your home movies — check out Chapter 19 for ten essential moviemaking extras.

Capture hardware

A digital camcorder and a powerful computer equipped with Adobe Premiere Elements won't do you much good if you can't get video from the camcorder into the computer. For this, you need *capture hardware*, so called because it captures audio and video into your computer.

FireWire (IEEE-1394) devices

FireWire is a high-speed interface developed by Apple Computer and first released in 1996. *FireWire* is actually Apple's trademark name for the technology officially known as IEEE-1394, named for the international standard to which it conforms. Sony and a few other companies call the interface *i.Link*. Many digital camcorders — especially tape-based camcorders — have a FireWire interface. Although Apple originally developed FireWire with digital video in mind, the IEEE-1394 interface is also used by other devices, including external hard drives, disc burners, and networking devices.

A FireWire interface makes capturing digital video really easy. You just connect a cable between the FireWire port on your computer and the FireWire port on your camcorder, and then capture video by using Premiere Elements. It's easy because all Premiere Elements really has to do is copy digital video data from the camcorder onto your hard drive.

Why is the process of getting video from a camcorder tape onto your hard drive called *capturing* rather than just *copying?* Digital video is often recorded onto a camcorder tape in an endless stream of data. The tape doesn't contain data files like those found on a computer hard drive. When you capture video, you are basically taking a chunk of the video data and capturing it into a file that can be stored on your hard drive and used by your software programs (including Premiere Elements).

Many new Windows-based PCs come with FireWire ports, but some don't, so double-check your own PC. You should see a 6-pin FireWire port that resembles Figure 2-1. If you don't see one, you can purchase a FireWire expansion card from an electronics retailer. Installing a FireWire card in your PC has two indispensable prerequisites:

✔ A vacant expansion slot in your computer

✔ PC hardware expertise

Figure 2-1:
The
FireWire
port on your
computer
should look
something
like this.

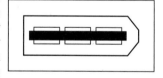

If you aren't familiar with expansion slots and don't have experience with hardware upgrades, consult a professional PC technician. If your computer is still under warranty, don't even *look* at a screwdriver until you've reviewed the warranty terms to determine whether — and how — upgrades should be performed.

USB 2.0 devices

Virtually all Windows PCs sold in the last several years have USB 2.0 ports. USB 2.0 is an upgrade to the original USB (Universal Serial Bus) specification. Premiere Elements cannot capture video from tape-based camcorders by using a USB 2.0 port, but you can use USB 2.0 to get video from DVD or flash-based camcorders.

Connect your camcorder directly to a USB 2.0 port on your computer; not to a USB hub. USB hubs are often slower and less reliable than the USB ports built in to your computer.

Analog video capture devices

Do you have a bunch of old home movies on VHS, 8mm, or Hi-8 tapes that you'd like to capture and use? The video stored on those older tape formats is analog. Analog video is a bit trickier than digital video because it must be digitized before you can work with it on your computer. Capture cards are available to help you do this bit of magic, but keep in mind that Adobe Premiere Elements cannot directly capture video from an analog capture card. Fortunately, analog capture cards almost always come with their own video capture programs to help you convert the analog video to AVI or MPEG files. As I describe in Chapter 5, you can easily import AVI or MPEG files into Premiere Elements for editing.

Whatever capture card you decide to use, review the specs carefully before you make a buying decision. Many FireWire cards are marketed as "video capture cards" even though they can capture video only from digital camcorders.

Another solution may be an external video converter that sits on your desktop and connects to your computer's FireWire or USB 2.0 port. The benefit of a video converter that connects to a FireWire/USB port is that you can capture video directly into Premiere Elements, because as far as Adobe Premiere is concerned, the video streaming in from the port is digital video. Video converters are described in more detail in Chapter 19.

Storage options

Video files consume lots and lots of storage space. This presents a challenge as you try to figure out the best way to reliably archive all your footage. The best solution is to archive copies in multiple formats. Archive and storage options include

- ✔ **Tape:** If your camcorder uses MiniDV/HDV tapes, I strongly recommend that you not reuse tapes and instead archive used tapes in a safe storage location. Tapes tend to deteriorate after about ten years, and if you ever get rid of your MiniDV camcorder, you may lose the ability to play back the tapes.

✔ **DVD:** Recordable DVDs are cheap and easy to store, and the technology to play DVDs is likely to be around for a while. There is disagreement as to how long DVDs last. Estimates range from as little as a decade to as long as 100 years. Blu-Ray discs have the same advantages as DVDs, but with greater storage capacity.

✔ **External hard drives:** An external USB or FireWire hard drive is a good place to archive footage that you plan to use again in the near future. External drives can be easily moved from one computer to another. But the lifespan of hard drives (external and internal) is short, so this should not be counted on as a long-term archiving solution.

Although external drives are good for short-term storage, video should be copied back to your computer's internal hard drive before you edit it in Premiere Elements. USB and FireWire ports can present a speed bottleneck as you try to perform advanced video edits.

✔ **Internal hard drives:** Your computer's internal drive is the best place to store video that you're currently editing. But it's the worst place for long-term storage because hard drives are notoriously short lived, and a full hard drive deteriorates your computer's overall performance.

✔ **The Internet:** If you upload a movie to YouTube, it's there forever, right? Maybe. YouTube was just born in February 2005, which wasn't very long ago. Things change fast online, and what's here today may or may not be there tomorrow. Web server space can serve as a useful backup, but don't rely on it as your only archive source.

Blu-Ray burners

One way to share high-def video is to record it onto high-definition Blu-Ray discs. But to do this you need a Blu-Ray burner, and your audience must have Blu-Ray players. Earlier in this chapter, I recommend that if you're buying a new computer, choose one that includes a Blu-Ray burner as well as a standard DVD burner. If your computer doesn't have a Blu-Ray burner, you need to add one.

Although you may see a Blu-Ray logo on the front of your computer's disc drive, double-check the computer's specs to make sure that it's actually a Blu-Ray recorder, and not just a Blu-Ray player. Some drives can play Blu-Ray discs and record regular DVDs, but they can't record Blu-Ray discs.

Several companies, including Lacie, LG, Lite-On, Pioneer, and Sony, make both internal and external Blu-Ray burners for under $300. Internal drives usually cost less money, but they require some computer hardware upgrading expertise and there could be warranty ramifications if you modify your computer. External burners cost a little more, but they are usually much easier to install and use.

Chapter 3

Introduction to Moviemaking

. . . .

In This Chapter

▶ Mastering the basics of digital video and movie editing

▶ Comparing camcorder formats

▶ Understanding video codecs

▶ Shooting better video

. . . .

*H*igh-def camcorders and Blu-Ray discs are the hot video technologies today, but home movies aren't exactly a new concept. Portable hand-cranked 16mm film cameras first appeared in the 1920s, and in 1932 Kodak introduced the 8mm film format. By the 1950s, 8mm film cameras had become downright affordable, and the milestones ticked by with every passing year. Home movie cameras sprouted zoom lenses in the late 1950s; in 1964, Kodak introduced the Super 8 format, with its easier-to-handle film cartridges; in 1973, a magnetic audio recording system was added to Super 8 cartridges.

Despite many advances, film-based movie cameras still had important disadvantages. The film had to be developed before it could be viewed, and watching movies required special movie projectors and a projection screen (or a big blank wall). In 1976, JVC introduced the VHS videotape format, and by the 1980s most home movie enthusiasts had replaced their antiquated film cameras with video camcorders. Digital video camcorders appeared in the 1990s, and the rest, as they say, is history.

While movie camera technology has evolved steadily over the last 85 years or so, home movie editing is still a relatively new concept. Sure, you could always "edit" your old film movies by cutting and splicing the film with a razor blade and cellophane tape. And home videos could be edited by creatively juggling the pause and record buttons on a VCR and camcorder. But professional-style movie editing wasn't really practical for the low-budget enthusiast until about the year 2000. That's when digital camcorders prices became semi-affordable, and it's also when the average consumer was finally able to afford a personal computer powerful enough to edit video.

If you're new to video, this chapter is for you. Here I introduce you to digital video technology, and I help you sort through the confusing morass of high-definition formats and terminology. This chapter also introduces you to video technologies and concepts to help you make more effective use of Adobe Premiere Elements.

What Is Digital Video?

Computers, as you probably know, aren't very intelligent. They don't understand the serene beauty of a rose garden, the mournful song of a cello, or the graceful motion of an eagle in flight. Computers only understand ones and zeros. And yet, we force computers to show us pictures, play music, and display moving video. Humans perceive light and sound in infinitely variable waves. These waves are *analog* data. For a computer to understand this data, it must be converted into the language that computers understand: ones and zeros. This conversion process is called *digitizing*. Digital video is (you guessed it) video that has been digitized.

To fully understand the difference between analog and digital data, suppose that you want to draw the profile of a hill. An analog representation of the profile (see Figure 3-1) would follow the contour perfectly, because analog values are infinitely variable. A digital contour of that same hill would not be able to follow every single detail of the hill because, as shown in Figure 3-2, digital values are made up of specifically defined individual bits of data.

Figure 3-1:
Analog data
is infinitely
variable.

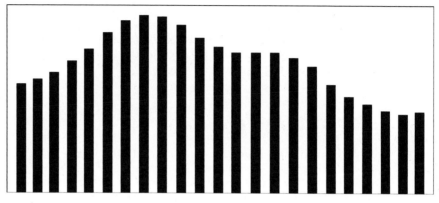

Figure 3-2:
Digital data
contains
specific
values.

It could be said that a digital recording will always be theoretically inferior to an analog recording because the analog recording can contain more values. But the truth is that major advances in digital technology mean that this "limitation" really doesn't matter. Yes, a digital recording must have specific values, but modern recordings have so many unique values packed so closely together that human eyes and ears can barely tell the difference. In fact, casual observation often reveals that digital recordings appear to be of higher quality than analog recordings. Why?

One of the problems with analog recordings is that they are highly susceptible to deterioration. Every time analog data is copied, some of the original data is lost. This phenomenon is called *generational loss* and can be observed in that dark, grainy copy of a copy of a copy of a wedding video that was first shot 15 years ago. But digital data doesn't have this problem. A one is always a one, no matter how many times it is copied, and a zero is always a zero. Likewise, analog recordings are more susceptible to deterioration after every playback, which explains why your vintage *Meet the Beatles* LP pops, hisses, and has lost many of its highs and lows over the years.

When you consider the implications of generational loss on video editing, you begin to see what a blessing digital video really is. You will constantly be copying, editing, and recopying content as you edit your movie projects — and with digital video, you can edit to your heart's content, confident that the quality won't diminish with each new copy you make.

Video Basics

Before getting into a detailed description of what video *is,* take a look at what video *is not.* Video is not film. What's the difference? In film, an image is captured when chemicals on the film react with light. In modern video, an image is captured by a sensor called a *charged-coupled device* (CCD) or a *complementary metal-oxide semiconductor* (CMOS). The image sensor is a sort of electronic eye that records the image digitally. Many "films" today are actually shot by using high-def digital video, even though they are output and distributed to movie theaters on film.

Converting light to video

Little Jenny picks a dandelion on a sunny afternoon. She brings the fluffy flower to her lips and with a puff, the seeds flutter gently away on the breeze (they land in the neighbor's immaculate yard and spawn dozens more of the unappreciated yellow flowers). As this scene unfolds, light photons bounce off Jenny, the dandelion stem, the seeds, and anything else in the shot. Some of those photons pass through the lens of your camcorder. The lens focuses the photons on transistors in the light sensor. The transistors get excited, and this excitement is converted into data which is then digitally recorded by the camcorder. This process is repeated approximately 30 times per second.

The prehistoric ancestors of modern camcorders (those portable video cameras of about 25 years ago) used video-pickup tubes rather than image sensors. Tubes were inferior to CCD or CMOS sensors in many ways, particularly in the way they handled extremes of light. With pickup tubes, points of bright light (like a light bulb or reflection of the sun) bled and streaked across the picture, and low-light situations were simply too dark to shoot.

Reviewing analog video standards

Several new terms have entered the videophile's lexicon in recent years: NTSC, PAL, HDTV. These terms identify a variety of broadcast television standards. Until the advent of digital HDTV broadcasting, you could find three main broadcast video standards throughout the world: NTSC, PAL, and SECAM. Table 3-1 gives technical details for each standard and lists where they were used. The important thing to know about these standards is that NTSC video was not compatible with PAL televisions, and vice versa, so make sure that you export movies that use the local standard for your audience.

All three video standards listed in Table 3-1 are *interlaced*. This means that the horizontal lines are drawn in two passes rather than one. Every other line is drawn on each consecutive pass, and each of these passes is called a *field*. On a PAL display, which shows 25 fps, there are actually 50 fields per second.

Table 3-1	Analog Broadcast Standards		
Standard	*Frame Rate*	*Resolution*	*Where Used*
NTSC (*National Television Standards Committee*)	29.97 fps	525 lines	North America, Japan, Philippines
PAL (*Phase Alternating Line*)	25 fps	625 lines	Western Europe, Southeast Asia, South America, Australia
SECAM (Sequential Couleur Avec Mémoire)	25 fps	625 lines	France, Russia, Eastern Europe, Central Asia, Africa

Mastering HDTV formats

When digital HDTV came along, the world hoped that it would once and for all end the problem of incompatible video standards. Alas, countries still couldn't agree on the details, particularly frame rates. And so digital broadcasting has caused the list of worldwide video standards to grow from three to four. They are listed in Table 3-2.

Table 3-2	Digital Broadcast Standards
Standard	*Where Used*
ATSC (*Advanced Television Systems Committee*)	North America
DVB (*Digital Video Broadcasting*)	Europe, India, Southeast Asia, Australia
ISDB (*Integrated Services Digital Broadcasting*)	Brazil, Japan
DMB (Digital Multimedia Broadcasting)	China, Korea

Adding to the confusion surrounding digital TV are the various technical details supported by each format. Resolutions can range from just 480 horizontal resolution lines up to 1080, and the frame rate can be 24, 25, 29.97, 30, 50, or 60 frames per second. And among the various resolutions and frame rates, digital TV can use interlaced or progressive scanning.

It seems like a lot to remember! Fortunately, most HDTVs support all the common resolutions and frame rates. And manufacturers have standardized on several common resolutions for HDTVs and HD camcorders. The most common resolutions are

✔ **480i:** 480 lines, interlaced, 25 or 30 fps. If you have a standard-definition digital camcorder, it probably uses this resolution.

✔ **720p:** 720 lines, progressive, 50 or 60 fps. The high frame rate makes 720p great for sports or high-action video.

✔ **1080i:** 1080 lines, interlaced, 25 or 30 fps. Higher resolution makes this good for shots with lots of detail, but interlacing makes it less ideal for fast-moving subjects. Confusingly, some vendors call this format 1080i60, because there are 60 interlacing fields but only 30 actual frames per second.

✔ **1080p:** 1080 lines, progressive, 24, 25, or 30 fps. Progressive scanning makes 1080p superior to 1080i for fast motion, although 720p still offers a higher frame rate. High-def Blu-Ray discs use 1080p, sometimes (but not always) with a 24 fps frame rate to mimic film.

The many aspects of aspect ratios

Different moving-picture displays have different shapes. The screens in movie theaters, for example, look like long rectangles, whereas older TV and computer screens were almost square. The shape of a video display is called the *aspect ratio*.

The aspect ratio of a typical television screen used to be 4:3. This means that for any given size, the display was four units wide and three units high. To put this in real numbers, if you measure a 4:3 display and find that it's 40 cm wide, you should notice that it's also 30 cm high. If a picture completely fills this display, the picture is also said to have an aspect ratio of 4:3.

Different numbers are sometimes used to describe the same aspect ratio. The 4:3 aspect ratio is sometimes expressed as 1.33:1. Likewise, the 16:9 aspect ratio is sometimes expressed as 1.78:1. But do the math and you'll see that these different numbers still equal the same basic shape.

Most new TVs now come in a *widescreen* format. The aspect ratio of a widescreen TV picture is 16:9. This aspect ratio is now standardized in all worldwide HDTV systems. Most movies are now distributed in a widescreen format as well. If you watch a widescreen movie on a 4:3 TV screen, you will see black bars — sometimes called *letterbox* format — at the top and bottom of the screen. Widescreen movies are popular because they more closely match the aspect ratio of the movie-theater screens for which the movies were originally shot. Figure 3-3 illustrates the difference between the 4:3 and 16:9 aspect ratios.

Figure 3-3:
The two
most com-
mon image
aspect
ratios.

4:3   16:9 (widescreen)

Whatever aspect ratio you shoot video in — 4:3 or 16:9 — you will need to be aware of your video's aspect ratio as you edit your movies. This becomes important when preparing still images for use in movies, or when choosing settings for a new movie project.

Understanding timecode

A video image is actually a series of still frames that flash rapidly on the screen. Every frame is uniquely identified with a number called a *timecode*. The location and duration of all edits that you perform on a movie project use timecodes for reference points, so a basic understanding of timecode is critical. You'll see and use timecode almost every time you work in Adobe Premiere Elements. Timecode is usually expressed like this:

```
hours:minutes:seconds:frames
```

Thus the 14th frame of the 3rd second of the 28th minute of the 1st hour of video is identified like this:

```
01:28:23:13
```

"But wait," you say. "Why is the 14th frame noted with the number 13?" The frame portion of a timecode starts with zero and counts up from there. In video with a 25 fps frame rate (such as PAL or SECAM), frames are counted from 00 to 24. In video with a 30 fps frame rate (such as NTSC), frames are counted from 00 to 29.

"Hey!" you exclaim. "Zero to 29 adds up to 30 fps, but Table 3-1 says that the frame rate for NTSC video is 29.97."

You're an observant one, aren't you? As mentioned earlier, the frame rate of NTSC video is 29.97 fps (refer to Table 3-1). NTSC timecode actually skips frame codes 00 and 01 in the first second of every minute — except for every tenth minute. Work it out (let's hear it for calculators!), and you see that this system of reverse leap-frames adds up to 29.97 fps. This is called *drop-frame* timecode. In Premiere Elements and most other video-editing systems, drop-frame timecode is expressed with semicolons (;) rather than colons (:) between the numbers.

Why does NTSC video use drop-frame timecode? Back when everything was broadcast in black and white, NTSC video was an even 30 fps. For the conversion to color, more bandwidth was needed in the signal to broadcast color information. Dropping a couple of frames every minute left enough room in the signal to broadcast color information, while at the same time keeping the video signals compatible with older black-and-white TVs. (Clever, those earthlings . . .)

Decoding codecs

To deal with the massive bandwidth requirements of video, digital video is compressed by using compression schemes called *codecs*. The term codec is short for *compressor/decompressor*. High-def video uses an MPEG codec to compress video down to about 3MB per second (depending on the resolution and frame rate; mileage may vary; please drive responsibly).

Why do codecs matter to you? Premiere Elements enables you to choose from a variety of codecs when you output movies for a variety of uses (see Part IV for more on preparing movies for distribution). For example, video for the Internet needs a codec that compresses the data more, while outputting for DVD or Blu-Ray means less compression to maintain picture and sound quality. Usually, Adobe Premiere automatically picks a codec for you based on your output options, but it's good to know what codecs are and how they work.

The nonlinear editing method

My grandfather is a tinkerer. Over the years, he has tinkered with wood, old lawn mowers, and even 8mm film. He wasn't content to simply shoot home movies with his old 8mm film camera, so Grandpa actually edited his source footage into interesting films. He performed edits by cutting the 8mm film with a razor blade and then splicing scenes together in a different order, using cellophane tape (Scotch tape) to hold the splices together.

The process described above is what professional video editors call *linear editing,* and once upon a time all motion pictures were edited this way. It's linear because you perform all your edits in order *in a line,* from beginning to end. Linear editing is terribly inefficient. If you dub a program and then decide to perform another edit, subsequent video usually has to be redubbed.

What is the alternative? *Nonlinear editing,* of course! As the name implies, *non*linear edits can be performed in any order. Nonlinear editing is made possible by the miracle of computer programs like Premiere Elements. Suppose (for example) that you have a program in which Scene 1 is followed by Scene 2, as shown in Figure 3-4. But later you decide that you want to squeeze in another scene — call it Scene 1.5 — between Scenes 1 and 2. In Premiere Elements, you simply click-and-drag Scene 1.5 into the Sceneline or Timeline between Scenes 1 and 2. As shown in Figure 3-5, Premiere Elements automatically moves Scene 2 over to make room for Scene 1.5.

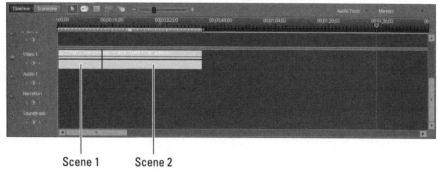

Figure 3-4:
Two unsuspecting scenes sit beside each other in the Timeline.

Scene 1   Scene 2

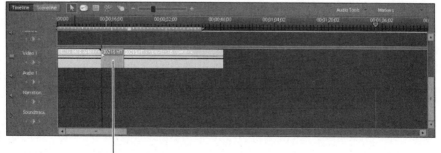

Figure 3-5:
Click-and-drag a new scene to insert it between two existing scenes.

Scene 1.5

Shooting Better Video

Editors have always been called upon to create movies that are worth watching. But an editor can wield only so much magic. If you want to make a great movie, you need to start with great source footage, because there is only so much improvement that an editing program like Premiere Elements can do. And if you don't think "great" video footage is possible (yet) with your entry-level equipment and novice talents, think again! You *can* improve your techniques enough to make your results a lot more watchable. The following sections offer simple tips to help you shoot video like the pros.

Planning the shot

Modern camcorders are so simple that they encourage seat-of-the-pants videography. And by all means, if you see a UFO flying overhead, please just grab your camcorder and start shooting! But for most situations, you can plan many aspects of the shot to achieve the desired results in your final edited movie:

- ✔ **Make a checklist of shots that you need for your project.** Even when you're recording events like a family vacation, take the time to get establishing shots of signs and panoramas. While you're at it, make an equipment checklist, too.

- ✔ **Survey the shooting location.** Position yourself to record the action, and make sure that passersby won't trip over your tripod legs.

- ✔ **Talk to property owners or other responsible parties.** Make sure that you have permission to shoot; identify potential disruptions (wandering livestock, air traffic near an airport, scheduled mud-wrestling matches — the usual).

- ✔ **Bring more charged batteries and blank tapes or memory cards than you think you'll need.**

Composing the shot

Like a photograph, a great video image must be thoughtfully composed. Start by evaluating the type of shot you plan to take. Does the shot include people, landscapes, or some other subject? Consider what kind of tone or feel you want to achieve. Figure 3-6 illustrates how different compositions can affect a shot. In the left-hand shot, the camera looks down on the subject, as is often the case when video is taken of children. In the right-hand shot, the camera is held level with the subject. This might mean that you have to bend over, but the shot is much more interesting and flattering.

Dressing your cast for video success

Most of your video "shoots" will probably be pretty informal affairs, where you basically record an event that was scheduled to happen whether you brought your camcorder or not. Thus, you may have a hard time convincing all who are attending that they should dress appropriately for video. But there definitely are some types of clothes that work better than others in video — and if you have any control at all over what the people in your video wear, make these suggestions:

✔ **Avoid clothes with lots of thin parallel lines or stripes.** Thin parallel lines (like those you'd find on coarse corduroy or

pinstripe suits) don't get along well with TV screens; they create a crawling or wavy visual effect called a *moiré pattern.*

✔ **Limit the use of very bright shades of red and blue.** Red is especially problematic because it tends to bleed into neighboring portions of the video image. This doesn't mean everyone in your movie should wear dark, drab colors, however. Black is another good color to avoid. Ideally, your subjects' clothing should be bright enough to lend some interest, but contrasts with the background somewhat so they don't get lost in the video image.

Your camcorder's LCD screen swivels for a reason! If you swivel the screen to face up, you can more easily hold the camera at chest or waist level for more pleasing shots. Some prosumer camcorders have handles to make waist-level video shooting easier.

Figure 3-6: Composition affects how your subject is perceived; the left-hand shot is much more flattering.

Panning effectively

Another important aspect of composition is *panning,* or moving the camera. A common shooting technique that snapshot enthusiasts use with home camcorders is to pan the camera back and forth, up and down, either to follow a moving subject or to show a lot of things that don't fit in a single shot. This technique is called *firehosing* and is generally discouraged. Firehosing screams "Amateur!" and can be disorienting to the viewer. Practice these rules when panning:

✔ **Pan only once per shot.**

✔ **Start panning slowly, *gradually* speed up, and slow down again before stopping.**

✔ **Slow down!** Panning too quickly — say, over a landscape — is a common mistake.

✔ **If you have a cheap tripod, you may find it difficult to pan smoothly.** Try lubricating the tripod's swivel head. If that doesn't work, limit tripod use to stationary shots. Ideally, you should invest in a higher-quality tripod with a fluid head for smooth panning. See Chapter 19 for help with choosing a tripod.

✔ **Keep the camera level with the horizon.** A tilting horizon is very disorienting.

✔ **If you're shooting a moving subject, try moving the camera with the subject, rather than panning across a scene.** This reduces out-of-focus issues with the camera lens, and it also helps to keep the subject in frame.

Like all the other video shooting tips in this book, the advice given on panning should be taken as guidelines, not hard-and-fast rules. Valid exceptions do exist; for example, imagine shooting video of your kid's soccer game. As you keep the camera on a moving subject, you'll naturally end up panning back and forth multiple times. If the shot ultimately looks right to you, that matters more than standard videography advice from a book.

Using (not abusing) the zoom lens

Most camcorders have a handy zoom feature. A *zoom lens* is basically a lens with an adjustable focal length. A longer lens — also called a *telephoto lens* — makes faraway subjects appear closer. A shorter lens — also called a *wide-angle* lens — allows more of a scene to fit in the shot. Zoom lenses allow you to adjust between wide-angle and telephoto views.

Because the zoom feature is easy to use and fun to play with, amateur videographers tend to zoom in and out a lot. I recommend that you avoid zooming during a shot as much as possible. Overuse of the zoom lens disorients the viewer, and it creates focal and light problems whether you're focusing the camera manually or using the auto focus option. Zoom-lens tips include the following:

✔ **Avoid zooming whenever possible.** Consider your purpose before you touch that dial. Wide-angle shots often provide the audience with a better view of the overall scene and action. Zooming in too much can make otherwise great scenes feel claustrophobic.

✔ **If you must zoom while recording, zoom slowly.** You may need to practice a bit to get a feel for your camera's zoom control.

✔ **Consider repositioning the camera instead of using the zoom lens to compose the shot.** Wide-angle shots usually provide greater *depth of field*. This means that more of the shot is in focus if you're zoomed out. If you shoot subjects by zooming in on them from across a room, they may move in and out of focus. But if you move the camera in and zoom the lens out, focus will often be less of a problem.

Lighting the shot

Light can be subdivided into two basic categories: good light and bad light. Good light allows you to see your subject, and it flatters the subject by exposing details that you want shown. Shadows aren't completely eliminated, but the shadows don't dominate large portions of the subject either. Bad light, on the other hand, washes out color and creates lens flares — the reflections and bright spots that show up when the sun shines across the lens — and other undesired effects.

Shedding some light on the subject

How do you light video shots effectively? Remain ever aware of both the good light and the bad. If you don't have control over lighting in a location, try to compose the shot to best take advantage of the lighting that is available. Here are additional lighting tips that may come in handy:

✔ **Bounce intense lights off a reflective surface.** Light reflecting from a surface, such as a white wall or sheet, is more diffused, providing more flattering lighting than shining bright light directly on the subject.

✔ **Use multiple light sources of varying intensity.** Light on the front of the subject brings out facial details, while light from above and behind (called *key* lighting) highlights the subject relative to the background.

✔ **Watch for backlight situations.** *Backlighting* occurs when your subject appears in front of a bright background, such as an open window, as shown in Figure 3-7. This is one of the most common lighting mistakes in video and photography. If you can't avoid backlit shots, one solution may be to increase the exposure setting on your camera. Unfortunately, this can cause the background to be overexposed and washed out, as shown in the bottom left of Figure 3-7. The automatic backlight compensation features in many camcorders cause this problem. A better solution is to put extra light on the foreground subject, as I've done on the bottom right in Figure 3-7. Now I have good exposure of both my subject and the background.

Backlit shot

Increasing exposure to fix backlighting

Adding extra light to fix backlighting

Figure 3-7: Increasing exposure is better than backlight-ing, but adding extra light to the subject is the best solution.

✔ **Shield your lens from bright light sources, particularly the sun.** Intense light can reflect on the lens glass and cause flares that only show up later on video. If your camera lens doesn't have a black hood, you can use your hand or black tape to make a temporary shield (check the viewfinder to ensure that your shield doesn't appear in the shot).

✔ **Check your camera's documentation.** Your camcorder might include built-in features to help you deal with special lighting situations, such as sporting events or a sun-washed beach.

✔ **Use lens filters.** A neutral-density filter, for example, reduces light in bright outdoor settings, reducing depth of field and making colors appear more vivid. A polarizing filter controls how reflective surfaces (like water or glass) appear, and reduces haze on landscape shots. See Chapter 18 for more on using lens filters.

Controlling exposure

Cameras with automatic exposure control have been around since the 1950s, and all modern camcorders can detect light and set exposure automatically. Automatic exposure usually works pretty well, but there will be times when you'll want to adjust exposure manually for a more pleasing shot.

Exposure is actually determined by two things: the size of the *aperture* in the lens, and the *shutter speed.* The aperture opens or closes to let in more or less light, much like the pupil in the human eye. Smaller numbers such as f1.8 indicate a large aperture opening, while larger numbers like f16 or f22 mean a smaller, almost pinholelike aperture. The shutter opens and closes at varying speeds to change how long the light sensor is exposed. Shutter speeds are expressed in fractions of a second, so "100" means 1/100th of a second.

Every camcorder is different, so you'll need to spend time studying your camera's manual to find out exactly what settings are available and how to use them. Still, most camcorders offer four common exposure control modes:

- ✔ **Automatic (A):** This mode usually means that everything is set automatically and no manual controls are available. This is the boring, "play it safe" mode for using your camera.

- ✔ **Program (P):** This is similar to Auto mode, but there are usually sub-options for things like sports, portraits, or the beach. Choose the sub-option that best matches what you plan to shoot, and the camera will choose exposure settings that work best for your video.

- ✔ **Shutter Priority (TV):** In this mode, you manually set the shutter speed and the camera automatically adjusts the aperture to match. Shutter speeds of 1/30 or slower usually result in blurry, jerky video.

  If your video image includes a TV or computer screen, you may notice that the screen appears to flicker in your recorded video. Increase the camcorder's shutter speed to 1/90 or higher to eliminate the flickering.

- ✔ **Aperture Priority (AV):** In this mode, you manually set the aperture, and the camera automatically adjusts the shutter speed to match.

Knowing how to use the P, TV, and AV modes on your camcorder is great, but they all still involve automatic exposure control. What if your video subject is still too dark or too bright? In that case, use the Exposure (EXP) setting to manually increase or decrease the *exposure value* (EV) to get the desired light levels.

More advanced prosumer camcorders usually also offer a Manual (M) mode where you set both the shutter speed and aperture manually. This gives you the greatest level of control over exposure, but many consumer-level camcorders lack a fully Manual mode.

Exposure controls don't just affect how much light is in your video images — they can also change the entire character of your subjects. Adjusting the size of the aperture gives you control over depth of field. Small apertures such as f11 or f16 give a broad depth of field, meaning that more of the shot is in focus. Large apertures like f1.8 or f2 yield a shallow depth of field, making the subject in focus and the background blurry. In Figure 3-8, I shot video of a hummingbird. I used a large aperture to shorten the depth of field, which blurs the background and makes the bird stands out better.

Figure 3-8:
A shallower depth of field causes the background to be out of focus.

Shooting the shot

Perhaps the most important tip I can give you before you shoot your video is this: *Know your camera.* Even today's least-expensive digital camcorders are packed with some pretty advanced features. For example, most digital camcorders include image stabilization, in-camera effects, and the ability to record 16-bit stereo audio. But these advanced features won't do you much good if they aren't turned on or are configured improperly. Spend a few hours reviewing the manual that came with your camcorder and practice using every feature and setting.

All modern camcorders include automatic exposure and focus control. But no matter how advanced this automation may seem, it isn't perfect. Get friendly with the manual exposure and focus controls on your camera (if it has them) and practice using them. (I describe how to manually control exposure in the preceding section.) If you always rely on auto focus, inevitably your video will show the queasy effects of the focus "hunting" for the right setting during some shots — especially if you shoot moving subjects or in poor light. If your camera has a manual focus mode, you can avoid focus hunting by turning off auto focus.

Chapter 4

Revving Up Premiere Elements

Computer software designers work hard to make sure that their programs are easy to use. When you open a new program for the first time, you often see a tutorial or a wizard screen that helps you get started without adjusting a lot of settings or mastering a bunch of cryptic menu commands. Adobe Premiere Elements is easier to use than pro-oriented video-editing programs, but you should still spend time configuring Premiere Elements before you start working.

Premiere Elements is an advanced program that accommodates a variety of editing styles, and you can configure Premiere Elements to use your preferred style. I recommend that you review the Premiere Elements options to ensure that your movie comes out right. And with that in mind, this chapter helps you configure Premiere Elements for making movies your way, take charge of important program and project settings, and get familiar with useful options.

Adjusting Premiere Preferences

Adobe Premiere Elements offers a plethora of settings, and you could easily spend a day or two sorting through them all. Some settings are immediately relevant to your work; others won't be used until you perform more advanced work. The next few sections show you key settings that help you effectively use Premiere Elements on a daily basis.

Setting up your scratch disks

I hear some of you scratching your heads. "What in the Wide, Wide World of Sports is a scratch disk?" A *scratch disk* is the disk on which you store all your video stuff. When you capture video onto your computer, you capture it to the scratch disk. Likewise, many transitions, effects, and edits must be *rendered* — that is, they are actually applied to the clips — before those clips can be exported as part of a movie. The rendered clips are stored as *preview files* on the scratch disk. The scratch disk is your Premiere Elements storage place — your video data bucket, so to speak.

If your computer has just one big hard drive, you don't necessarily have a separate scratch disk. Your scratch disk may actually be a folder on your main hard drive. But if you can get a separate hard disk to use exclusively as a Premiere Elements scratch disk, I strongly recommend it. Because big and fast hard drives are so cheap these days, there is almost no reason to *not* have a separate hard drive dedicated to serve as your scratch disk.

A scratch disk must be both big and fast. Those digital video files can take up a lot of space, and if your disk isn't fast enough, you'll drop frames during rendering and when you try to burn DVDs. I recommend a 7200 RPM internal hard drive. See Chapter 2 for more on selecting hard drives.

You can choose different scratch disks and folders for different types of files. Premiere Elements always uses the location you specify. To set up your scratch disks, follow these steps:

1. **On the Premiere Elements menu bar, choose Edit⇨Preferences⇨ Scratch Disks.**

   The Scratch Disks section of the Preferences dialog box appears, as shown in Figure 4-1.

2. **Use the Captured Video and Captured Audio menus to adjust the scratch disk settings for the video and audio that you capturewith Premiere Elements.**

   When you capture movies from a camera, video deck, or other source, the location specified in the Captured Video menu is where the video files are stored. The default location for all scratch disks is a setting called Same as Project — which means the same location where you save your project file when you create a new project. If you have a separate hard drive that you want to use as a video scratch disk, choose Custom from the drop-down menu next to each item, and then click Browse to choose a specific drive and folder. In Figure 4-1, I have chosen the custom location D:\Video for all my scratch disk locations.

3. **Choose a scratch disk for previews and other files used by Premiere Elements from the Video Previews, Audio Previews, and Media Cache drop-down menus.**

   Whether you want to preview or export part or all of your project, Premiere Elements usually must render several preview files. Just as with Captured Video and Captured Audio, the default location for these preview files is Same as Project, which as the name suggests is the folder where your Premiere Project (. PREL) file is saved. You can select a different folder if you want.

4. **Choose a scratch disk location in the Disc Encoding drop-down menu.**

   When you burn a DVD, Premiere Elements needs a wide-open expanse of hard drive space in which to build the DVD image. This process is called *disc encoding,* and you should select an encoding scratch disk that is fast and has lots of free space.

5. **Click OK when you're done adjusting your Scratch Disk settings.**

   The Preferences dialog closes. From now on, whenever you capture audio or video, it's stored in the locations that you specified in the Scratch Disk settings.

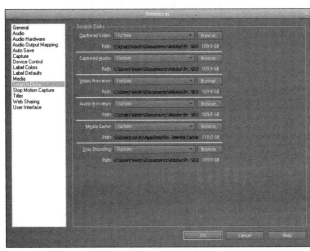

Figure 4-1:
Configure
your
storage
space by
using the
Scratch
Disks
settings.

If your computer is part of a network, you can choose network drives on other computers when you set up your scratch disks. However, I strongly recommend against using network drives as scratch disks. Most networks are not fast enough or reliable enough to adequately handle large video files without dropping frames and causing other problems.

Reviewing other options

Premiere Elements has many options and preferences that you can fiddle with to make the program work the way *you* want it to. The Preferences dialog box (refer to Figure 4-1) lets you quickly jump to different groups of settings by simply clicking a category in the list on the left side of the dialog box. To open the Preferences dialog box, choose Edit➪Preferences, and then choose any item from the submenu that appears. Preferences are organized into the following groups:

- ✔ **General:** The most important General settings are the Default Duration settings for video and audio transitions — these determine how long a transition takes when you first apply it to an audio or video clip. Of course, you can always adjust the duration for any transition; you may find it useful to change the default settings. The duration for video transitions is expressed in *frames,* and the default duration for audio transitions is expressed in *seconds.*

- ✔ **Audio:** The main option you see here is called Play Audio While Scrubbing. This option has nothing to do with listening to music while washing dishes (sorry, dish-washing advice is beyond the scope of this book). Moving slowly or frame by frame through a video clip in Premiere Elements is called *scrubbing.* You'll scrub video a lot as you identify exact locations for edits. But because you aren't playing at full speed, you may find that audio sounds funny or even annoying while you scrub video. If so, deselect the Play Audio While Scrubbing check box. The other important options to review here are SmartMix options. SmartMix automatically adjusts the levels of main and background audio to give the perfect mix of dialog, soundtrack music, and other audio elements. I show how to use SmartMix in Chapter 8.

- ✔ **Audio Hardware:** If you have multiple audio input/output sources on your computer, you can tell Premiere Elements which ones to use by setting the Audio Hardware preferences.

- ✔ **Audio Output Mapping:** If your computer has multiple speakers, click-and-drag the speaker icons here to map sound to different speakers.

- ✔ **Auto Save:** Choose whether Premiere Elements automatically saves your projects, and control how often those auto-saves occur. I recommend that you keep the default settings, which automatically save your work every 20 minutes. This way, you won't lose hours of work simply because your dog tripped over the computer's power cord; at most you'll lose 20 minutes of work. And remember, you can manually save your work at any time by clicking Save on the Premiere Elements toolbar.

- ✔ **Capture:** Here you can tell Premiere Elements to abort video capture if any frames are dropped. (I recommend that you leave the Report Dropped Frames option checked; if frames get dropped, you'll want to know.)

✔ **Device Control:** Set control options for your video-capture and output hardware here. (See Chapter 5 for more on working with device control.)

✔ **Label Colors:** Do you like to color-code your work? Then you're in luck, because Premiere Elements lets you apply color-coded labels to all kinds of program elements such as video clips, audio clips, titles, and other types of media. Use this preferences group to choose label colors.

✔ **Label Defaults:** Different types of media and elements are given different colored labels by default. Control those default colors here.

✔ **Media:** The media cache stores files that Premiere Elements creates during editing, such as audio preview files and video indexing files. Stick with the default settings here; if you want to change the storage location for media files, use Scratch Disk preferences.

✔ **Scratch Disks:** Determine where the video files for your project are stored on your computer. (See the preceding section for more on adjusting Scratch Disk settings.)

✔ **Stop Motion Capture:** Adjust settings related to stop motion video capture here. See Chapter 17 for more on using Stop Motion Capture in Premiere Elements.

✔ **Titler:** The Adobe Title Designer includes a font browser that lets you preview the appearance of fonts. The preview usually just shows the letters Aa in various font faces. If you don't like those letters, choose different letters in the Titler preferences.

✔ **Web Sharing:** Premiere Elements has built-in YouTube support, but Adobe wants to keep its options open for the future. Keep the Automatically Check for Services option enabled to allow Premiere Elements to periodically check for new video sharing sites that have partnered with Adobe to be supported directly by Premiere Elements. Click Refresh to manually check for new services.

✔ **User Interface:** Does the Premiere Elements program window look too dark? Use the slider control here to adjust the window's brightness.

Customizing Premiere Elements

Premiere Elements users share something in common: We're all individuals! This means you probably want to personalize Adobe Premiere to make it better suit your needs. We don't all have the same work habits, and what works for me may not be ideal for you. The programmers at Adobe have given you quite a bit of control over some of Premiere Elements' windows. You can even customize keyboard commands.

Arranging the workspace

If you don't like the default arrangement of the Premiere Elements workspace, you can easily customize it. This capability is especially useful if your computer has a high-resolution display or multiple monitors. To play around with the Premiere Elements workspace, follow these steps:

1. **Choose Window⇨Show Docking Headers.**

   Docking headers appear at the top of the Monitor, Task pane, and Timeline/Sceneline windows (the header for the Timeline/Sceneline says My Project). You can hide the docking headers by choosing Window⇨Hide Docking Headers, but you may find that the headers are pretty useful.

2. **Click the header menu in the upper-right corner to choose window-specific options.**

   The header menus — shown in Figure 4-2 — are unique to each individual window in Premiere Elements, and they contain useful window-specific commands. I frequently refer to the header menus throughout this book.

3. **To move a window, click and hold on the header and drag the window to a new location.**

   The capability to tear off windows (as I've done with the Monitor window in Figure 4-2) from their default locations is especially useful if your computer has multiple displays. Move the Monitor window over to your second monitor and then click-and-drag the corners of the Monitor to make it bigger. This allows you to see a full-size preview of your video while leaving lots of working space in the rest of Premiere Elements. A secondary display is also a good place to put the History and Info windows, which I show you how to use in Chapter 7.

   After you tear off a window from its default location, you can close the window by clicking its Close (X) button in the upper-right corner. For example, if you're organizing and tagging video clips (see Chapter 6) you can tear off and close the Timeline window to give you more working space in the Monitor and Organizer.

4. **To revert back to the default Premiere Elements workspace, choose Window⇨Restore Workspace.**

Click and drag headers to tear off windows.   Click to see header menu.   Close

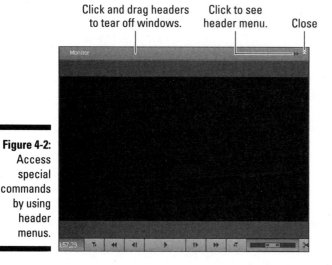

Figure 4-2:
Access
special
commands
by using
header
menus.

Modifying the Timeline

Throughout this book, I show the Timeline with default view settings.
However, you can adjust some useful view options by using a couple of different tools. If the Sceneline is currently shown, click the Timeline button to
open the Timeline. (The Sceneline doesn't offer many customization options.)
Timeline customization tools include:

✔ **The Header menu:** Open this menu in the upper-right corner of the
Timeline. Here you can choose Track Size and select a new size for
tracks from the submenu. Or you can choose Add Tracks to add audio
or video tracks to the Timeline. A dialog box appears, enabling you to
add tracks to the Timeline. I show you how to work with Timeline tracks
in Chapter 7. Premiere Elements supports up to 99 video tracks and 99
audio tracks in a single Timeline.

The Timeline header menu also includes an option called Snap. Snap
is kind of handy sometimes because when you click-and-drag a clip or
other item to the Timeline, the item automatically snaps into place on
the edit point or next to an adjacent clip. If you find this behavior annoying, choose Snap from the Header menu to disable the Snap option.

✔ **The Set Display Style button for video tracks:** Click this button on the
track header for a video track to toggle between display styles. The
default setting for video tracks only shows the first frame of the clip as a
thumbnail at the beginning of the clip. In Figure 4-3, I've chosen the display style that shows a visual progression of frames across the clip.

✔ **The Set Display Style button for audio tracks:** Click the Set Display Style button on the track header for an audio track to toggle between audio view options. When the line on audio tracks is yellow, waveforms of the left and right channels of the audio clip appear in the background. A *waveform* is a visual line-graph representation of the audio levels in an audio clip. Moving the line adjusts audio volume, also called *gain*.

✔ **The Zoom slider:** Use this slider, located at the top of the Timeline window, to zoom in or out on the Timeline. The plus (+) and minus (–) keys on your keyboard also let you quickly zoom in or out.

Set display style   Zoom slider   Header menu

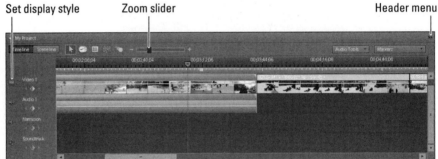

Figure 4-3: Change the way clips appear in the Timeline window.

Customizing keyboard commands

Adobe Premiere Elements follows the same basic design paradigm as most other modern software programs. The Premiere Elements workspace is designed as a GUI (*graphical user interface,* often pronounced "gooey"), which means that program elements are laid out graphically. You navigate program windows and execute editing commands by using the mouse to click buttons, drag and drop items, and choose menu items. You can do almost anything in Premiere Elements with a mouse.

Still, don't throw away that keyboard just yet. Many Premiere Elements users find that the mouse just doesn't have enough buttons to quickly perform important actions. Thankfully, many common commands are accessible by using keys on the keyboard. In fact, Adobe worked hard to ensure that Premiere Elements uses some of the same industry-standard keyboard commands as other professional editing programs. An example is the use of J, K, and L to reverse, pause, and play video, similar to the shuttle controls used by many other professional video-editing programs.

To view some of the most common keyboard commands in Premiere Elements, choose Help➪Keyboard (sorry, you'll have to use the mouse for this one). A help page at Adobe's Web site opens with links to keyboard shortcut lists. If you want to customize keyboard commands, choose Edit➪Keyboard Customization. The Keyboard Customization window appears, as shown in Figure 4-4.

This window has two drop-down menus at the top. The first drop-down menu lets you choose a set of keyboard commands. The default set is the Adobe Premiere Elements Factory Defaults (which you can return to anytime by choosing it from the Set menu). The second menu displays different items for which you can set your own keyboard shortcuts. The choices in this menu are

- ✔ **Application:** The majority of keyboard commands can be found here. Virtually all Premiere Elements program commands can be found in the Application group.

- ✔ **Windows:** This group contains commands that are specific to the various windows in Premiere Elements.

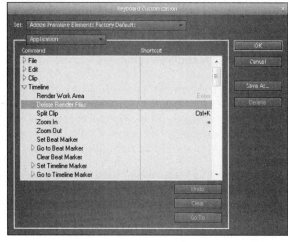

Figure 4-4: Use the Keyboard Customization window to set your own keyboard commands.

Scroll down the lists to see the keyboard shortcuts assigned to each Premiere Elements command. To change a command, click the shortcut in the Shortcut column and type a new shortcut. If your new shortcut is already used by another command, that fact is noted at the bottom of the window.

If you make a lot of changes, I recommend that you save your keyboard-command set. To do so, click Save As and give your command set a descriptive name like Keyboard Commands. Afterward, your custom keyboard-command set is available as a choice in the Set menu.

Installing Plug-Ins for Premiere Elements

One of the things I really like about Adobe software — from the ubiquitous Acrobat Reader all the way up to Premiere Elements — is that the company designs its programs so that new features can be added through the use of plug-ins. Some third-party software companies get pretty creative with the capabilities they add. Plug-ins for Premiere Elements can add new special effects, video transitions, video export options, advanced title appearance options, image filtering tools, and more. Adobe provides a list of select plug-ins for Premiere Pro and Premiere Elements online at

```
www.adobe.com/products/plugins/premiere/main.html
```

When you obtain a Premiere Elements plug-in, make sure that the plug-in is designed to work specifically with Premiere Elements (some plug-ins listed on Adobe's third-party plug-ins page are only for Premiere Pro). Installation instructions *should* be provided by the publisher. Ideally, the plug-in comes with a setup program or installer that takes care of everything for you. Keep in mind, however, that many plug-in publishers assume that you know a thing or two about how Premiere Elements is installed and configured on your system. Therefore, you may not receive installation instructions, and you may need to do some manual installation procedures. Oh, joy!

Don't worry. The main thing to know is that all plug-ins for Adobe programs are stored in a program-specific plug-ins folder somewhere on your hard drive. When you obtain a new plug-in, often you're expected to copy the plug-in file to that specific folder manually. Of course, it helps to know where the folder *is.* No problem. The folder should be right about here:

```
C:\Program Files\Adobe\Adobe Premiere Elements\Plug-ins
```

Make sure that Premiere Elements is completely closed *before* you install a new plug-in. If Premiere Elements is running when you try to install a plug-in, the program may crash and you may lose unsaved work.

Again, carefully read the documentation that comes with the plug-in (there might be a `Readme` file) for specific installation instructions. After you place the plug-in file in the folder mentioned here, it should be available the next time you open Premiere Elements. For example, if the plug-in adds a new transition, look for that transition to appear as an option in the Transitions group on the Effects tab when you restart Premiere Elements.

Optimizing the Windows Operating System

Premiere Elements can weave some seriously high-tech movie magic, but Premiere Elements is only as capable as the computer on which it runs. If your PC can't keep up, you won't be able to truly harness Adobe Premiere's power. To optimize Windows and your PC for the performance, check the following:

- ✔ **Make sure that your PC exceeds the system requirements I outline in Chapter 2.** Premiere Elements needs lots of RAM, a good video card, and a fast hard drive.

- ✔ **Do some hard drive housekeeping.** Try to keep at least 50 percent of your hard drive available as free space. A full hard drive performs slowly and may not be able to keep up with high-def video. Back up large files to an external hard drive or a DVD to clear space, and empty the Recycle Bin. About once per month, click Start⇨All Programs⇨Accessories⇨ System Tools⇨Disk Defragmenter and run Defragmenter to optimize the hard drive's performance.

- ✔ **Close other programs.** E-mail, Web browser, music player, and other open programs use up RAM and processor cycles that should be devoted to Premiere Elements. Those distractions also use up creative juices you should be saving for your movies! When you're working on your videos, close everything except Premiere Elements.

- ✔ **Disable animations.** Windows Vista and 7 come with window and menu animations that look cool, but they also detract from system perfor-mance. Choose Start⇨Control Panel, open the System icon, and then click Performance in the lower-left corner. Click Adjust Visual Effects to open the Performance Options window shown in Figure 4-5. Select Adjust for best performance, and then click OK.

- ✔ **Disable superfluous startup items.** Every time you restart your PC, lots of unnecessary utilities and tools launch and run in the background, under the guise of "helping" you. Some of these tools — such as anti-virus programs — are actually pretty important. But others — media players, extra toolbars, and so on — are just a big waste of RAM. To dis-able undesirable startup items, choose Start⇨Run, type `msconfig`, and click OK. In the System Configuration dialog box that appears, click the Startup tab and remove check marks next to items you don't recognize, as shown in Figure 4-6. Click OK, and then restart your computer to dis-able the unchecked items. If you want any of the Startup items back, open System Configuration again and simply re-check the items.

If you experience persistent performance problems, you can also disable anti-virus and security programs, but do this only as a last resort. If you disable your anti-virus and Internet security, first disconnect the network or modem cable that connects your computer to the Internet. Make sure that security is restored *before* you reconnect to the online world.

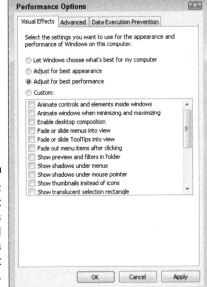

Figure 4-5:
Set
Windows
visual
effects
to best
performance.

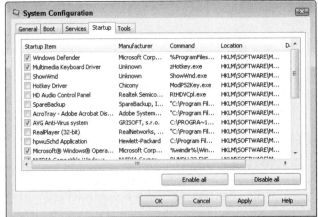

Figure 4-6:
Disable
unneces-
sary startup
items.

Starting New Projects

An ancient proverb says, "A journey of a thousand miles begins with a single step." I believe that whoever wrote this proverb — thousands of years ago — must have been an Adobe Premiere Elements user. The journey of movie editing often feels like a thousand miles because there are so many creative possibilities that you never want to stop editing. And of course, this editing journey must begin with a single first step: creating a new project. The next section shows you how to create a new project. I also show how to customize project settings so that your new project matches the source footage from your camera.

When you first launch Adobe Premiere Elements, you see a welcome screen. The easiest way to create a new project is as follows:

1. On the Welcome screen, click the New Project button.

The New Project dialog box appears, as shown in Figure 4-7.

Figure 4-7:
Give your
new project
a filename.

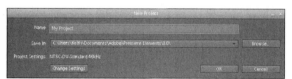

2. Give your project a name, and choose a location in which to save the project file.

The default location for project files is a special Premiere Elements sub-folder of your Documents folder.

3. Take a look at the Project Settings noted in the New Project window, and then click OK or Change Settings, depending on what you see.

If they match the video you plan to capture and work with, click OK to create the project. But if the Project Settings are incorrect — or if you just aren't sure — click Change Settings to open the Setup window shown in Figure 4-8. Here you find presets for different kinds of projects.

• **PAL or NTSC:** When you first install Premiere Elements, the setup program asks where you live and decides what your default video standard should be. As I describe in Chapter 3, if you live in North America, your default video standard should be NTSC. Many other parts of the world use PAL video systems instead.

- **Camera recording format:** Check the documentation for your camcorder to see what format it uses. The four basic categories are AVCHD (used by most high-def camcorders that use hard drives, flash memory, or DVDs); DV (standard-def camcorders that use MiniDV or Digital8 tapes and have a FireWire interface); Hard Disk, Flash Memory Camcorders (most tapeless standard-def camcorders); and HDV (MiniDV tape-based high-def camcorders).

- **Camera settings:** Some SD camcorders (and most HD camcorders) can record video in widescreen format (16:9). (See Chapter 3 for more on aspect ratios.) If you recorded widescreen video and want to produce your movie in widescreen format, choose a widescreen preset in Premiere Elements. If you have an HD camcorder, choose a preset that matches your recording mode, such as 1080i or 720p (again, Chapter 3 describes these modes in detail).

The video standard and screen aspect ratio settings for a Premiere Elements project can't be changed after the project has been created. You *must* use the correct preset to start your project if you need to work with widescreen video or a foreign video format.

If none of the presets seem to match your source video — suppose, for example, you plan to work primarily with Web cam or VGA (640 x 480) video — you can create a custom preset as described in the next section.

Figure 4-8:
Choose a
project pre-
set here.

Reviewing and Changing Project Settings

When you click the New Project button to create a new project in Premiere Elements, default settings are automatically applied to your project. These settings describe the format of your movie project, specifying such things as the size of the video picture, the number of frames per second, and the default appearance of some of the Premiere Elements program windows when your project opens. Some of these settings can be changed, and some cannot.

To review project settings for an open project, choose Edit⇨Project Settings⇨General. The Project Settings dialog box appears, as shown in Figure 4-9. The Project Settings dialog box includes three categories of options. Click a category in the list on the left to review options on the right. The options in each category are described in the following sections.

Figure 4-9: Create your own custom preset here.

General settings

General project settings (refer to Figure 4-9) in the Project Settings dialog box determine the basic audio and video format for your project and other settings of a, well, *general* nature. Important General settings include

✔ **Playback Settings:** Click the Playback Settings button to open the Playback Settings dialog box, as shown in Figure 4-10. The settings in this dialog box control how your media plays on a video device connected to your computer, such as a camcorder. Playback settings are divided into three basic categories:

• **Realtime Playback:** As you edit video, you constantly play it back to see how your edits look. If you select the Desktop Video Display During Playback check box, video from your project will play both in the Premiere Elements window and on your external device, if the device happens to be connected to your computer and turned on. In Chapter 14, I explain the benefits of previewing video on an external monitor.

Also choose whether you want audio to play back on your computer's audio hardware (Desktop Audio) or your external device (External Device Audio).

Figure 4-10:
This dialog
box controls
how your
project is
played back
on external
hardware.

- **Export:** If you have more than one camcorder or video-recording device connected to your computer, select the one you want to use for video export from the External Device drop-down menu.

- **24p Conversion Method:** If you're working with 24p footage (see Chapter 2 for more on 24p shooting), select a conversion method for that footage here.

  Some HD camcorders have a cinema mode that records HD video at 24 frames per second (fps), the same frame rate as cinematic film. Premiere Elements converts 24p footage to a standard frame rate of 25, 30, or 60 fps by using either the Repeat Frame or Interlaced Frame pull-down method. The Interlaced Frame method provides the smoothest motion, but it can introduce interlacing artifacts (called *combing* because it creates fleeting lines that look like comb teeth). The Repeat Frame method avoids interlacing artifacts, but you may observe motion flaws when some frames are repeated.

✔ **Display Format (under Video):** This menu controls how timecode is displayed while you work in your project. (See Chapter 3 for a detailed explanation of timecode.) If you're working with NTSC digital video, I strongly recommend that you keep the 30 fps Drop-Frame Timecode setting.

✔ **Title Safe Area:** As I explain in Chapter 13, most standard-def TVs cut off portions of a video image at the edges of the screen. This problem is called *overscan.* To make sure that titles don't get cut off by overscan, this setting enables Premiere Elements to temporarily display Title Safe margins in the Monitor window. The margins are just lines that appear over the video image to show which parts of the image may get cut off by TV overscan. Don't worry: The lines aren't permanent and won't show up when you export your video; they're just there to help you while you work. You can adjust the size of the Title Safe Area.

✔ **Action Safe Area:** This setting is similar to the Title Safe Area and is designed to ensure that important action on the screen isn't cut off by overscan. The Action Safe Area is usually a little closer to the edges of the screen than the Title Safe Area.

✔ **Display Format (under Audio):** Control how audio appears in the Premiere Elements timeline by using this menu. I find that the Display Audio Samples option is easiest to work with.

A bunch of other settings appear in the General Project Settings, but you can't change them. These settings include the Editing Mode, Frame Size, Timebase, Audio Sample Rate, and more. Adobe Premiere Pro allows you to change those settings, but in Premiere Elements, the fields are provided merely for informational purposes.

Capture settings

Capture settings control the default source from which you capture video. The choices available depend on your system's hardware. The Capture Format menu gives you three options:

✔ **DV Capture:** Choose this for SD capture, using a FireWire/IEEE-1394 port.

✔ **HDV Capture:** Choose this for HD capture, using a FireWire/IEEE-1394 port.

✔ **WDM Capture:** Choose this for capturing any video, using a USB port.

Video Rendering settings

As you edit a project and add transitions and effects to your video, Premiere Elements must apply your edits by using a process called *rendering* (building preview files for video). When Premiere Elements renders your work, it creates temporary files on your hard drive that allow your edits to play properly. Video Rendering settings control the format of these *render files.* Premiere Elements doesn't allow you to change the format of render files, but that isn't exactly a huge tragedy in my opinion, because render files are only temporary files anyway. The Video Rendering options screen does contain two check boxes that you can adjust:

✔ **Maximum Bit Depth:** Enable this option to render previews with the maximum possible bit depth for better image and color quality. Preview quality will be improved, but render file sizes will be larger.

✔ **Optimize Stills:** If your project has a lot of still images, choose this option to reduce rendering time. Optimizing stills could cause playback problems, however. If you encounter problems when the stills play, disable optimization.

Saving a Project

Saving a project in Adobe Premiere Elements is pretty straightforward. Just choose File➪Save from the menu bar and you're done. As with most Windows programs, pressing Ctrl+S on your keyboard quickly saves your project. Or better yet, just click the toolbar button that looks like a floppy disk. That's the Save Project button. If you want to save the project with a different name, choose File➪Save As, and if you want to save a backup copy of your project file, choose File➪Save a Copy.

You probably could have figured out how to save a project on your own, so why this section? One of the interesting things about Premiere Elements is that although video files tend to be very large, project files are actually quite small. Indeed, the project file for a 30-minute movie may be smaller than 50 kilobytes (KB). This is because the project file doesn't contain any actual audio or video. But the project file *does* contain

- ✔ Edit points that you create
- ✔ Pointers to the original source clips
- ✔ Information about effects that are applied to the project
- ✔ The layout of Premiere Elements windows from the last time you worked on the project

Because Premiere Elements project files are so small, it's a good idea to frequently save backup copies of a project. This way, you can easily go back to an earlier version of your project if you don't like some of the changes that you've made.

So where *are* all the big files? Not only do the source files for your audio and video take up a lot of disk space, but the process of rendering work for playback or output creates huge render files as well. All these big files live on your *scratch disk.* I explain how you find and specify a scratch disk earlier in this chapter.

Chapter 5

Capturing and Organizing Your Media

. . . .

In This Chapter

▶ Capturing video to edit

▶ Importing video, audio, and other media

▶ Organizing your multimedia files

. . . .

*I*f you have a word processing program like Microsoft Word, you simply launch the program and start typing to compose something new. Likewise, you can open most graphics programs and start drawing freehand to create a new picture. But Adobe Premiere Elements is different, because you can't just open the program and create a movie from nothing. To really put Premiere Elements to use, you must capture video from your camcorder and import other kinds of media such as music and photos.

This chapter guides you through the process of capturing audio and video, using Premiere Elements, whether you're capturing video from your digital camcorder or importing it from another source. This chapter also shows you how to organize your media. Organization becomes increasingly important as you build a collection of dozens or even hundreds of video clips, audio clips, still images, and more.

Capturing Video

Before you can make movies in Premiere Elements, you have to capture or import video from your camcorder. What's the difference between *capturing* and *importing* video? They're slightly different processes that depend on the type of camera you have:

✔ **Capture:** Capturing is what police do to fugitives from justice. It's also what you do with video that has been recorded onto a tape. Premiere Elements can capture video from DV camcorders that use MiniDV or Digital8 tapes, or MiniDV-based high-def (HDV) camcorders. The process of getting video from tapes and turning it into files on your computer's hard drive is called capturing. Recording live images from a Web cam is another form of video capture.

✔ **Import:** Importing is the process of buying goods produced overseas, and it's what you do with video from tapeless camcorders. Tapeless camcorders may use DVDs, hard drives, or memory cards to store digital video. Because the videos are already saved as files on your camera, those files simply need to be imported onto your computer's hard drive.

Don't worry too much about the difference between capturing and importing; it won't be on the test later! For the sake of simplicity, I often use the term "capture" to refer to the process of getting video from any digital camcorder, as well as digital still cameras, cell phones, and Web cams.

To start capturing video from your camera, launch Premiere Elements and start a new project as described in Chapter 4. Then follow these basic steps:

1. **Connect your camera to your computer's FireWire or USB 2.0 port.**

   Check your camera's documentation if you aren't sure which port to use.

2. **Turn the camera on to Playback or VTR mode.**

   Make sure that the camera has a charged battery. Some cameras must be plugged into AC power for video capture.

   Windows will probably detect your camera as soon as you turn it on, and a dialog box will appear asking you what you want to do. It'll probably ask you if you want to capture video or make a DVD by using Windows components rather than Premiere Elements. Click Cancel to close the dialog box.

3. **In Premiere Elements, click the Organize tab in the Task pane, and then click Get Media.**

   A list of device types appears, as shown in Figure 5-1.

4. **Click the button that most closely matches your camcorder.**

   What happens next depends on the type of camera you have. If you have a tape-based camcorder, you should click "DV Camcorder" for a standard-definition camera, or "HDV Camcorder" for a high-definition unit. Now visit the next section, "Capturing video from DV or HDV tapes," for your next steps. If your camcorder uses DVDs, a hard drive, or memory cards, or if you want to get video from a still camera or cell phone, see the section titled, "Copying video from tapeless cameras." Visit "Capturing Web cam video" if you have a Web cam.

Figure 5-1:
Choose your
camera for-
mat to start
capturing.

As I describe in Chapter 4, video capture (particularly from tapes) requires a lot of system resources. Before you start capturing, close all other open applications, disable unnecessary Windows startup utilities, and make sure that your scratch disk has plenty of empty space.

Capturing video from DV or HDV tapes

If your digital camcorder stores video on tapes (either MiniDV or Digital8), the process of transferring that video onto your computer's hard drive is called capturing. Premiere Elements supports capture from three different types of tape-based digital camcorders:

- **MiniDV:** This tape format — sometimes also called DVC — was first developed for digital camcorders in the 1990s and is the most common camcorder tape format today. Most MiniDV camcorders have FireWire ports for video capture. Some MiniDV cameras have USB 2.0 ports, but FireWire is required for capture in Premiere Elements. Standard-definition MiniDV-based camcorders use the DV codec.

- **HDV:** This is simply a high-definition video codec that records onto MiniDV tapes.

- **Digital8:** These camcorders record digital video onto Hi-8 tapes. Digital8 camcorders have FireWire ports and use the DV codec, so in Premiere Elements they work exactly like MiniDV cameras.

If your camera uses Sony's short-lived MicroMV tape format, I have some bad news: Premiere Elements doesn't support MicroMV. If you own a MicroMV-based camcorder, use Sony's included software to capture video, and then export it in MPEG2 format for easy import into Premiere Elements.

Setting up device control

If you connect your DV or HDV camcorder to a FireWire or USB 2.0 port, Premiere Elements should recognize it automatically. But as with all things in the computer world, what *should* happen and what *does* happen aren't always the same thing. Before you try capturing video from a DV or HDV camcorder, I recommend that you manually configure Device Control in Premiere Elements. Device Control allows Premiere Elements to take control of and synchronize with your camcorder. To enable Device Control:

1. **Connect your DV or HDV camcorder to your FireWire or USB port with an appropriate cable, and turn the device on to playback mode.**

2. **In Premiere Elements, choose Edit⇨Preferences⇨Device Control.**

   The Preferences dialog box appears, displaying Device Control options.

3. **In the Devices menu, choose DV/HDV Device Control for FireWire devices.**

4. **Click Options.**

   The Device Control Settings dialog box appears, as shown in Figure 5-2.

5. **Choose the appropriate video standard (NTSC or PAL) from the Video Standard drop-down list.**

   See Chapter 3 for more on video standards.

6. **Choose the brand of your camcorder from the Device Brand menu.**

7. **Choose a type or model number from the Device Type menu.**

   If your DV device isn't listed, click Go Online for Device Info. Premiere Elements checks Adobe's online hardware database and updates as necessary.

8. **Choose a format from the Timecode Format menu.**

   I recommend that you keep the default or Auto Detect setting. See Chapter 3 for a detailed explanation of timecode formats.

9. **If you see the word Offline next to the Check Status button, click Check Status to see if Premiere Elements can detect your camera.**

   If the Offline mode remains, make sure that the camera is turned on to playback mode, the battery is charged, and your FireWire/USB cable is properly connected.

10. **Click OK twice to close the dialog boxes when you're done.**

Figure 5-2:
Tell
Premiere
Elements
what kind of
camcorder
you have.

Capturing video

Your computer is ready to capture video. The camcorder is turned on and ready. Premiere Elements is ready. What about you? If you're ready to capture video, follow these steps:

1. **Connect all the necessary cables, turn on your hardware, launch Premiere Elements, start a new project, and perform all the other preparatory steps described earlier in this chapter.**

   As described earlier in this chapter, click Organize and then click Get Media to open the list of device types (refer to Figure 5-1).

   If you want your captured video to be stored in a particular folder or hard drive, choose Edit➪Preferences➪Scratch Disks and adjust scratch disk settings as described in Chapter 4.

2. **Click either DV Camcorder or HDV Camcorder.**

   Choose DV if you have a standard-definition MiniDV or Digital8 camcorder; choose HDV if you have a high-def camcorder.

3. **Type a name for your video clips in the Clip Name field.**

   The Clip Name field is located in the upper-left corner of the Capture window. You can give a descriptive name to your clips, or you can just accept the default name.

4. **Decide whether you want to capture video straight to the Timeline.**

   The right side of the Capture window has options, and one of them is called Capture to Timeline. If you keep this option enabled, your captured video will be automatically dumped onto the Timeline when you're done. This is helpful if you just want to make a movie quickly, but if you want to pick and choose scenes later, uncheck the Capture to Timeline option.

5. **Enable the Split Scenes option if you want Premiere Elements to automatically detect scenes.**

   This feature creates separate clips for each scene on the tape and makes editing a lot easier later. I recommend that you leave the Split Scenes option enabled.

6. Enable the Auto-Analyzer.

Auto-Analyzer is one of the coolest features of Premiere Elements. When you're done capturing, Premiere Elements analyzes your clips and then labels them with tags that tell you if the clips are in focus, if they include faces, whether the video is shaky or in focus, and other things. Auto-Analyzer adds a lot of time to the capture process, but if you aren't in a hurry, I recommend that you keep this feature enabled. The information that Auto-Analyzer provides will be useful later.

7. Use the controls located beneath the viewer section of the Capture window to review the tape.

To identify the exact frame at which you want to start capturing, use the left- and right-arrow keys on your keyboard. Figure 5-3 details the various playback controls. The Step Back and Step Forward buttons enable you to move back or forward a single frame at a time.

8. Click Capture to start capturing video.

9. Click Pause to stop capturing.

When you stop capturing, Premiere Elements reviews your captured video to detect clips and analyze content, if you enabled those features. A progress bar tells you how long the analysis will take.

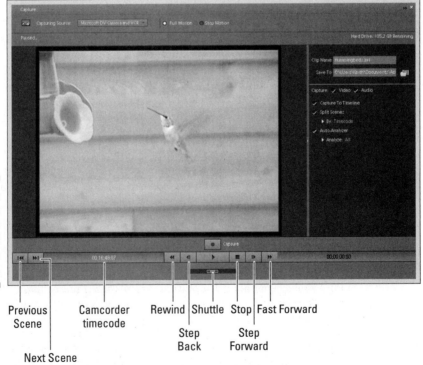

Figure 5-3:
Use these controls when you capture video.

Previous Scene   Camcorder timecode   Rewind   Shuttle   Stop   Fast Forward

Next Scene   Step Back   Step Forward

10. Close the Capture window when you're done capturing.

When the capture job is done, your clips are loaded into the Organizer, and if you opted to capture directly to the Timeline, clips are placed there too. Visit Chapter 7 for more on deleting and moving clips in the Timeline.

Troubleshooting DV configuration mishaps

If you got hung up on Step 7 in the preceding section, there is probably something wrong with your DV device, your computer, or both. If your camcorder doesn't respond to the playback controls in the Capture window, follow these troubleshooting tips:

✔ **Close and restart Adobe Premiere Elements:** While you're at it, restart your computer, too. Make sure that the camcorder's power is turned on to playback mode *before* you restart Premiere Elements.

✔ **Double-check the physical connection to your computer:** Is the FireWire cable properly installed and secure? The small ends of FireWire cables, which connect to camcorders, are prone to slipping out; I run into this problem even during professional video projects.

✔ **Be sure that the DV device recognizes the FireWire connection:** The display or viewfinder on your camcorder may show an indication such as "DV IN" if the connection is detected.

Dealing with dropped frames

The most common problem to afflict the video capture process is the infamous *dropped frame.* If something in the computer gets choked up during capture, Premiere Elements may miss, or *drop,* one or more frames. Dropped frames create unacceptable quality problems for captured clips in Premiere Elements, because essential digital data is gone — poof.

But how do you know whether a frame has been dropped? Glad you asked. If you finish capturing a clip and a Properties dialog box appears, that is a bad sign. Review the statistics in this dialog box. If you see a line that says, `This movie appears to have DROPPED FRAMES,` you almost certainly dropped frames during capture — and that usually means that you have to redo the capture.

Determining the cause of dropped frames can be challenging, but here are a few possible causes:

✔ **A timecode break:** A timecode break on the tape can confuse Premiere Elements into thinking it dropped frames when it really didn't. Timecode breaks often occur when you reuse tapes by recording new footage over old footage you no longer want. When you reach the end of the new recorded footage, the timecode may change and thus confuse Premiere Elements. If you have been reusing tapes — not something I recommend — you might want to consider this as a possible cause of dropped-frame reports.

> ✔ **A hard drive error:** The most common cause of dropped frames is that the hard drive can't maintain the required data rate during capture. Usually this isn't a problem on computers that match even the minimum system requirements for Adobe Premiere Elements, but it isn't beyond the realm of possibility either. Common causes include
>
> • Programs other than Premiere Elements were open during capture.
>
> • The hard drive has not been defragmented recently.
>
> • Another computer was trying to access the hard drive over your network (if you have one) during capture.
>
> If your hard drive does appear to be the culprit, you can try to correct the problem by methodically repreparing your computer for capture as described earlier in this chapter. Close unneeded programs, defragment your hard drive, buy more RAM, or consider upgrading your drives. If your capture card came with its own capture software, you may want to try using that software to capture, and then import the captured clips into Premiere Elements for editing.
>
> ✔ **A problem with the DV device:** If your Date Rate/Sec graph is a straight line but frames are still dropped, the cause is more likely your DV device or the tape.

If you have a separate hard drive used primarily for video capture, and you have a network, make sure that the hard drive isn't shared with your network. To check, right-click the drive in My Computer, and then choose the Sharing and Security option from the menu that appears. In the dialog box that appears, disable sharing if the drive is shared, and then click OK.

Copying video from tapeless cameras

Early versions of Adobe Premiere Elements only supported camcorders that used MiniDV and Digital8 tapes. But tapeless video cameras are increasingly popular, and Adobe has flowed with the changes. The latest versions of Premiere Elements support nearly all digital camcorders, including those that record video on DVDs, hard drives, or solid-state memory. You can even import video shot with digital still cameras and cell phones.

Solid-state memory is just a fancy technical term for data storage media that doesn't have any moving parts. This includes built-in flash memory as well as removable memory cards like SDHC cards.

Tapeless cameras make the capture process a *lot* easier. With tapes, you have to play the video in real time while your computer records it to files. But with tapeless cameras, the video is already saved into files, so all you have to do is copy those files from the camera to your hard drive. Follow these easy steps:

1. **Connect the camcorder to your USB 2.0, turn it on to video playback mode, and prepare your computer as described earlier in this chapter.**

2. **In Premiere Elements, click Organize; then click Get Media, and choose the type of camera you have.**

   Choose DVD if you have a DVD-based camcorder (including miniature DVDs), or AVCHD or other hard disk/memory camcorder for most other tapeless camcorders. You can also choose Digital Still Camera or Mobile Phone and Players from the list of device types. The steps for importing video from those devices are the same as for importing from other tapeless camcorders.

3. **In the Media Downloader that appears, shown in Figure 5-4, choose your camera in the Get Media From menu.**

   If your camera isn't listed, make sure that it's connected and turned on. You may need to adjust settings on the camcorder itself to specify PC output; check the camera's documentation to be sure.

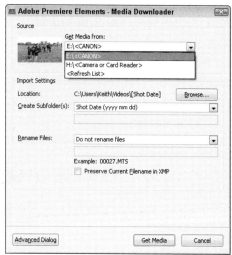

Figure 5-4:
Choose your camera.

4. **Select a subfolder option for your video in the Create Subfolders menu.**

   The default option creates separate folders for each date on which video was shot. This option is useful, but only if your camcorder's internal calendar and clock are set correctly.

5. **Click the Advanced Dialog button.**

   The advanced Media Downloader dialog — shown in Figure 5-5 — lets you preview clips before you capture them. For some reason, Adobe thinks this step is optional, but I think it's pretty important.

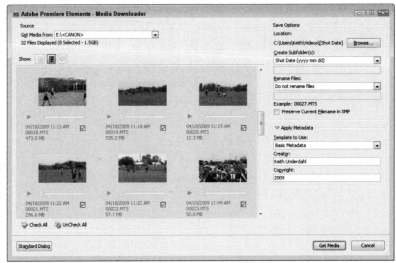

6. **Place check marks next to clips you want to download.**

   Use the three Show/Hide buttons in the upper-left corner to show or hide video clips, still images, or audio clips.

7. **Click Get Media to import media from your camera.**

   When the import is complete, clips appear in your Organizer and are ready to use.

8. **After the import is finished, close Premiere Elements, and then open My Computer or Windows Explorer.**

   Choose Start⇨My Computer (Windows XP) or Start⇨Computer (Windows Vista or 7) to open My Computer.

9. **Right-click the icon for your camcorder, and then choose Eject from the menu that appears, as shown in Figure 5-6.**

   The Eject command ensures that the camcorder can be safely disconnected from your PC. Although this step may seem unnecessary, failure to "Eject" the camera from Windows could cause data corruption and loss on the camera's memory.

10. **Turn off the camcorder's power and disconnect the USB cable.**

Some camcorders use SD memory cards for storage, and many computers have built-in SD card readers. You may be tempted to simply insert your SD cards directly into the card reader to try to copy video, but that may not work too well. Use the camcorder and the Media Downloader to ensure that your clips are imported properly and stay organized in Premiere Elements.

Figure 5-6:
Eject the camera before disconnecting it.

Capturing Web cam video

If you have a Web cam connected to your computer, Premiere Elements can record directly from that camera. Capturing video from a Web cam is a lot like capturing video from a tape-based camcorder. You should close other open programs to make sure that your computer runs efficiently. Then you can start to capture:

1. **Connect the Web cam to your computer's USB port and make sure that the camera is powered on.**

2. **In Premiere Elements, click Organize, click Get Media, and then click Webcam or WDM Device.**

3. **In the Capture window that appears (refer to Figure 5-3), make sure that the video image is framed the way you want it to appear.**

4. **Give your clip a name in the Clip Name field.**

   Entering a clip name for Web cam video is important, because Premiere Elements can't automatically generate a name based on information from a camcorder.

5. **Click Capture to start recording, and click Pause when you're done.**

That's it! You can now plop your smiling mug (or whatever your Web cam was pointed at) into your movies.

Importing Media Files

There is no doubt in my mind that all the video you record with your camcorder is indescribably perfect just the way it is. But, if I may be so bold, wouldn't it be *even better* if you enhanced it a bit with music, or perhaps illustrative stills? Good, I'm glad you agree. Premiere Elements can import all kinds of media, even video produced by other applications. Supported formats include

✔ **Video:** 264, 3G2, 3GP, ASF, AVC, AVI, DV, FLM, M1V, M2P, M2T, M2TS, M2V, M4V, MOD, MOV, MP2, MP4, MPD, MPE, MPEG, MPG, MPV, MTS, SWF, TOD, VOB, WMV

✔ **Audio:** AAC, AC3, AIF, AIFF, M2A, M4A, MOV, MP3, MPA, MPE, MPEG, MPG, WAV, WMA

✔ **Still graphics:** AI, BMP, CR2, CRW, DIB, DNG, EPS, GIF, ICB, ICO, JFIF, JPE, JPEG, JPG, MRW, NEF, ORF, PCT, PCX, PIC, PICT, PNG, PRTL, PSD, PXR, RAF, RAW, RLE, TGA, TIF, TIFF, VDA, VST, WMB

You can import any format in this list and use it in your Premiere Elements projects, although cell phone videos in the 3GP or MP4 formats require you to have Apple QuickTime installed. (A free QuickTime download is available at www.apple.com/quicktime; if you have an iPhone or iPod, you already have QuickTime.) The following sections show you how to import audio from an audio CD or another source and how to prepare still graphics for use in Premiere Elements. After you've done that, you can move to the last section, which describes how to actually import files (stills or not).

Importing files of any kind (still images, video, or audio files) that don't belong to you can get you in hot water if you don't have permission from the originator or owner of the files. I'm no copyright expert, so the best I can do is advise you that if you have any questions about whether you're using files inappropriately, err on the side of caution. For general information about copyright and the Internet, check out www.whatiscopyright.org. For more specific information about technology law in the United States, check out www.bitlaw.com.

Capturing audio clips

If you want to use audio from a music CD, you have to first rip the track(s) you want onto your hard drive by using third-party software. Adobe Premiere Elements can easily import AAC, MP3, and WMA files. You can rip CDs into one of these formats, using many common media player programs such as iTunes or Windows Media Player. To rip WMA files with Windows Media Player, follow these steps:

1. **Place an Audio CD in your CD-ROM drive and launch Windows Media Player by choosing Start➪All Programs➪Windows Media Player.**

2. **In Windows Media Player, click Rip.**

   After a few moments, a list of tracks on the current audio CD appears. Usually Windows Media Player automatically identifies the album, songs, and artist by using an online music database, but if your musical selections are more obscure, Media Player displays the songs as Unknown. You can manually enter song names, the name of the artist, and other information about the song if you want.

3. **To manually enter a song or artist name, click the field, wait for a second, and then click again. Type a name.**

   Entering a descriptive name and artist name for the song helps you find it later.

4. **Use the playback controls to play the tracks and identify songs that you want to copy.**

5. **Place check marks next to each song that you want to copy.**

6. **Click Start Rip at the top of the Windows Media Player window.**

   Windows Media Player shows the copying in progress. When the desired files are copied to your hard drive (Windows Media Player displays the message, `Ripped to Library`), go ahead and close Windows Media Player.

7. **In Premiere Elements, click Organize, click Get Media, and then click PC Files and Folders.**

8. **Browse to the folder containing the song that you copied.**

   Unless you've changed Windows Media Player's default settings, the copied songs appear in the My Music folder of your Documents folder. Folders are automatically created to organize music by artist and album.

9. **Choose the song you want to import and click Open.**

   The imported song appears in the Adobe Organizer.

When you import a song, Premiere Elements converts the song so that it has the same sample rate and number of channels as your project. The converted version is saved as a copy in the Premiere Elements media cache (see Chapter 4 to find out where the cache is located). This audio conversion is called *conforming,* and you'll see a Conforming... message in the Premiere Elements status bar at the bottom of the screen during the process. But don't worry: Conforming your favorite punk rock tracks will not make the music *conformist.*

Preparing still images for your movie

Using still photos in your movies seems like a simple enough task, but it isn't. Still photos can get distorted when they're used in videos, appearing stretched or squished. Either that, or they don't fit the whole screen and have to be "letterboxed." The reason for this is that pesky matter of image aspect ratios I talk about in Chapter 3.

Fortunately, changing your still photos to the correct aspect ratio is easy if you have an image-editing program like Photoshop Elements. To resize images in Photoshop or Photoshop Elements, follow these steps:

1. **Determine the image aspect ratio of your project.**

   Standard video images have an aspect ratio of 4:3, while widescreen images are 16:9. All the high-definition presets in Premiere Elements are 16:9 widescreen. See Chapter 4 for more on selecting project presets.

2. **Open the image in Photoshop and save it as a Photoshop document (PSD) before performing any edits.**

   Make sure that you save a new copy of the image so that the original is preserved. Photoshop documents can be imported directly into Premiere Elements. If you have a different image-editing program, save the document in TIFF format.

3. **Find your project format in Table 5-1, and then decide which image size you want to use.**

   The sizes in the Small column of Table 5-1 should be considered minimums. Images that are smaller than these minimums will appear pixilated in your videos. In most cases, it's safe to use the Small size, but if you want to use any of the image panning and zooming effects described in Chapter 17, select a size from the Medium or Large columns instead. Large sizes allow more zooming.

4. **In Photoshop, choose Image⇨Image Size.**

   The Image Size dialog box appears, as shown in Figure 5-7.

5. **Make sure that the Resample Image option is checked, and choose Bicubic from the Resample options menu.**

6. **In the Pixel Dimensions section of the Image Size dialog box, choose Pixels from the drop-down menu, and then make sure that both the width and height exceed the dimensions you want to use from Table 5-1.**

   If either dimension is under the size you want to use, select a smaller dimension from the Small or Medium columns of Table 5-1 instead.

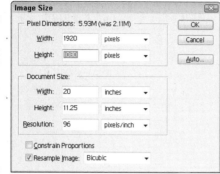

Figure 5-7:
Adjust
the size of
your still in
Photoshop
before
importing it
into a video
project.

If you're working with high-definition video, you need to start with higher resolution still graphics. The dimensions for the Small high-def image size listed in Table 5-1 require that you start with an image that is approximately 3 megapixels. You'll need a 7 megapixel image to achieve the Medium size, and the Large size requires about 12 megapixels.

7. **Enter a new width or height from Table 5-1.**

   For example, if you're using the Small size for high-def widescreen, enter 1920 for the width, but make sure that the height isn't below 1080. If the height is below 1080, enter 1080 for the height. The width should still exceed 1920.

8. **Click OK to close the Image Size dialog box.**

   The image should shrink down to the new dimensions.

9. **Choose Image⇨Canvas Size.**

10. **In the New Size section of the Canvas Size dialog box, select pixels in width and height menus.**

    At this point, one of the measurements — width or height — should match the size you want from Table 5-1, while the other measurement is bigger.

11. **Change the Width and Height so that they both match the size you chose in Table 5-1, and then click OK to close the Canvas Size dialog box.**

12. **Click Proceed in the warning message that appears.**

    The image is cropped down to the appropriate size.

13. **Choose Filter⇨Video⇨NTSC Colors.**

    The NTSC Colors filter ensures that the colors in your still graphic are compatible with video displays. You may notice that some colors appear less saturated after using this filter, but the NTSC Colors filter is necessary to prevent other problems in your movies. Photoshop doesn't offer a PAL Colors filter, but the NTSC Colors filter should be adequate for images destined for PAL video.

14. **Save and Close the image.**

Table 5-1	Still Image Sizes for Video		
Project Format	*Small (width x height)*	*Medium (width x height)*	*Large (width x height)*
High definition 16:9 wide-screen (NTSC or PAL)	1920 x 1080	2880 x 1620	3840 x 2160
Standard definition 16:9 widescreen (NTSC)	960 x 534	1440 x 801	1920 x 1068
Standard definition 16:9 widescreen (PAL)	1024 x 576	1536 x 864	2048 x 1152
Standard definition 4:3 (NTSC)	720 x 534	1080 x 801	1440 x 1068
Standard definition 4:3 (PAL)	768 x 576	1152 x 864	1536 x 1152

You can do a lot of cool things with still photos in Premiere Elements, like zoom in on details or pan across an image while the video plays. Visit Chapter 17 for advanced techniques that help you bring still photos to life in your movies.

Importing stills and other media

Importing still graphics, audio files, and other neat things into Premiere Elements is really easy. If you're importing a still image into a project that is based on NTSC or PAL video, first adjust the image size as described in the preceding section. Then follow these steps:

1. **In Premiere Elements, click Get Media on the Organize tab, and then click PC Files and Folders.**

   The Add Media dialog box appears.

2. **Browse to the file that you want to import.**

   Note that All Supported Files is selected in the Files of Type menu by default. If you want to search for files of only a certain type, choose the desired type from this menu.

   You can also import an entire folder into Premiere Elements. Browse to the folder you want to import, and then click Add Folder in the Add Media dialog box.

3. **Select the file and click Open.**

   The imported file appears in your Organizer.

If the file you want to import doesn't show up in the Add Media window — and you're certain that you're looking in the correct folder — the file may be of a type that isn't supported by Premiere Elements. (To double-check, see the "Importing Media Files" section earlier in this chapter for my list of supported file types.)

Keeping Your Media Organized

When most people think of Adobe Premiere Elements, they think mainly of video, but this is truly a multimedia-rich program. You'll no doubt work with many different kinds of media in Premiere Elements — audio, video, still graphics, and even text. You'll wind up using files from all over your computer, and possibly even your network. Keeping track of all this media stuff can be a challenge, but Premiere Elements can help in several ways:

- ✔ **Tags:** You can apply tags to any piece of media in Premiere Elements. These tags may tell you that the clip includes people, places, events, or other tags that you create. Tags can tell you at a glance if a clip has problems like poor lighting or shaky video, and you can rate clips from one to five stars. Best of all, Premiere Elements can analyze your clips and apply many tags automatically, saving you hours of work reviewing and evaluating every clip in your library.

- ✔ **Organizer:** The Organizer window displays nontechnical details of clips, such as tags and ratings. You can sort and filter clips by date, tags, ratings, or media type.

- ✔ **Edit window:** If you're the kind of person who likes to read spec sheets, you'll appreciate the Edit window. Like the Organizer, the Edit window lets you sort or filter clips by media type, and you can organize clips into folders. But the Edit window also shows you technical details about each item, including the frame rate, duration, and more.

The first time you launch the Premiere Elements Organizer, you are asked if you want to specify the location of media you want organized. If you already have some videos, pictures, music, or other media that you want to use in Premiere Elements, click Yes. Browse to a folder containing media, click the folder name once to select it, and then click Get Media. The Organizer searches for and imports compatible media in the selected folder.

Using the Organizer

As you work in a project, any media that you import or capture is added to your Organizer. The Organizer, shown in Figure 5-8, displays a lot of information about your clips. Key functions you can perform in the Organizer include

✔ **Filter clips by album:** Use the Albums menu to show only clips from a specific album. Premiere Elements creates separate albums for each new project, and you can also create your own albums. (I show you how to create albums later in this chapter.)

✔ **Filter clips by tag:** Under Keyword Tags, place check marks next to tags you want to display. I show you how to tag clips in the next section.

✔ **Apply and use ratings:** You can rate clips from one to five stars by simply clicking the appropriate star under a clip. Then use the Ratings option at the top of the Organizer to filter clips by rating.

✔ **Change the thumbnail size:** Use the thumbnail slider to change the size of thumbnails to show more or fewer clips on-screen.

✔ **Sort by date:** Click the Date menu, and then enter a date range if you only want to see clips from a certain time period. Use the Media Arrangement menu to sort clips by newest or oldest first.

✔ **Show/hide details:** Deselect the Details check box at the top of the interface if you don't want to see details under each clip icon. Hiding details lets more clips fit on the screen.

Change the thumbnail size   Sort by date   Show/hide details   Filter by album

Figure 5-8:
Use the
Organizer to
make sense
of your
media clips.

Ratings   Filter by tag

Click Show All to remove filters and redisplay all clips. This truly does show *all* your clips from *all* your projects, so you may need to refilter a bit after clicking Show All.

Tagging your clips

For years, I mentally subdivided my media clips into categories. I tried to remember which clips showed soccer games, which ones showed people, and which ones showed holidays or school events. Adobe must have been reading my mind because they created an excellent tagging system that means users no longer have to remember which clips fit into what categories.

As I show earlier in this chapter, Premiere Elements can analyze clips and apply many tags automatically during video capture. You can also use automatic tagging later, and you can manually change tags or create your own. You can then use these tags to categorize, review, and sort clips in the Organizer, as shown in Figure 5-9. Some important things to know about tags in the organizer include

- ✔ **Tag icons:** A tag icon under a clip means that the clip has been tagged, either manually or automatically. With larger thumbnails, the tag icon is purple and appears under the clip, as shown in Figure 5-9. If you make the thumbnails smaller, the tag icon turns yellow and appears on top of the clip thumbnail.

- ✔ **Tag ToolTips:** Hover the mouse pointer over a tag icon to reveal a ToolTip, as shown in Figure 5-9. The ToolTip lists tags assigned to that clip.

- ✔ **Tag categories:** Click the arrow next to SmartTags on the right side of the Organizer, and use the check boxes next to each SmartTag category to filter clips. If a category has an arrow next to it, click the arrow to reveal subcategories. You can, for example, filter your media so that you only see clips that are high quality, in focus, with dialog, and panning quickly to the left. Alas, it isn't yet possible to view only clips that are high quality, in focus, with dialog, panning to the left, and shot on the second Tuesday of the month during a lunar eclipse. Maybe in the next version of Premiere Elements.

As you can see, SmartTags are pretty, uh, smart. The next few sections show you how to apply and use tags, as well as how to create new albums to help keep clips organized.

Figure 5-9:
Use tags
to sort
clips in the
Organizer.

Tag icon indicates a tagged clip   Click arrows to expand tag categories

Clip tags appear in ToolTips

Adding SmartTags automatically

Premiere Elements can intelligently analyze your clips. Premiere Elements detects quality issues such as dark or blurry video, and it also detects the content. For example, Adobe Premiere can detect human faces in clip, and even distinguish between close-ups, long shots, or large groups of people.

To automatically apply SmartTags, first select the clips you want to tag in the Organizer. You can select a single clip, click-and-drag around a group of clips, or press the CTRL key on your keyboard and click on individual clips. Each selected clip has a blue border. Then right-click the selected clip (or clips) and choose Run Auto Analyzer, as shown in Figure 5-10. At this point you can probably go take a coffee break. SmartTagging takes awhile, especially if you selected a lot of clips.

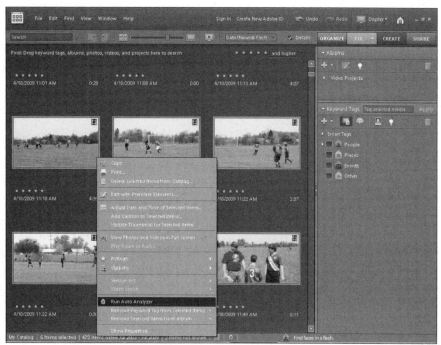

Figure 5-10:
Apply
SmartTags
automati-
cally.

You may notice a button on the right side of the Organizer called Start People Recognition. This feature recognizes individuals in images. When you first run it, the Organizer finds a face and then asks you, "Who's this?" Type in "Jane Smith" and the software searches for and finds other images showing Jane. Cool, huh? Unfortunately, People Recognition only works with still images, not video. Adobe isn't trying to tease us; they just include this feature because the Organizer is shared by both Premiere Elements and Photoshop Elements.

Applying your own keyword tags

The SmartTag feature in Premiere Elements saves you a lot of work, but there is only so much that a computer program can do. Fortunately you can add tags to or remove tags from your clips — even tags of your own creation.

When you use the Organizer, notice the four additional tag categories listed directly under SmartTags: People, Places, Events, and Other. These tags aren't SmartTags because they aren't applied automatically by the Organizer software, but don't call them dumb tags because they're applied manually by you (and like I say in this book's intro, you're no dummy).

The four categories of manually applied tags are overly broad. You can create your own subcategories and tags, and even create whole new categories. To create and apply your own tags, follow these steps:

1. **In the Organizer, click the green plus (+) sign under Keyword Tags and choose New Category.**

2. **Type a name for your new category in the Create Category dialog box that appears.**

3. **Click Choose Color, and then use the color picker to choose a tag color.**

4. **Choose a category icon, and then click OK to create the category.**

   To create subcategories, click the green plus (+) sign in the Organizer and choose New Sub-Category. Enter a name for the subcategory in the dialog box that appears, and decide where you want to create the sub-category by using the Parent Category or Sub-Category menu.

5. **Click the green plus (+) sign again, and choose New Keyword Tag.**

6. **In the Create Keyword Tag dialog box that appears, choose a category in the Category menu, and then type a name for the new tag.**

   In Figure 5-11, I am creating a tag called Single Bird within the Hummingbirds category, which I also created.

   The Create Keyword Tag dialog box includes a button called Place on Map. Unfortunately, as of this writing, the map feature only works for still photos because the Organizer is shared with Photoshop Elements. Some still cameras automatically assign locations to photos by using a built-in GPS function, and the Organizer can use that data.

7. **To apply a tag to a clip, click-and-drag the tag from the Keyword Tags menu and drop it directly on the clip.**

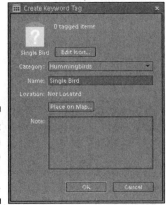

Figure 5-11:
Tags can
be tied to
geographic
locations.

When you apply a tag to a clip, a little tag icon appears with the clip details. To remove a tag, right-click a clip's tag icon, and then choose the tag you want to remove from the context menu that appears.

Although the Auto-Analyzer that applies SmartTags is pretty powerful, you can manually apply SmartTags as well. Simply click-and-drag tags from the SmartTags category and drop them on clips, just like with keyword tags.

Creating new albums

Whenever you create a new project in Premiere Elements, a new album is created for all the media you capture or import into that project. These albums are handy because — as shown earlier in this chapter — you can easily view the albums of other projects while you work in Premiere Elements.

Although albums are normally associated with specific projects, you can create new albums if you wish, and then add files to those albums either manually or automatically. To create a new album:

1. **In the Organizer, click the green plus sign (+) under Albums and choose New Smart Album from the menu that appears.**

2. **In the New Smart Album dialog box that appears, type a name for the new album in the Name field.**

3. **Under Search Criteria, select search options.**

   Choose a search criteria in the first criteria menu. You can search based on almost any imaginable criteria, including tags, filenames, map locations, media types, video formats, and much more. The remaining fields and menus vary, depending on what you choose in the criteria menu. Figure 5-12 shows examples of several different types of search criteria.

4. **Click the Add Additional Criteria button to add more criteria.**

   In Figure 5-12, I have created four search criteria. The first two specify files from a couple of video projects. The third criteria searches for clips that have a Hummingbirds keyword tag. The fourth criteria searches for any clips that have Sledding somewhere in the filename.

5. **Choose whether clips in the album must meet one or all of the search criteria.**

   In Figure 5-12, I've selected the first option, which means that clips can meet any of the criteria. If I only want clips that meet all four criteria, I would choose the second option. The options work like the OR and AND search commands used in Boolean searches.

6. **Click OK to create the album.**

To manually add a clip to an album, click-and-drag the album from the Albums list and drop it on a clip in the Tagging window.

Name the album

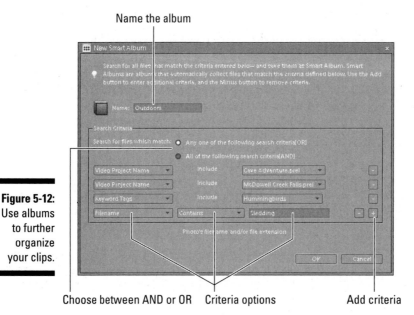

Figure 5-12:
Use albums
to further
organize
your clips.

Choose between AND or OR   Criteria options   Add criteria

In the Organizer, click the name of an album on the right side of the screen to only view clips within that album. Click Show All at the top of the Organizer to remove the album filter and reveal all clips.

Managing clips in the Task pane

The Adobe Organizer lives up to its name because it does a great job of helping you organize all your media files. But the Organizer is really a separate program from Premiere Elements, and sometimes you don't want to launch a second program. The Premiere Elements Task pane gives you access to useful tools to help you quickly gather info about your clips.

Open a project in Premiere Elements, click the Organize tab in the Task pane, and then click the Project button. You see a window similar to Figure 5-13, listing details for all the clips associated with your current project. This includes video clips you have captured, as well as other imported media files. The Project view gives access to some useful features:

✔ **View detailed information about clips.** The Project view indicates whether clips have already been used in your movie (and if so, how many times). It also lists the media type, frame rate, and duration.

Using the Organizer rather than Premiere Elements

If you look at the upper-right corner of the Organizer, you see four tabs called Organize, Fix, Create, and Share. In this chapter, I mainly show you how to use the features on the Organize tab. These tabs give you access to a surprising array of editing and sharing features, although not all of them apply to video. The Fix tab, for example, provides tools for cropping and improving still photos, but none of the features found on this tab work for video. The only video-related button on the Fix tab is the Edit Videos button, which launches Premiere Elements.

The Create tab is also primarily intended for working with still photos, with options for making prints, calendars, photo books, and slideshows. The Instant Movie and DVD with Menu buttons both launch Premiere Elements. I show how to use the Instant Movie feature in Chapter 1, and DVD creation is covered in Chapter 16.

The Share tab is a little more versatile, with sharing options that apply to both still photos and video. The options are self-explanatory, with most of them simply launching Premiere Elements. The Online Album button helps you share photos and videos online by using Photoshop.com or another Web service, and the E-mail Attachments and Photo Mail buttons launch your e-mail program. Chapter 15 describes your online sharing options, as well as the implications of sending large video files through e-mail.

✔ **Organize clips into folders and subfolders.** Click the New Folder button at the bottom of the Task pane, and then type a name when the new folder appears. Click-and-drag clips into folders to organize them.

✔ **Click New Item to quickly create a title, black video, bars and tone, color matte, counting leader, or a SmartSound audio file.**

   I show you how to add titles to your movies in Chapter 13. Black video, bars and tone, color mattes, and counting leaders are elements that you often add to the beginning or end of a video for technical purposes. I briefly explain these technical elements in Chapter 14. SmartSound is a handy soundtrack creation tool that I describe in Chapter 8.

✔ **Add comments to your video clips.** In Figure 5-13, you can see that I've added comments to a couple of clips. For example, next to the clip 00024.MTS I've added the comment, Post game huddle. I may find this information useful later.

✔ **In List view, click a column head to sort clips by that heading.**

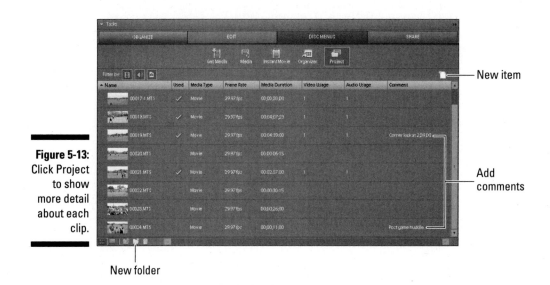

New item

Add comments

Figure 5-13: Click Project to show more detail about each clip.

New folder

Part II
Editing Video and Sound

The 5th Wave   By Rich Tennant

THE LEVINES EDIT THEIR AFRICAN SAFARI VIDEO

"Do you think the 'Hidden Rhino' clip should come before or after the 'Waving Hello' video clip?"

In this part . . .

*V*ideo editing can be broken down into three basic steps: Capture, edit, and export. The chapters in this part of *Premiere Elements 8 For Dummies* cover the first two steps. First, you start by creating new movie projects. Then you find out how to capture video from your digital camcorder and how to import other kinds of media.

When you have some media to work with, I show you how to perform basic editing to turn your media into a basic movie. I also cover adding transitions between video clips, and I show how to work with music and other audio.

Chapter 6

Trimming and Editing Video Clips

. . . .

In This Chapter

▶ Reviewing your clips

▶ Setting In points and Out points

▶ Marking your place with clip markers

▶ Fine-tuning your clips

. . . .

*L*ike plays, movies are made up of scenes you put together in a certain order so that the show makes sense and is enjoyable to watch. Before you can turn scenes into a movie in Premiere Elements, you need to identify which scenes you want to use. Each scene — called a *clip* in video-editing parlance — should be previewed for both video and audio content. After you decide to use a clip, you then determine which portions of that clip you want to keep. Sometimes you may want to leave virtual sticky-notes on scenes to remind yourself later of an important spot in the scene.

After you've captured some video as described in Chapter 5, this chapter leads you through the next steps — previewing your video clips, selecting portions of clips to use in projects, and performing other tasks to make your clips ready for use in your movies.

Reviewing Your Clips

Clips that you capture or import into Premiere Elements all wind up on the Task pane and in the Organizer (see Chapter 5 for more on capturing and organizing clips). Clips come in many flavors: video, audio, still graphics, titles, and more. And that's just the tip of the iceberg. (For more on working with titles, see Chapter 13.)

Getting the details on your clips

The Premiere Elements Task pane displays thumbnail images of clips, but not much else. It also usually displays every clip you've ever captured or imported, making it harder to find just the clips associated with your current project. To view basic details about clips in your current project, click the Project button on the Organize tab. A list of clips appears, displaying details such as the media type, frame rate, and clip duration. If you need even more technical detail about a clip, right-click a clip and choose Properties from the menu that appears. A Properties window appears, as shown in Figure 6-1. The Properties window lists some important clip details, including:

- ✔ **File path:** You know the files are somewhere on your hard drive, but *where* exactly are they? The File Path field tells you the exact folder in which a clip resides.

- ✔ **Image size:** Does the frame size of the video clip or still image match your project? Clips that you imported into Premiere Elements may not have the same frame size as clips that you captured from your camcorder. For example, if you import a clip with the frame size 320 x 240, the image quality of that clip may appear blocky and pixilated when it's inserted into a project that consists mainly of standard- or high-definition video.

  You should also be wary of mixing standard- and high-def video in the same project. If you use a standard-def clip with an image size of 720 x 480 in a high-def project with a size of 1920 x 1080, the lower-quality standard-def clips will stick out like sore thumbs.

- ✔ **Frame rate:** Does the frame rate for all your video clips match? If you mix frame rates in a single project, jerky video may be the sad result.

  If you have a clip with a frame rate that doesn't match the rest of your video, import that clip into a new Premiere Elements project. Place the clip in the Timeline and export it as an MPEG or AVI file with a frame rate that matches your original project. Then import the new clip into your original project.

- ✔ **Pixel aspect ratio:** A pixel aspect ratio of 1.0 means that the pixels are square. A number above or below 1.0 indicates rectangular pixels. NTSC video often has a pixel aspect ratio of 0.9, and PAL footage usually has a pixel aspect ratio of 1.067. So-called full HD video with an image size of 1920 x 1080 usually has square pixels (1.0) in either NTSC or PAL formats. I explain pixel aspect ratios in Chapter 3.

  As with image size and frame rates, avoid mixing video clips with different pixel aspect ratios in the same project. Still images used to be problematic too, but newer versions of Premiere Elements automatically compensate for mismatched pixel aspect ratios in still images. (See Chapter 5 for more on preparing still images for use in your movies.)

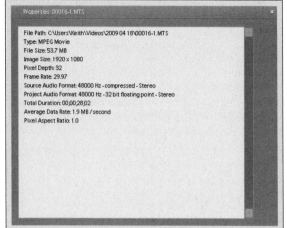

Figure 6-1:
View clip properties to get detailed information.

The Properties dialog box, shown in Figure 6-1, is for a clip recorded by an AVCHD tapeless camcorder. If you view properties for a clip from a tape-based camcorder (either standard or high-def), the Properties dialog will also show a Data Rate Analysis graph for the clip. In most cases, this graph is just interesting to look at, but if your captured video doesn't play back smoothly and you suspect dropped frames, check the clip properties. Dips in the clip's Data Rate Analysis graph indicate dropped frames, whereas a straight line indicates no dropped frames. See Chapter 2 for more on camcorder formats, and Chapter 5 for tips to prevent dropped frames during video capture.

Previewing clips

When you view a list of clips in the Task pane, the thumbnail images that appear show only one frame of the clip. You need to play the whole clip to see what it contains. After you preview the clip, you can decide whether you want to use that clip (the whole thing or just small chunks of it) in your movie.

Previewing a clip is pretty easy. Just double-click it to open the clip in a separate Preview window like the one shown in Figure 6-2. The Preview window includes the following controls:

✔ **Playback controls:** Like the controls on a VCR or DVD player, these let you play, pause, rewind, or fast-forward the clip. Use the Step Back or Step Forward buttons to move a single frame at a time.

- ✔ **Clip timeline:** This is like a ruler that represents the clip as it plays from beginning to end. The clip timeline shows timecode in hours, minutes, seconds, and frames (see Chapter 3 for more on timecode). Color coding is used on the clip timeline to show In and Out points, which I explain later in this chapter.

- ✔ **Current Time Indicator (CTI):** The CTI shows where the current video frame is along the clip timeline. The CTI moves as you play a clip, and you can click-and-drag the CTI to move it. The CTI is an important editing tool that I refer to often throughout this book.

- ✔ **Current timecode:** This lists the current timecode of the CTI. Click-and-drag left or right on the timecode to shuttle the video backward or forward. Or click once on the timecode and type a new number to quickly jump to a specific location.

- ✔ **Clip duration:** No big surprises here; this shows the duration of the clip. If you set In and/or Out points as described later in this chapter, the duration shrinks to reflect the duration between the In and Out points rather than the whole clip.

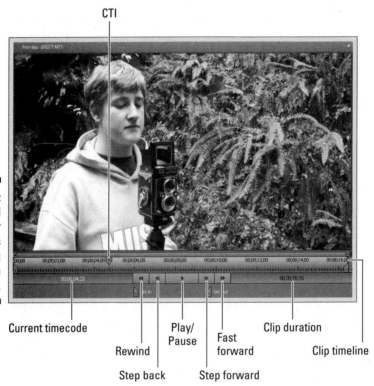

Figure 6-2:
Preview and trim your video clips before using them in projects.

If you want to reveal safe margins in the Preview window (shown in Figure 6-3), right-click the video picture and choose Safe Margins from the menu that appears. As I explain in Chapter 13, safe margins help ensure that titles and important action appear properly on different TVs and displays. Action that happens outside the larger safe margin is too close to the screen edge and may not be visible on some TVs.

Edit faster using the keyboard

The Preview window gives you a lot of options for playing, pausing, and moving around in your clips. But the more you work with video, the more you will find that clicking buttons with a mouse pointer is not an efficient way to work. You'll start to wish for an easier way. Good news! There is an easier way: keyboard shortcuts. Professional video editors rely heavily on keyboard shortcuts when they edit video, because those shortcuts make life easier. As you play with the Preview window, practice these handy keyboard shortcuts:

- ✔ **J, K, and L:** These three keys are good friends who live next to each other on your keyboard, and you'll want to move in next to them, too. Press L to play forward. Press L again to double the speed. Press L again to double the speed again. Keep pressing L to make your video play forward so fast that all the action is a blur! Press K to pause playback, and then get ready for something really cool: Press J. The J key works just like the L key, but in reverse.

- ✔ **Spacebar:** The spacebar is not where astronauts order cocktails. Press the spacebar to play or pause your clip.

- ✔ **Left and right arrows:** The left- and right-arrow keys are, if anything, even more important and valuable than the J, K, and L keys. Press the left-arrow key to step back one frame, and press the right-arrow key to step forward one frame.

The arrow keys are the best way to position the CTI on the *exact* spot where you want to make an edit.

- ✔ **Home and End:** There's no place like home, except at the beginning of every video clip. Press Home to jump to the beginning of a clip, and press End to jump straight to the end.

- ✔ **Q and W:** After you set In and Out points (see the next section of this chapter), press Q to move to the In point and W to go to the Out point.

- ✔ **I and O:** In the next section, I show you how to use In and Out points. Press I to set the In point at the current CTI location, and press O to set the Out point.

Working with Clip Markers

In a perfect universe, there would be peace on Earth, we'd all be eating free rainbow stew, and every clip of video would start and end at exactly the right time. Alas, this world isn't quite perfect yet. But at least with video you can provide the illusion of perfection by using *In points* and *Out points.* In and Out points are critical in video editing because they let you control which portions of a clip appear in the video program and which portions don't appear. The following sections serve up steps for perfecting your clips by using In points, Out points, and other markers.

Setting In and Out points

The In point is the spot where the clip begins playing in the project, and an Out point is, of course, the spot where you want to stop using the clip. Setting In points and Out points on a clip is pretty easy, and Premiere Elements gives you a couple of different methods to choose from. Before you get started, you need to understand a few basics to make your editing go smoothly:

- ✔ I strongly recommend that you set In and Out points on a clip *before* you insert it into your project's Timeline. You can adjust In and Out points later in the Timeline, but that process is a little more cumbersome.

- ✔ In general, do not set the In point at the very beginning of the clip if you can avoid it. The main reason for not doing so is to facilitate transitions between clips. *Transitions* — described in Chapter 9 — are ways to smooth out or dress up the changes between scenes in a movie. Suppose (for example) you want to apply a Cross Dissolve transition to the beginning of a clip, and you set it to last for one second — during this one-second period, the preceding clip fades out and the new clip fades in. By default, Premiere Elements facilitates such a transition by using the "extra" material just beyond the In and Out points of the adjacent clips.

- ✔ As with In points, Out points should not be set at the very end of a clip if you can avoid it. As with In points, this gives some leeway for transitions.

When you're ready to set In and Out points, follow these steps:

1. **Double-click a clip in the Task pane to open it in a Preview window, as described earlier in this chapter.**

2. **Use the preview controls to position the CTI where you want to set an In point or Out point.**

3. **Mark the point in your desired spot.**

Premiere Elements provides a couple of methods for setting these points (see Figure 6-3 for control locations):

- In the Preview window, click the Set In Point or Set Out Point button.
- Press I (In point) or O (Out point) on your keyboard.

After you've marked In and Out points on a clip, the duration of your marked clip portion appears to the right of the playback controls. As you can see in Figure 6-3, I have set In and Out points to select just over nine seconds of this clip.

Action Safe Margin

Figure 6-3:
Mark In and Out points before editing clips into the Timeline.

In point   Set in   Set out   Out point   Current duration

Using clip markers

In points and Out points usually get all the attention in books like this, but you can use other markers in your clips as well. Markers come in handy because they can serve as virtual sticky-notes, marking specific events or spots in a clip. To set a marker at the current position in the clip, right-click the CTI (refer to Figure 6-2) and choose Set Clip Marker from the menu that appears. A submenu offering several different kinds of markers appears. Different kinds of markers include

✔ **In, Out:** These are your basic In points and Out points, as described in the preceding section.

✔ **Video In/Out, Audio In/Out:** Use these if you want audio and video to go in or out at separate points. Figure 6-4 shows that I am setting a separate audio Out point so that the audio from this clip continues to play for another five seconds after the video Out point. You might use this technique to insert an audio track (or narration that explains the scene), while several different video or still images appear on-screen.

✔ **Unnumbered:** If you want to mark only a single spot in the clip, add an unnumbered marker. I like to use these to mark the location of visual events, which I later match with an audio soundtrack.

✔ **Next Available Numbered, Other Numbered:** Use numbered markers if you want to set more than one marker in the same clip. Choose Next Available Numbered if you just want Premiere Elements to select a number automatically. For example, if you've already set markers named `Marker 1` and `Marker 2`, Premiere Elements uses the name `Marker 3` when you choose Next Available Numbered. Choose Other Numbered if you want to set a specific number yourself.

Figure 6-4:
You can set separate In and Out points for audio and video.

When you right-click the CTI, you see two other options in addition to the Set Clip Marker. You can choose Go to Clip Marker or Clear Clip Marker. Choose Go to Clip Marker to open a submenu of markers that you have already set. Click one of the markers to jump directly to that location.

If you want to delete a marker, right-click the CTI and choose Clear Clip Marker. Select an option from the submenu that appears. As you can see, you can clear the current marker, all markers, In points and Out points, or specific numbered markers.

Changing the Speed and Duration of Clips

What *is* a clip, really? When you see a list of clips in Premiere Elements, you're looking at references to actual files on your hard drive. When you set markers on clips or perform edits, you're not editing the original files; you're actually editing the references to those files in Premiere Elements. This is important because it leaves the original source file undisturbed for future use. It also saves storage space because you don't have multiple copies of the same material all over your hard drive.

You can even duplicate clips without eating up extra disk space. Duplicate clips come in handy when you have a really long clip containing a lot of material, some of which you might use in different parts of your project.

To duplicate a clip, right-click it in the Organizer or the Task pane and choose Duplicate. A copy of the clip appears. If you want to give the copy a more useful name, right-click it and choose Rename.

You can also change the speed or duration of a clip without affecting the original source file. The next couple of sections show you how to change the duration and speed of clips in Premiere Elements.

Adjusting clip duration

The duration of a clip is determined by the length of time between the In and Out points for the clip. For audio or video clips, I usually recommend that you adjust the duration of the clip only by setting In and Out points (as I describe earlier in this chapter). However, when you are working with still images or titles (I explain how to create titles in Chapter 13), you may want to change the duration of the clip. You can safely change the duration of a title or still image and not worry about playback speed, because the clip isn't moving to begin with. (If you want to change the speed of audio or video clips, see the next section in this chapter.)

Avoiding repetitive stress injuries with the Preferences dialog box

Do you ever feel like you keep repeating yourself? Do you find yourself performing the same redundant tasks? Do you ever get the feeling that you do the same thing over and over? And again and again? Before you form any habits that might lead to a repetitive stress injury, try adjusting the default settings in Premiere Elements to save yourself a lot of repeated effort.

Take still graphics, for example. If you use a lot of stills in your movie projects, you may find that you adjust the duration repeatedly for each still — by the same amount almost

every time. Premiere Elements has a default duration for still graphics, and you can adjust that default if you want. To do so, choose Edit⇨Preferences⇨General, and locate the Still Image Default Duration field. The default duration for a still image is 150 frames, which works out to about five seconds in NTSC video, or six seconds in PAL video. If that doesn't work for you, simply enter a new number in the Default Duration box, using the frame rate of the video that you work with as a guide. To find out what other Adobe Premiere Elements preferences can be adjusted, check out Chapter 4.

You can set the duration of a still clip by entering a numeric duration value. The duration of a still clip determines how long the picture plays when it's inserted in a movie. To adjust the duration of a clip, follow these steps:

1. **Select a clip in the Task pane.**

2. **Choose Clip⇨Time Stretch.**

   The Time Stretch dialog box appears. As you can see in Figure 6-5, when you adjust the duration of a still clip, some options that pertain only to audio and video clips (Speed, Reverse, and Audio Pitch) are unavailable.

3. **Enter a new duration for the clip in the Duration field.**

   Clip duration is expressed in the same format as timecode, so it looks like this:

   ```
   hours:minutes:seconds:frames
   ```

   To enter a new duration, either type a new number or click-and-drag left or right on the timecode number. As you drag the mouse pointer left, the duration decreases. As you drag the mouse pointer right, the duration increases.

4. **Click OK when you're done.**

   The clip in Figure 6-5 is set to play for exactly five seconds.

Figure 6-5:
Set the
duration of a
still clip
by using
timecode.

You can also adjust a clip's duration in the Timeline. See Chapter 7 for more on changing the duration of clips in the Timeline.

Changing playback speed

Besides adjusting the duration of a clip, you can also adjust the speed at which it plays. Speed adjustments can give you a fast motion or slo-mo effect. Before you dismiss speed adjustment as gimmicky, consider some useful applications of this feature:

- ✔ **Fix holes:** You can adjust the length of the clip without reshooting it. If you have a specific period of time in your project that a clip must fill, but the clip is shorter than the gap, slow the clip down slightly.

- ✔ **Fix bad pans:** You can use speed adjustments to correct shots that are too slow or too fast. For example, if you aren't happy with the speed at which the camera pans across a scene — say, across a landscape — adjust the speed of the clip to speed up or slow down the pan as desired.

- ✔ **Set the tone:** You can use speed adjustments to change the mood or feel of a shot. If an action scene doesn't seem quite as exciting as you would like, speed it up just a bit. Conversely, if two lovers are bounding across a grassy meadow toward each other's embrace, slow it down to increase the drama.

- ✔ **Create an audio effect:** You can create interesting voice effects by adjusting playback speed of audio clips. A faster speed makes the voice sound small and wacky (like Alvin and the Chipmunks), and a slower speed makes the voice sound large and ominous (like Darth Vader).

Just be aware of the potential negative effects of speed adjustment. While moderate speed adjustments to video may be imperceptible to the eyes of most viewers, even slight speed adjustments to audio tracks are almost always immediately obvious.

Also, you may find that your video doesn't seem to play smoothly when you slow it down or speed it up. When you slow down a clip, Premiere Elements must duplicate some frames so the clip still fills the required duration. When you speed up a clip, some frames are removed. Choose your speed-change percentage carefully to ensure that frames are added or removed evenly. Table 6-1 lists percentages that will give reasonably smooth speed changes in Premiere Elements. If you plan to change the speed of a clip, use one of these percentages for the smoothest possible playback.

Table 6-1	Safe Speed-Change Percentages for Video Clips
Safe Slow-Motion Speeds	**Safe Fast-Motion Speeds**
50%	100%
33.33%	200%
25%	300%
20%	400%
16.67%	500%

If you do a little math, you can see a pattern in the speed-change percentages in Table 6-1. If you turn all the Safe Slow Motion percentages into ratios, you would see that they all start with the number one. The 50% speed gives a ratio of 1:2, which means that every single frame turns into *two* frames when Premiere Elements adjusts the speed. With a speed change of 25% (1:4), each frame becomes four frames. Likewise, all the Safe Fast-Motion percentages end with 1 when converted to ratios. The 200% speed gives a ratio of 2:1, and the 300% speed gives a ratio of 3:1.

Adjusting the speed of a clip in Premiere Elements is pretty easy. Follow these steps:

1. **Select a clip on which you want to adjust the speed.**

   You can choose a clip in the Task pane, or one that has already been edited into the Timeline. I recommend that you work with a duplicate of the original.

2. **Choose Clip⇨Time Stretch.**

   The Time Stretch dialog box appears, as shown in Figure 6-6.

3. **Enter a new percentage number in the Speed field.**

   To make the clip play at double its original speed, enter **200**. To make the clip play at half its original speed, enter **50**. The duration of the clip is adjusted automatically, based on your percentage change. Again, I strongly recommend that you use a percentage from Table 6-1.

Figure 6-6:
Changing
the play-
back speed
of your clips
is easy.

4. **If you want the clip to play in reverse, place a check mark next to the Reverse Speed option.**

   This option can be handy if you're going for a "fast rewind" look for the clip.

5. **Place a check mark next to Maintain Audio Pitch to, er, maintain the audio pitch of the clip.**

   This is another one of those really cool features that sets Premiere Elements apart from lesser video-editing programs. If you maintain the audio pitch, you can make speed adjustments to video without making the accompanying audio sound like Alvin and the Chipmunks or Darth Vader (see my earlier comment on this subject). This feature is especially handy if you want to maintain with a clip ambient sounds such as crashing waves or chirping birds. Experiment with this setting, trying the clip with and without the Maintain Audio Pitch setting enabled. Play the clip each way and see how this option affects the audio.

6. **Click OK to close the Time Stretch dialog box.**

7. **Play the clip to preview your speed changes.**

Chapter 7

Making Movies with the Timeline

Consider all the tools of the trade for a painter: brushes, scrapers, a palette, containers of paint, and cleaning supplies. All these tools are necessary, but ultimately the painter's entire work centers around the canvas, where the tools are put to use to create a work of art.

The Timeline is your canvas in Premiere Elements. The other parts of Premiere Elements — the Task pane, the Monitor, the Capture window, and others — all serve crucial purposes, and that purpose is to put together movies in the Timeline. This chapter shows you how to turn your clips into movies worth watching, using the Premiere Elements Timeline. Here I show you how to insert clips in the Timeline, move clips around and modify them, and how to insert DVD chapter references and other markers in the Timeline. I also show you how to undo mistakes that you make in the Timeline — don't feel bad; it happens to all of us — or even revert to previous versions of a project.

The Premiere Elements Timeline is indeed a powerful canvas, but sometimes you may find that you don't need all that power. If you just want to throw some clips together and output a basic movie fast, Premiere Elements also offers the Sceneline. The Sceneline doesn't allow a lot of fine-tuning of your movies, but it is easy and fast to use. The first part of this chapter shows you how to use the Sceneline rather than the Timeline.

Working Quickly on the Sceneline

Remember all that spare time you used to have? If you're like me and free time on your calendar is a distant memory, you'll appreciate the Sceneline. The Premiere Elements Timeline offers a lot of editing power, but if you're in a hurry, the Sceneline is quicker and easier to use.

Even if you aren't in a hurry, you may find that the Sceneline is a good place to start any movie project. You can use the Sceneline to pick and choose which clips you want to use in your movies, and then fine-tune those clips later by using the Timeline. When you add clips to the Sceneline, they are automatically added to the Timeline. The next couple of sections show you how to make movies in just a few minutes by using the Sceneline.

The Sceneline and Timeline share the horizontal space at the bottom of the Premiere Elements program window. You can view either the Sceneline or the Timeline, but not both. Click the Sceneline button in the upper-left corner of the Timeline/Sceneline area to reveal the Sceneline.

Dropping clips on the Sceneline

To start using the Sceneline, first capture or import video clips as described in Chapter 5. When you have clips to work with, click the Sceneline button in the upper-left corner of the Timeline/Sceneline window. Adding clips to the Sceneline is pretty straightforward:

- ✔ **Add clips automatically by using InstantMovie.** I show how to use InstantMovie in Chapter 1.

- ✔ **Click-and-drag clips to the Sceneline, as shown in Figure 7-1.** On the Task pane, click the Organize tab and then click the Media button. Drag clips from the Task pane and drop them in the Sceneline in the order you want scenes to appear in the finished movie.

- ✔ **Click-and-drag clips between existing clips to insert them.** You can also click-and-drag clips left or right in the Sceneline to change the order in which they will play in the finished movie.

After you add clips to the Sceneline, click the Play button in the Monitor to preview the movie. If you're happy with the results, you can export your finished movie to DVD or the Internet as described in Part IV of this book. If you want to trim some clips or make other changes, see the next section.

Drop clips from the Task pane

Figure 7-1:
Make
movies
fast in the
Sceneline.

Drop new clips between existing clips to insert them   Drop clips on Sceneline

Editing Sceneline clips

If you plan to do a lot of editing in your movie, the Sceneline isn't the best place to do it. The best place for editing is the Timeline. But if you have only one or two clips you want to trim, you can do it in the Sceneline. Here's how:

1. **In the Sceneline, click the clip you want to trim to select it.**

   The selected clip appears in the Monitor and has a blue border in the Sceneline. A small time ruler appears at the bottom of the Monitor. Black lines indicate the beginning (In point) and end (Out point) of the current clip (see Figure 7-2). The Current Time Indicator (CTI) shows the current playback location.

2. **Click-and-drag an edit point in the Monitor to trim the clip.**

   To trim the beginning of the clip, click-and-drag the edit point at the In point. To trim material from the end of the clip, click-and-drag the edit point at the Out point. In Figure 7-2, I am moving the edit point at the In point to trim some video from the beginning of the clip.

Clip in point   CTI   Clip out point

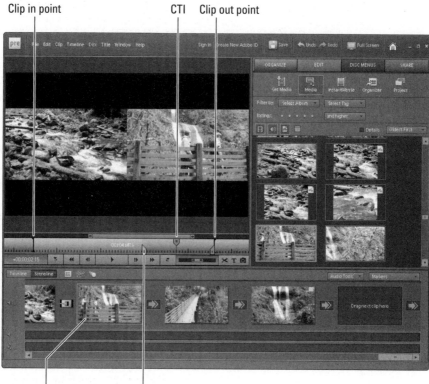

Figure 7-2:
You can
easily trim
clips while
work-
ing in the
Sceneline.

Select the clip   Click-and-drag
you want to trim   the edit point

3. Click Play in the Monitor to review your trimming.

You can also quickly add transitions between clips in the Sceneline. Simply right-click one of the arrows between clips in the Sceneline, and then select a transition from the menu and submenus that appear. See Chapter 9 for more on working with transitions.

Making Sense of the Timeline

As I mention in Chapter 3, video is considered a *linear* medium because when you watch video, one scene follows another from start to finish. You can think of a movie as being laid out along a line through time. When you create a movie in Adobe Premiere Elements, the Timeline is the primary tool you use to assemble the various elements of your movie. Here you lay out all the different scenes and portions of the movie in order from start to finish (as shown in Figure 7-3).

Video tracks   Zoom slider   CTI   Timeline ruler   Work area bar

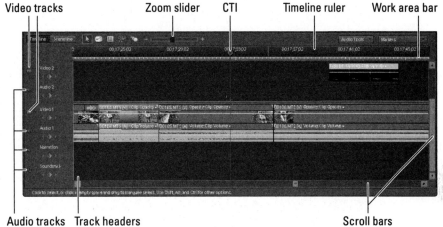

Figure 7-3:
The
Timeline is
where you
assemble
your movies.

Audio tracks   Track headers   Scroll bars

As you can see in Figure 7-3, the Timeline shows a lot of useful information and is easy to navigate. Key features of the Timeline include

✔ **Track headers:** Tracks are layered atop each other, with video and audio tracks paired together, as shown in Figure 7-3. Additional audio tracks for narration and soundtrack music can be found at the bottom of the Timeline. Scroll bars on the right side of the Timeline allow you to scroll through the various tracks. Each video and audio track has a header on the left side of the Timeline. The track headers remain visible even as you scroll the Timeline. Track headers contain important controls (described in the following section). The Premiere Elements Timeline can have up to 99 separate video tracks, as well as 99 unique audio tracks. I show how to add Timeline tracks later in this chapter.

✔ **Ruler and CTI:** Your current location in the Timeline is indicated by the CTI (Current Timecode Indicator) and Timeline ruler. When you play the Timeline, the CTI moves to show your location. The CTI's current time-code is shown in the bottom-left corner of the Monitor window.

✔ **Work Area bar:** The light gray bar just below the Timeline ruler is the Work Area bar. This bar covers your entire project by default, but you can resize the Work Area bar so that it only covers part of your project. I show how to do this — and explain why you might do this — later in this chapter.

✔ **Zoom and scroll controls:** Use the zoom slider near the top of the Timeline to zoom the view in or out. You can also use the plus (+) and minus (–) keys on your keyboard to zoom in or out. Use the scroll bar at the bottom of the Timeline to scroll left or right.

Adding and renaming Timeline tracks

Tracks are perhaps the most important feature of the Premiere Elements Timeline because they allow tremendous versatility and control over the sound and pictures in your project. For example, one audio track might contain the sound that goes with a certain video clip, a second audio track may contain background music, and a third may contain voice-over narration. With multiple video tracks, you can perform special compositing effects, picture-in-picture effects, overlay titles, and more.

Adobe Premiere Elements allows you to have up to 99 separate video tracks, as well as 99 audio tracks. Although it is difficult to imagine what you might do with 99 video tracks, it's definitely better to have too many tracks than not enough. Many other affordable video-editing programs give you only one or two tracks to work with, severely limiting your creative control over movie projects. Premiere Elements is limited only by your imagination.

If you need more tracks in your Timeline than those already present, you can add them by following these steps:

1. **Choose Timeline⇨Add Tracks.**

   The Add Tracks dialog box opens, as shown in Figure 7-4.

2. **Enter the number of tracks you want to add under Video Tracks or Audio Tracks (as appropriate).**

3. **Choose an option from the Placement menu.**

   In most cases, you'll want to just stick with After Last Track.

4. **Click OK to close the dialog box and add your tracks.**

You can also add, delete, or rename tracks by right-clicking a blank area of any track header in the Timeline. You may find it handy to give some tracks more descriptive names, to better reflect what you put in that track. Track names won't appear in the final movie, so you can choose any name that you find useful as you edit.

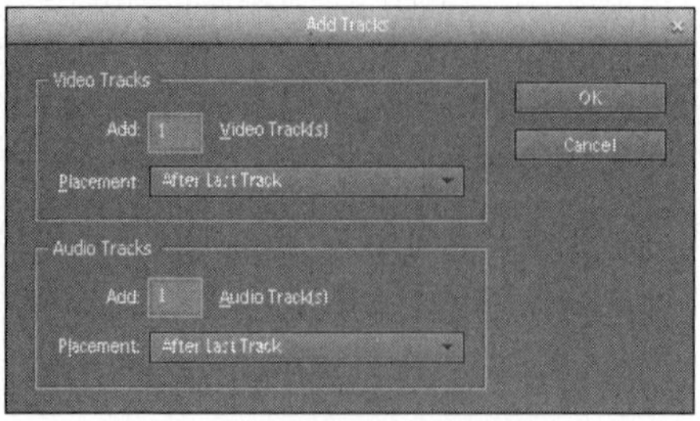

Figure 7-4:
You can have up to 99 video and 99 audio tracks on the Premiere Elements Timeline.

Do you have empty, unused tracks taking up space in your Timeline? If so, right-click a track header and choose Delete Empty Tracks from the menu that appears. Only empty tracks can be deleted. If a track won't delete itself, scroll back and forth through the project to check the entire length of that stubborn track. Chances are there's a clip hiding somewhere on that track.

Working with the Work Area bar

As you look at the Timeline, you'll notice a light gray bar near the top of the Timeline, just underneath the Timeline ruler. This bar is called the Work Area bar, and by default it spans the entire length of your movie project. However, you can shrink the Work Area bar so that it covers only part of your project, as shown in Figure 7-5.

When you resize the Work Area bar so that it covers only part of your project, Premiere Elements only renders effects, transitions, and other edits that are covered by the Work Area bar. You may want to shrink the Work Area bar if you want to export only a portion of your movie project, for example. As I describe in Chapters 14 through 16, when you export your movie project, you can choose to export the entire project or just the area spanned by the Work Area bar.

To change the size of the Work Area bar, click-and-drag on either end of the Work Area bar. After you adjust the Work Area bar, hover the mouse pointer over the Work Area bar to view details like the new duration, as shown in Figure 7-5.

Click-and-drag   Work Area bar   Click-and-drag

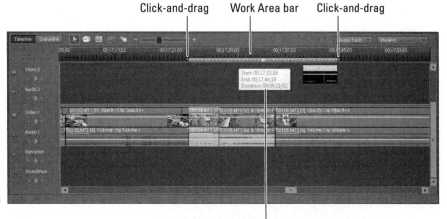

Figure 7-5:
Use the
Work Area
bar to select
portions
of a movie
project.

Hover over Work Area bar for details

Using Timeline tools

Somewhere in a garage, closet, basement, or shed, you probably have a tool-box full of tools. In Premiere Elements, you find editing tools on a toolbar in the upper-left corner of the Timeline, as shown in Figure 7-6. To use a tool, simply click it on the toolbar. The available tools are:

- ✔ **Selection tool:** Use this tool to select clips for click-and-drag edits, or to perform ripple edits (described later in this chapter) to lengthen or shorten clips. You can also activate the Selection tool by pressing V on your keyboard.

- ✔ **Time Stretch tool:** Use this to change the playback speed of a clip. See the section on changing clip speed later in this chapter. To activate the Time Stretch tool, click the Time Stretch toolbar button, shown in Figure 7-6, or press X on your keyboard.

- ✔ **Properties:** Click a clip in the Timeline to select it, and then click the Properties toolbar button. Important clip controls and properties appear in the Organizer. These controls and properties are used for various advanced edits described throughout this book.

- ✔ **Smart Trim mode:** I hesitate to call other programs "dumb," but Smart Trim mode is one of the features that definitely makes Premiere Elements a smart choice. Smart Trim quickly identifies which portions of your clips are most interesting and have the best image quality. Clips are then trimmed — either manually by you or automatically by Premiere Elements — down to just the best video. I show how to use Smart Trim mode later in this chapter.

- ✔ **Motion Tracking mode:** This feature identifies moving subjects in video, and then tracks the motion of those subjects. The applications for motion tracking are as limitless as your creativity. You could use motion tracking to put a clip art speech bubble over a person, cover up an airplane flying across an otherwise unblemished sky, or apply special effects to moving objects. I show how to use Motion Tracking mode in Chapter 12.

When you perform edits in the Timeline, the mouse cursor changes to show the tool that is currently active. Sometimes you may see a red slash across the mouse pointer when you try to perform some edits. If you see a red slash on the mouse pointer, this means you can't use the currently selected tool on whichever clip happens to be under the pointer.

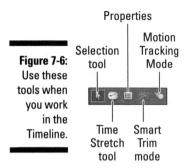

Figure 7-6:
Use these tools when you work in the Timeline.

Properties

Selection tool

Motion Tracking Mode

Time Stretch tool

Smart Trim mode

Adding Clips to the Timeline

Before you start assembling stuff into the Timeline to make your movie, make sure that you've marked In points and Out points for your clips. (Chapter 6 explains how.) After you've completed that process, you can start putting clips in the Timeline. The following sections show you how to add clips to the Timeline, and then figure out what to do with those clips after they're there.

The bottom portion of the Premiere Elements program window toggles between the Sceneline (described earlier in this chapter) and the Timeline. Click the Timeline button in the upper-left corner of the Timeline/Sceneline window to reveal the Timeline.

Inserting clips

A lot of the work you do in Adobe Premiere Elements requires you to simply drag and drop items onto new locations. So it won't surprise you that adding clips to the Timeline requires the same technique. After you have set In and Out points for a clip, the easiest way to add that clip to the Timeline is to simply drag and drop it from the Task pane to the Timeline, as shown in Figure 7-7. You *can* drop clips on the Timeline before setting In and Out points, but I find it easier to set those points first.

Set In and Out points   Click-and-drag clip from Task pane

Figure 7-7:
Drag and
drop clips
from the Edit
tab to the
Timeline.

Drop clip in a Timeline track

Premiere Elements provides two other methods for placing a clip in the
Timeline as well. These editing methods — called *insert* and *overlay* — are
usually more precise and efficient ways to place clips in the Timeline at
exactly the desired location. Each type of edit is a little different:

- **Insert edit:** The incoming clip is inserted at the current location of the
  CTI (Current Time Indicator). Clips that fall after the CTI are moved over
  to make room. Figure 7-8 shows an insert edit. I inserted a clip showing
  some people between two landscape shots.

- **Overlay edit:** The incoming clip is inserted at the current location of
  the CTI, but instead of moving subsequent material over, the new clip
  simply replaces the old material. Figure 7-9 shows an overlay edit. My
  close-up shot of people sledding has replaced a portion of the wide landscape shot. A cutaway scene such as this is a good time to use overlay
  edits.

Figure 7-8:
Insert edits
insert clips
between
exist-
ing clips,
shifting
subsequent
material to
make room.

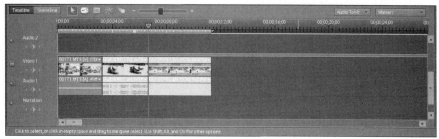

Figure 7-9:
Overlay
edits insert
clips and
replace
subsequent
material.

An important thing to keep in mind about insert and overlay edits is that in Premiere Elements they can only insert clips into the Video 1 track. To perform an insert or overlay edit, follow these steps:

1. **Use the Preview window to set In and Out points for a clip (as described in Chapter 6).**

2. **Place the Timeline CTI at the exact location where you want the incoming clip to start.**

   Use the left- and right-arrow keys to fine-tune the location of the CTI, one frame at a time. Alternatively, press Page Up to move to the preceding edit point in the Timeline, or press Page Down to move to the next edit point.

3. **Click once in the Preview window to make that window active.**

4. **Choose Clip⇨Insert or Clip⇨Overlay to perform an insert or overlay edit.**

   The clip is inserted into track Video 1 of the Timeline.

You can also quickly perform insert or overlay edits by using keyboard shortcuts. To do an insert edit, press the comma (,) key. To perform an overlay edit, press the period (.) key.

The clip is added to the Timeline. Using this method of placing clips in the Timeline is usually more precise than dragging and dropping because you can pick an exact location for the edit by using the CTI. Dragging and dropping clips can seem downright clumsy by comparison.

Premiere Elements analyzes your clips for potential quality problems, such as poor lighting or shaky video. If you add a clip to the Timeline and Premiere Elements thinks your clip could be improved, you are asked if you want to automatically fix quality problems. If you click Yes, Premiere Elements automatically applies fixes such as image stabilization or color correction. I describe how to improve your video images — either manually or automatically — in Chapter 10.

Moving clips in the Timeline

After you have some clips in the Timeline, it's time to move them around. Moving a clip is so easy that you've probably already figured out how: You simply click-and-drag clips to new locations. You can drag clips back and forth in a track, or drag them to a different track altogether.

If you're trying to move a clip in very small increments, you may get frustrated by the tendency of clips to snap to the nearest adjacent clip edge or to the CTI. To disable this snapping, choose Timeline⇨Snap to remove the check mark. This disables the snap-to-edges feature. Click Timeline⇨Snap again to enable snap-to-edges.

Performing ripple edits

No hip waders required. Honest. One of the changes you can make to clips in the Timeline is to make them longer or shorter. This kind of edit is called a *ripple edit* and basically just changes the In point or Out point for the clip. Consider the diagram in Figure 7-10. I want to trim material off the end of Clip B, so I perform a ripple edit on the Out point for Clip B.

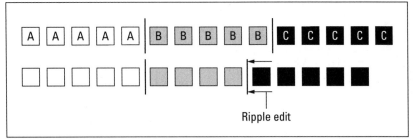

Figure 7-10: A ripple edit changes the duration of a clip.

Ripple edit

You can trim a clip to a smaller size by using a ripple edit, or you can extend the length of the clip. However, if you want to make the clip longer, the original source clip must contain sufficient material. For example, suppose you started out with a clip that was five seconds long. In the Monitor window, you cut one second off the end of the clip before editing it into the Timeline. Using a ripple edit, you can add some or all of that second you trimmed off, but nothing more. To perform a ripple edit, follow these steps:

1. **Choose the Selection tool in the Timeline.**

2. **Hover the mouse pointer over the edit point of the clip you want to ripple.**

   The mouse pointer changes to a bracket facing toward the affected clip.

3. **Click-and-drag the edit point.**

   As you drag the edit point, a ToolTip appears next to the mouse pointer showing how much material you are adding or removing.

Why did slip, slide, and roll edits slip, slide, and roll away?

If you have used Adobe Premiere Pro or an earlier version of Premiere such as Adobe Premiere 6, you may be familiar with several other editing methods in addition to ripple edits. Other editing methods include roll edits, slip edits, and slide edits. Unfortunately, as part of Adobe's efforts to simplify Premiere Elements, these editing methods were removed.

Three-point edits and four-point edits didn't make the cut either. These editing methods are favored by many video-editing professionals who edit video on a daily basis and need advanced editing tools and features to work efficiently. I've always been a big fan of three-point edits myself, but I have to admit that they can be a little complicated to do at first. If you're a video-editing professional and you absolutely need to be able to do three-point edits, roll edits, and other such techniques, you'll need to step up to Premiere Pro.

Deleting gaps in the Timeline

As you move, delete, and reorganize clips, you'll wind up with gaps in your Timeline. You may be tempted to try filling the gaps by using any number of difficult methods: dragging over each subsequent item in the Timeline (a time-consuming endeavor that can mess up any advanced edits you've already made), pecking around for an alternate clip, or, inserting a black matte with the word "Intermission" splashed across it (yeah, you meant to leave the space blank).

A better idea is to simply delete the Timeline gap and automatically shift all subsequent material over. Ahh, genius! The great thing about deleting gaps is that Premiere Elements can automatically shift all clips in *all* tracks. This is important if you've done a lot of editing later in the Timeline that involves titles, compositing, or other effects that involve multiple Timeline tracks.

To properly delete a gap, right-click the undesired void in the Timeline and choose Delete and Close Gap from the little menu that appears, as shown in Figure 7-11. If you don't like right-clicking, click the void once with your left mouse button, and then choose Edit⇨Delete and Close Gap.

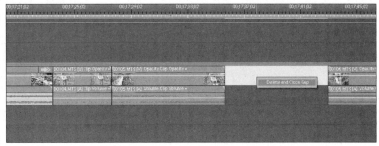

Figure 7-11:
Premiere
Elements
helps you
clean up
gaps in the
Timeline.

Selecting clips in the Timeline

Most of your editing is probably done one clip at a time. You can also select and work with multiple clips in the Timeline, a feature that often comes in handy. For example, if you want to select a portion of your movie and move it somewhere else, you can select all the clips in that section and then click-and-drag them to the new location. Premiere Elements gives you two methods for selecting multiple clips:

✔ Hold down the Shift key on your keyboard and click individual clips to select them. This method works best when selecting noncontiguous clips. Premiere Elements differs from other Windows programs, which usually use the Ctrl key for selecting noncontiguous items.

✔ Click-and-drag a box around the clips you want to select, as shown in Figure 7-12. This method works best when selecting contiguous clips.

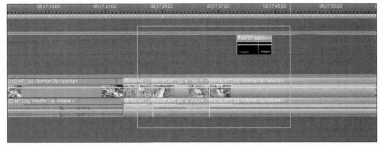

Figure 7-12:
Click-and-
drag around
a group
of clips to
select them.

Splitting clips

If you want to buy a soft drink from a vending machine, a $20 bill is probably too large a denomination. You'll need to make change. Likewise, you'll sometimes find that you need to make change (so to speak) with clips in Premiere Elements. To split a clip in the Timeline, follow these steps:

1. **Place the CTI on the exact frame where you want to split a clip.**

   You can use the left- and right-arrow keys to move forward and back a single frame at a time.

2. **Click the clip you want to split to select it.**

   The selected clip turns purple in the Timeline.

3. **Click the Split Clip button in the Monitor window.**

   The Split Clip button is in the lower-right corner of the Monitor and it looks like scissors. What was a single clip just a moment ago is now two clips, as shown in Figure 7-13.

   If you're a fan of keyboard shortcuts, press Ctrl+K to quickly split the currently selected clip at the CTI. If you prefer to use menu commands, choose Timeline ⇨ Split Clip.

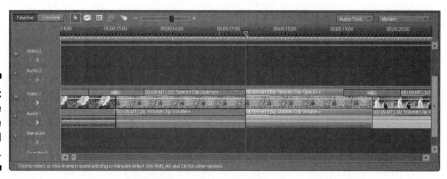

Figure 7-13: Split the clip at the desired location.

Changing playback speed

If you watched much TV in the 1970s, you probably remember a series called *The Six Million Dollar Man.* The show revolved around a former test pilot named Steve Austin (played by Lee Majors) who, after a horrific plane crash, was rebuilt by using cybernetic enhancements (we assume that those enhancements cost about $6 million, including installation). The cybernetics gave Steve super strength and speed, abilities he used to fight crime and battle the forces of evil. Several times in each episode, Steve Austin would run somewhere. In order to show that Steve was running inhumanly fast, we would see the hero running . . . in slow motion. (It seemed to make sense at the time.)

Video technology has progressed a great deal since the '70s, but few computer-generated special effects provide the same dramatic effect as slo-mo video and some well-chosen music. Changing the speed of your own clips in Adobe Premiere Elements is an effective (yet often overlooked) visual effect you can apply to video. You can adjust the speed of clips in the Timeline to create your own fast- or slow-motion effects.

Premiere Elements gives you two methods for changing the speed of clips in the Timeline. The old-fashioned way involves entering numbers in a dialog box, like this:

1. **Select a clip in the Timeline for which you want to adjust the playback speed.**

2. **Choose Clip⇨Time Stretch.**

   The Time Stretch dialog box appears, as shown in Figure 7-14.

3. **Enter a new percentage in the Speed field.**

   If you want to slow the clip down, enter a rate that is below 100%. If you want to speed it up, enter a rate above 100%. Leave the Duration field alone for now.

4. **Click OK.**

The other method for changing playback speed is to use the Time Stretch tool in the Timeline. This tool is located in the upper-left corner of the Timeline, next to the Razor tool. Click this tool and then click-and-drag on the edges of clips in the Timeline. As you stretch and squeeze clips with the Time Stretch tool, you change their playback speed. This method doesn't give you precise control over the rate of the time change, but it does come in handy if you have a specific block of time to fill.

If you ever decide to restore the clip to its original playback speed, simply open the Time Stretch dialog box, described earlier in this section, and reset the Speed to 100%.

You may need to experiment a bit with the rate that you choose. In Figure 7-14, I cut the speed of the clip in half to 50%. You may find that some speed changes result in rough or jerky playback. (See Chapter 6 for specific recommendations on speed changes that should provide smoother playback.)

Figure 7-14:
Use the
Time
Stretch
dialog box
to change a
clip's play-
back speed.

Using Smart Trim mode

You've probably noticed by now that video editing can eat up a lot of your time. Sure, fine-tuning your movie masterpieces is fun, but as editing hours turn into days, your personal hygiene suffers, your boss leaves messages wondering when you'll be coming back to work, and friends express concern about your "Video-editing problem."

Smart Trim mode is a new feature in Premiere Elements that helps you make better movies without letting the video-editing process take over your life. Smart Trim identifies portions of your video clips that have quality problems, and then recommends which sections of bad quality video should be trimmed. You can even let Premiere Elements do the trimming for you if you're in a hurry. To use Smart Trim mode:

1. **Click the Smart Trim mode button on the top of the Timeline.**

   Blue crosshatch boxes appear over portions of video that have quality problems, as shown in Figure 7-15. These areas can be trimmed manually by you, or automatically by Smart Trim.

   Smart Trim mode works only on clips that have been analyzed by Premiere Elements. See Chapter 5 for details on how to analyze clips when you capture or import video.

2. **Hover the mouse pointer over a trim area to see a summary of quality problems.**

   In Figure 7-15, Smart Trim has identified a portion of video that is blurred, shaky, and has poor contrast.

3. **Preview the video identified by Smart Trim.**

   Smart Trim is smart, but it isn't intelligent. Even though some video may have quality problems, you should review the video to make sure that it doesn't show something really important. Hastily shot video of Bigfoot may be shaky and blurry, but if that's your only Sasquatch footage, you probably want to keep it.

4. **Right-click a trim area, and then choose Keep to keep the video, or choose Trim to get rid of it.**

   If you choose to keep the video, the blue crosshatch disappears and the video clip remains intact. If you choose to trim the video, the trim area is removed from the Timeline.

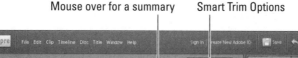

Figure 7-15: Smart Trim mode identifies lower-quality portions of your clips.

Suggested trim area

You can fine-tune Smart Trim if you feel that the trim suggestions are too aggressive (or not aggressive enough). Follow these steps:

1. **With Smart Trim mode enabled, click the Smart Trim Options button at the top of the Monitor window.**

2. **In the Smart Trim Options dialog box that appears, shown in Figure 7-16, adjust the options to your liking as follows:**

   • **Quality level:** Use the Quality Level slider to increase or decrease how sensitive Smart Trim is to quality issues.

   • **Interest level:** Smart Trim doesn't just look for quality problems. It can also analyze clips based on content. For example, if your video clip starts with an empty stage that is eventually filled by people, Smart Trim can identify the less interesting parts of the clip (the empty stage shots) and recommend them for trimming.

- **Mode:** Finally, choose either Manual or Automatic under Mode. If you choose Automatic, Smart Trim automatically trims clips for you. I recommend that you use Automatic Smart Trimming only when you're in a hurry.

3. Click Save to close Smart Trim Options.

Figure 7-16: Adjust Smart Trim's sensitivity.

Using Timeline Markers

In Chapter 6 I show how to add *markers* to clips. You can also add markers to the Timeline. Markers can be extremely helpful as you work in the Timeline. You can use markers as reference points for key events, visual indicators as you edit, or cues for items such as Web links or DVD scene references.

Clip markers that were added to a source clip *before* it was added to the Timeline appear directly on that clip in the Timeline. Markers that are added only to the Timeline appear on the Timeline ruler, as shown in Figure 7-17.

Timeline marker   Disc menu marker

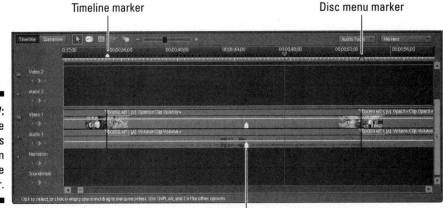

Figure 7-17: Timeline markers reside on the Timeline ruler.

Clip marker

Marking your place in the Timeline

Markers can serve various purposes. In Figure 7-17, I have added markers to indicate where specific visual events occur. You can use markers as references for later editing. For example, if you decide to add some audio and you need to time the audio to match certain visual events, you can use Timeline markers to line up the audio and video. To add a marker to the Timeline, follow these steps:

1. **Move the CTI to the location where you want to place a marker.**

   If necessary, use the left- and right-arrow keys on your keyboard to move frame by frame to the correct location.

2. **Choose Timeline⇨Set Timeline Marker⇨ and then choose a marker from the submenu that appears.**

   You can choose to set an unnumbered marker, the next available numbered marker, or choose Other Numbered and create a marker with a specific number.

   The only real difference between numbered and unnumbered markers is the way they appear on the Timeline ruler, so it's a matter of personal preference whether you use numbered markers, unnumbered markers, or a combination of both.

The marker now appears on the Timeline ruler. Pretty easy, huh? If you ever want to get rid of a marker, simply choose Timeline⇨Clear Timeline Markers and choose an option from the submenu to sentence a marker to the electronic ether. Choose Timeline⇨Go to Timeline Marker to quickly jump to a specific marker.

Using disc menu markers

Premiere Elements includes a special kind of marker called a disc menu marker, and as the name implies, these markers are designed to be used in movies that will be recorded to DVD or Blu-Ray discs. They can also serve as chapter markers if you export your movie in QuickTime or Windows Media format. Menu markers come in handy for several reasons:

✔ When you create a DVD or Blu-Ray disc layout in Premiere Elements, the Scene Selection portion of the disc menu uses the scene references that you create.

✔ When you watch the disc in almost any DVD or Blu-Ray player, you can quickly jump from scene to scene by pressing the Next Scene and Previous Scene buttons on the player's remote control. This feature also works for QuickTime and Windows Media videos.

✔ You can use menu markers to automatically stop playback or return the viewer to the disc menu.

✔ Menu markers serve as visual milestones between major scenes on the Premiere Elements Timeline.

Creating menu markers

You can create menu markers manually. I recommend creating menu markers at the beginning of major events or sections of your movie. To create a menu marker, follow these steps:

1. **Place the CTI where you want to place a marker.**

2. **Choose Disc⇨Set Menu Marker.**

   A Menu Marker dialog box appears, as shown in Figure 7-18.

3. **In the Menu Marker dialog box, enter a name for the marker in the Name field.**

   This name should be simple and in plain language, because viewers will see this scene name in the disc's scene selection menu.

4. **Choose a type from the Marker Type menu.**

   • A scene marker is the most common type of menu marker and simply marks the beginning of a new scene.

   • A main menu marker is similar to a scene marker, but it suggests a more important location. Also, when you use this kind of marker, Premiere Elements places a button linking to this marker in the disc's main menu (as opposed to placing it in the scene selection menu). Some DVD players call the main menu the Title menu.

   Use Main Menu markers if your movie project actually contains several unique "mini" movies that are meant to be viewed separately.

   • A Stop marker is usually placed at the end of a movie or wherever you want playback to stop and the main menu to reappear.

5. **Select a thumbnail image for the marker by clicking and dragging left or right on the timecode under the Thumbnail Offset control until you see a scene that would make an appropriate thumbnail.**

   The disc's scene selection menu includes thumbnail images for each scene, and by default, the thumbnail is always the first frame of the scene. Often, the first frame of a scene doesn't provide a good visual summation of the contents of the scene. In Figure 7-18, I have offset the thumbnail by 46 seconds.

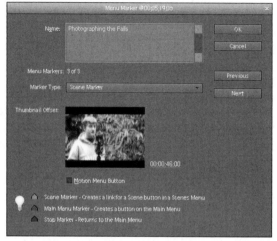

Automatically generating menu markers

If you're in a hurry, you can let Premiere Elements automatically generate menu markers for you. To do so, choose Disc⇨Generate Menu Markers. The Automatically Set Menu Scene Markers dialog box appears, as shown in Figure 7-19. You have several options:

✔ **At Each Scene:** This option sets a marker at every scene. In most cases, I don't recommend this option, because creating a menu marker for every single clip in your movie is probably overkill. Choose this option only if your movie consists primarily of a few long, unedited clips.

✔ **Every *x* Minutes:** You can automatically generate markers at specific time intervals. Use this option if your movie contains several hours of riveting footage of grass growing or paint drying.

✔ **Total Markers:** If you want to quickly create a few markers — say, five or six — choose this option and enter a number. Premiere Elements automatically creates markers and spaces them evenly.

✔ **Clear Existing Menu Markers:** Place a check mark next to this option if you want to get rid of the markers that you created earlier. Only do this if you know that the markers you created earlier are worthless.

Click OK to close the dialog box and automatically generate DVD markers.

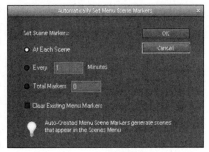

Figure 7-19:
Premiere
Elements
can auto-
matically
generate
menu mark-
ers for you.

Undoing Mistakes

Have you ever wished for a second chance to go back and undo life's mistakes? With Premiere Elements, going back in time is easy! If you make a mistake while editing your movie, you can quickly undo the mistake by choosing
Edit⇨Undo. The Edit menu lists the last action that was performed next to
Undo so you know exactly what you're undoing. You can also quickly undo
an action by using the keyboard shortcut Ctrl+Z.

Did you change your mind again? Perhaps that "mistake" wasn't such a bad
thing after all. If you want to redo the mistake that you just undid, choose
Edit⇨Redo (or press Ctrl+Shift+Z).

In addition to the beloved Undo/Redo commands, Premiere Elements offers
two additional tools to help you undo mistakes. The History panel displays a
complete editing history of your project, and Premiere Elements also offers
the ability to revert back to an earlier version of a project.

Using the History panel

One of the more useful features in Premiere Elements is the History panel, as
shown in Figure 7-20. The History panel is hidden by default, but you can display it at any time by choosing Window⇨History.

The Premiere Elements History panel is even more forgiving than the Undo/
Redo feature. It shows you a list of the last 100 edits you've made, in order,
with the most recent edit at the bottom of the list. To move back in history,
click an item in the list and then click the Trash bin icon at the bottom of
the panel. When you click OK to confirm the action, you undo the selected
item — *and all actions following it.* If you want to clear the history, click the
right-facing arrow in the upper-right corner of the History panel and then
choose Clear History.

Figure 7-20:
The History
panel keeps
a running
record of
your last 100
edits.

Reverting to previous versions

Sometimes your creative juices flow like a river and every edit you make just enhances the magic of your movies. Other times it seems like every change causes a train wreck. If you've ever said to yourself, "This movie looked better before I started editing today," then the Premiere Elements *Revert* feature is here to help. To quickly get rid of all the edits you have made during the current session, choose File➪Revert. When you click Yes to confirm the action, every edit you made since the last time you saved the project is discarded.

The only problem with the Revert option is that if you recently chose File➪Save to save your work, you may not be able to revert back very far. Fortunately, the Auto-Save feature may be able to help:

1. **Choose File➪Open Project.**

2. **In the Open Project dialog box, double-click the Adobe Premiere Elements Auto-Save folder to open it.**

   If you don't see this folder, choose your Documents folder in the Look In menu and then navigate to Adobe\Premiere Elements\8.0\Adobe Premiere Elements Auto-Save.

3. **Locate the backed-up .prel file for your current project, and then click it to select that file.**

   Premiere Elements numbers auto-save files sequentially. If your project is named "SuperMovie," you should see auto-save files called "SuperMovie-1," "SuperMovie-2," and so on. Higher numbers represent more recent versions.

4. **Click Open to open the auto-saved project.**

If the version that opens isn't the one you're looking for, repeat the steps above and open an earlier version of the same project.

Chapter 8

Adding Sound to Your Movies

· ·

In This Chapter

▶ Understanding audio fundamentals

▶ Recording good-quality audio

▶ Working with audio in the Premiere Elements Timeline

▶ Syncing your video to the beat of the music

▶ Making the best use of audio effects and transitions

· ·

*M*ost people think of movies as just moving pictures. When you edit your video clips together in a movie project, you probably spend most of your time working with the visuals by placing video clips in the Timeline, adding transitions, and even using a special effect or two. The audio portion of a movie is, sadly, often given the afterthought treatment.

Fortunately, you are reading this chapter, which means that you care about audio and you know that it matters. Many video experts claim that audiences are more forgiving of flaws and mistakes in video images, while poor-quality audio is immediately noticeable and off-putting. This speaks volumes (pun intended) about the importance of audio.

If you really want to create high-quality, well-rounded movies, you need to spend time tweaking audio levels, smoothing audio transitions between clips, and maybe adding narration or a musical soundtrack. This chapter introduces you to the basics of audio and shows you how to work with audio in your Premiere Elements projects. I also show you how to use the great audio tools that come with Premiere Elements. Those tools include SmartSound, which automatically generates royalty-free soundtrack music to match your project, as well as a beat-detecting tool that automatically synchronizes video clips to music beats. Another cool feature is called SmartMixer, which automatically adjusts the volume of different tracks to make sure that narration or other important audio isn't drowned out by a soundtrack or background audio.

What Is Audio?

Consider how audio affects the feel of a video program. Honking car horns on a busy street, crashing surf and calling seagulls at a beach, a howling wolf on the moors: These sounds help identify a place as quickly as images can, if not quicker. If a picture is worth a thousand words, well-done audio can be worth a thousand pictures.

Understanding sampling rates

For more than a century, humans have been recording sound waves by using analog devices, ranging from wax cylinders to magnetic tapes. But nowadays most audio is recorded digitally, just as with many modern video recordings. Because a digital recording can only contain specific values, it must approximate a continuous stream of sound. A digital recording device *samples* a sound many times per second. The more samples per second, the more closely the recording approximates the live sound.

The number of samples per second is called the *sampling rate.* As you might expect, a higher sampling rate provides better recording quality. CD audio typically has a sampling rate of 44.1 kHz — that's 44,100 samples per second — and most digital camcorders record at a sampling rate of 48 kHz. DVD movies also use an audio sampling rate of 48 kHz.

When you create a new project in Premiere Elements, the project always has a sample rate of 48 kHz, but when you export your project, you can sometimes choose a lower sample rate.

You may have to use a lower sample rate when exporting a movie for the Web because a small file size is usually more important than DVD-quality audio, especially when you're dealing with iffy and often-changing Internet connection rates. Higher audio sampling rates during export usually mean much larger movie files.

Delving into bit depth

A term you'll hear bandied about in audio editing is *bit depth.* The quality of an audio recording is affected by the number of samples per second, as well as the amount of information (or bit depth) in each of those samples. More bits equal more information. Many digital recorders and camcorders offer a choice between 12-bit and 16-bit audio; set your camcorder to the 16-bit audio setting whenever possible.

Conforming audio

When you first import audio into Adobe Premiere Elements — whether you're importing music from a CD or capturing audio and video from a DV tape — Premiere Elements *conforms* the audio to match the audio settings of your project. For example, when you start a new project in Premiere Elements, it always has an audio sample rate of 48 kHz (see Chapter 4 for more on starting a new project). But suppose you want to import audio from a music CD, which has a sample rate of 44.1 kHz. When you import that audio, Premiere Elements automatically converts the CD audio to 48 kHz (the sample rate of your project).

When you first import audio that doesn't conform to the project, Premiere Elements automatically starts creating conformed audio files. Conformed audio serves two important purposes:

  ✔ Audio quality remains consistent throughout your project.

  ✔ Conformed audio files are essentially rendered audio files, meaning that audio effects and other edits can be previewed in real time.

You may notice that some audio files won't play immediately after you import or capture them. That's because Premiere Elements isn't done conforming the audio. The process happens quickly, so you shouldn't have to wait long.

Conformed audio files are almost always huge, using up a lot of disk space. For example, when I recently imported a three-minute MP3 file, the resulting conformed audio file was 70MB, even though the original MP3 file was less than 3MB. If you're trying to clean up old files and recover some disk space, you may want to delete the conformed audio files left over from old, finished projects. Happily, if you decide to work on that project again later, Premiere Elements can automatically regenerate conformed audio files.

Making Better Audio Recordings

Recording great-quality audio is no simple matter. Professional recording studios spend thousands or even millions of dollars to set up acoustically superior sound rooms. You probably don't have that kind of budgetary firepower, but whether you're recording your sister's wedding or a YouTube documentary on the history of yodeling, you can get nearly pro-sounding results if you follow these basic tips:

✔ **Use an external microphone whenever possible.** The built-in microphones in modern camcorders have improved greatly in recent years, but they still aren't ideal. They often record undesired *ambient* (or background) sound near the camcorder, such as coughing or chatting audience members; some mics even pick up the mechanical whirring sounds from the camcorder's tape drive. If possible, connect an external microphone to the camcorder's mic input. Chapter 19 provides recommendations on finding a good-quality microphone.

✔ **Eliminate unwanted noise sources.** If you *must* use the camcorder's built-in mic, be aware of your movements and other possible causes of loud, distracting noises on tape. Problem items may include a loose lens cap banging around, your finger rubbing against the mic, wind blowing across the mic, and the *swish-swish* of those nylon workout pants you decided to put on this morning.

When you're recording audio in your studio (also known as your office), be aware of ambient noise. Subtle sounds like the cooling fans inside your computer, air rushing through heating ducts, and someone playing video games in the next room all create ambient noise that *will* show up on audio recordings. If you're using your computer to record narration, you won't be able to do much about the computer's fans, but if you have other computers in the room, you should shut those down.

Do not try to disable the cooling fans in your computer, not even for just a few minutes! Modern computer processors run so hot that they can be ruined in mere seconds if they aren't properly cooled.

✔ **Try to minimize sound reflection.** Audio waves reflect off any hard surface, which can cause echoing in a recording. Hanging blankets on walls and other hard surfaces is one way to significantly reduce reflection. If the floor isn't carpeted, cover it with blankets as well.

✔ **Obtain and use a high-quality microphone.** A good mic isn't cheap, but it can make a huge difference in recording quality. A high-quality mic may be worth the investment if your project necessitates it.

✔ **Watch for trip hazards.** In your haste to record great sound, don't forget that your microphone cables can become a hazard on scene. Not only are loose wires a safety hazard to anyone walking by, but if someone snags a cable, your equipment could be damaged as well. If necessary, bring along some gaffer tape (or duct tape) to temporarily cover cables that run across the floor.

Working with Audio in Your Movies

Premiere Elements offers two important tools to help you work with audio. These tools — accessible in the Window menu — include

✔ **Audio Meters:** Choose Window➪Audio Meters to open the meters, as shown in Figure 8-1. Audio Meters help you measure sound levels in your audio.

✔ **Audio Mixer:** Sometimes your movie will have multiple audio tracks. Besides the main audio that goes along with your video, you may add narration, background music, or additional layered audio/video tracks. To fine-tune which tracks are louder and which are less prominent, click Mix Audio on the Timeline or choose Window➪Audio Mixer. I show you how to use the Mixer later in this chapter.

I like to use a lot of different audio tracks in a project. If you like to use a lot of audio too, I suggest that you try to insert each new audio element on a different track. This trick gives you greater flexibility when you make adjustments to things such as volume. Different bits of audio get recorded at different levels, and you may find that one audio clip is too loud whereas another is not loud enough.

Figure 8-1: The Audio Mixer and Meters make audio work easy.

When you look at audio tracks in the Timeline, you'll notice a graph that visually illustrates the *waveform* of the audio track. The waveform shows two sets of waves (called *channels*) for stereo audio files. Waveforms are handy because large spikes show you where loud noises occur in audio tracks, whereas flat lines indicate quiet sections of audio.

Adjusting audio volume

When adjusting volume — also sometimes called *gain* — for an individual audio track, keep an eye on the audio meters. You can open the meters by choosing Window⇨Audio Meters. The volume of audio in movie projects is measured in *Volume Units* (VU), and the meters show you a VU measurement of audio. If the meters reach 0, you'll probably get audio distortion in the final program. If 0 is reached, the red indicator at the top of the VU meter lights up.

The audio meters in Premiere Elements may appear similar to the volume meters on a tape deck or other recording device you've used before. If you've ever recorded audio on an analog tape deck, you probably made sure that the audio levels got above 0 and into the red zone of the VU meter once in a while, but that the average volume stayed below 0. When you're working with digital audio, 0 is the maximum volume level you can have before distortion occurs. That's why if you look at the Audio Meters, you notice that the VU meter scales stop at 0.

Besides watching for audio peaks that are at or above 0, you should also keep an eye on the average audio levels. The VU meters dance up and down quite a bit as you play the project, and you should adjust volume so the average levels are between –12 and –18 on the VU meter.

When you adjust the volume of an audio clip, you can adjust the overall volume for the entire clip, or you can adjust specific segments throughout the clip. To adjust volume for a whole clip at once, follow these steps:

1. **Select the audio clip in the Timeline and choose Clip⇨Audio Options⇨Audio Gain.**

   The Clip Gain dialog box appears.

2. **Click-and-drag left on the dB number to reduce gain; click-and-drag right to increase gain.**

   Alternatively, click Normalize. Doing so automatically adjusts the gain to the highest possible level without creating distortion. To reset the clip to its original gain level, restore the gain value to 0 dB (decibels).

3. **Click OK to close the dialog box.**

In addition to adjusting the overall volume of an audio clip, you can also adjust volume at individual points within the clip. Here's how:

1. **Click an audio clip in the Timeline to select it.**

2. **Move the CTI to a spot in the Timeline where you want to start adjusting volume.**

3. **Click the Add/Remove Keyframe button.**

   A round keyframe appears along the yellow volume rubberband.

4. **Move the CTI to a new location in the clip, and click the Add/Remove Keyframe button again.**

   Repeat this step to create additional keyframes.

5. **Click-and-drag on keyframes to move the volume rubberband.**

   Moving the rubberband up increases volume, and moving it down decreases volume. In Figure 8-2, I have adjusted the volume rubberbands on two audio clips so that one fades out as the other fades in. The effect is barely noticeable to the listener and provides a seamless audio experience for the sequence. Also notice that audio waveforms appear on audio clips in the Timeline.

Figure 8-2:
Use volume rubberbands to dynamically adjust volume throughout a clip.

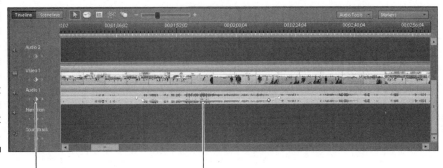

Add/Remove Keyframes   Click and drag rubberbands to adjust volume

If you adjust the volume rubberbands upward on any audio clips, make sure that you play the clip by using Audio Meters and keep an eye on the VU meters. If the audio levels exceed 0, you need to reduce volume a bit.

Setting audio In and Out points

When you first start putting a movie together, you begin by sorting through your captured video clips to decide which clips you want to use. For each clip, you also decide which portions of the clip you want to use. As I show in Chapter 6, you do this by setting In points and Out points for the clips.

Usually when you set an In point or Out point for a clip, you set them for both audio and video. However, you can set separate In points and Out points for audio and video. Why? Consider the video clip in Figure 8-3. In this clip, the subject throws a bowling ball down a bowling lane. My plan is to cut from this clip to the clip in Figure 8-4, which shows a ball traveling down the bowling lane and hitting some pins.

Figure 8-3:
This video clip will be shown first.

The audio portion of this bowling sequence presents an interesting editing challenge. I want the sequence to play the sound of one bowling ball rolling all the way down the lane and hitting the pins. To do this, I'm going to use the audio recorded with the clip in Figure 8-4 rather than the clip in Figure 8-3. This means that when I edit the clip in Figure 8-4 into the Timeline, I'm going to have to set separate In points for the audio and video. To set separate In points for audio and video, follow these steps:

1. **Open the clip with the desired audio in the Preview window.**

   Again, see Chapter 6 for more on opening clips in the Preview window and setting In points and Out points.

2. **Find the point where you want to start using the audio portion of the clip, and make sure that the CTI in the Preview window is stopped on that point.**

3. **Right-click the CTI and choose Set Clip Marker⇨Audio In.**

   An audio In point is set.

4. **Move the CTI to the spot where you want to start taking video.**

5. **Right-click the CTI and choose Set Clip Marker⇨Video In.**

   Separate In point markers for audio and video appear in the ruler, as shown in Figure 8-4.

6. **Repeat the above steps to set Out points for audio and video.**

To set the same In point or Out point for both audio and video, simply click the Set In or Set Out buttons at the bottom of the Preview window.

Figure 8-4:
This video clip contains the audio I will use in the whole sequence.

Unlinking audio and video in the Timeline

When you add a clip containing both audio and video to the Timeline, the audio and video tracks for that clip are usually linked together. This means that when you click the audio portion of a clip, you select both the audio *and* video portions. Usually this is a handy function, but sometimes you may want to unlink the two and edit them individually. For example, you may decide that you want to delete or ripple edit (see Chapter 7 for more on ripple edits) the audio portion of a clip, while leaving the video portion of the clip alone. To unlink audio and video for a clip, select that clip in the Timeline and choose Clip⇨Unlink Audio and Video. You can now select the audio and video portions of the clip individually.

A visual clue tells you which clips are linked and which ones are not: Linked clips have underlined names in the Timeline. The names of unlinked clips aren't underlined.

Mixing audio

When you bake chocolate chip cookies, you have to use just the right mixture of flour, butter, sugar, chocolate chips, and other ingredients. If you get the mix wrong, those cookies might not taste very good.

Similarly, if you don't get the audio mix *just right,* the end product will be unsatisfying. If your movie contains multiple audio tracks with narration, soundtrack music, and other sources, use the Premiere Elements Audio Mixer to make sure you're blending each track in the proper amounts.

Fortunately, the new SmartMix feature makes mixing audio tracks easier than ever. SmartMix analyzes your audio tracks and mixes the audio automatically so important sounds — such as narration — aren't drowned out by less critical sounds — such as soundtrack music. Follow these steps to use the Mixer:

1. **Choose Window➪Audio Mixer to open the Mixer.**

   You can also choose Audio Mixer from the Audio Tools menu on the Timeline.

2. **Position the Mixer so that you can see the Monitor and Timeline windows, as shown in Figure 8-5.**

3. **Click the arrow next to SmartMixer to expand the SmartMixer controls, as shown in Figure 8-5.**

4. **Choose whether each audio track should be in the Foreground, Background, or Disabled.**

   Foreground tracks have priority and are louder than Background tracks. Choose Disabled if you do not want SmartMix to disable a track.

5. **Click Apply in the SmartMixer.**

   SmartMix analyzes your audio tracks, making Foreground tracks louder and Background tracks softer when potential conflicts are detected. Audio keyframes (reference points for effects; see Chapter 12 for more on using keyframes) are automatically applied, as shown in Figure 8-5.

6. **Play the movie to hear the changes made by SmartMix.**

   If you're happy with the changes applied by SmartMix, you're done! Close the Mixer. But if you want to fine-tune the audio mix, or if you just prefer to do all your mixing manually, continue with the next steps.

7. **Place the CTI at the beginning of the section of your movie that you want to mix, and then click Play in the Monitor.**

   I recommend that you listen through the whole section first, and listen for which parts of the audio are too loud and which are too soft.

8. **Click-and-drag a slider up to increase the volume of a track, or down to decrease the volume.**

   Premiere Elements automatically creates audio keyframes in the audio track to adjust the track's volume dynamically while the Timeline plays.

   To avoid audio distortion, I recommend that you reduce the volume of tracks that you want to be less prominent rather than increase the volume of tracks that should be more prominent. Watch the audio level meters in the Mixer to ensure that audio levels aren't getting into the red portion of the scale. Red means distortion.

9. **Click Pause in the Monitor and close the Audio Mixer when you're done mixing audio.**

The Mixer also lets you adjust balance dynamically, which would be helpful in the unlikely scenario where you want to suppress or enhance a sound that is audible in one side of a stereo track but is not audible in the other side.

Adjustment sliders   Foreground tracks have priority

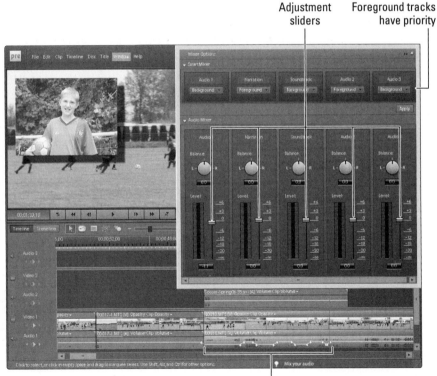

Figure 8-5:
Get the right audio mix.

Keyframes are created automatically

Narrating Your Movies

The great thing about video is that you can *show* people what happened, not just tell them about it. But sometimes you need to tell them about it too, and that's where narration comes in handy. Premiere Elements has a built-in recorder to help you quickly record narration. Here's how you use it:

1. **Plan your narration.**

   If your narration will consist of more than one sentence, write a script. Play the movie and practice your narration a few times before recording it to make sure that you have your timing perfected.

2. **Connect a microphone to your computer.**

   See Chapter 19 for microphone recommendations. If you have multiple microphones (for example, a built-in mic and an external mic), click the Mic Source button (it looks like a microphone) in the Narration dialog box and select the desired mic.

3. **Choose Add Narration in the Audio Tools menu on the Timeline.**

   The Record Voice Narration dialog box opens, as shown in Figure 8-6.

4. **In the Timeline, move the CTI to the beginning of the section you want to narrate.**

5. **Test your microphone to make sure it's working.**

   You should see the green audio meter in the Narration window move up and down as you talk.

6. **Decide whether you will mute the movie's audio while you record.**

   If you want to hear the movie's audio while you record narration, plug in some headphones and uncheck the "Mute audio while recording" check box. If you unmute audio and it plays through your computer's speakers while you record, your recording will be ruined by feedback.

7. **Click the Record button.**

   A three-second countdown begins, after which the movie starts to play. Speak to record your narration.

8. **Click Stop when you're done recording.**

   A new narration clip appears in the Narration track of the Timeline. If you aren't happy with the recording, click the Delete button (it looks like a trash can) and start again at Step 4.

Figure 8-6:
Narrating
your movies
is a snap!

Adding a Soundtrack

In the beginning there were silent movies. Of course, they weren't really silent because the theater almost always played music (live or recorded) to complement the mood and tempo of the movies. Even with the advent of *talkies* in the 1920s and '30s, soundtrack music has remained a crucial movie element. The next few sections show you how to automatically generate soundtrack music, using the SmartSound tool that comes free with Premiere Elements.

You don't have to use SmartSound for your soundtracks. You can also import and use songs in MP3, WMA, or other formats. See Chapter 5 for a list of compatible file types and instructions on how to import them. After you've imported an audio file into Premiere Elements, click-and-drag it to an audio track in the Timeline — you can use the Soundtrack track or any other open audio track if you want. Just keep in mind that music produced by others is protected by copyright law and should only be used for your personal enjoyment.

Generating a SmartSound soundtrack

You want to add some music to your movies, but you can't afford to hire John Williams and the London Symphony Orchestra to produce your soundtrack. Enter SmartSound, a tool that comes free with Adobe Premiere Elements. SmartSound automatically generates high-quality, royalty-free soundtrack music that almost perfectly matches the length of your movie.

To use SmartSound, edit your movie together and get it to a point where you consider it mainly finished. Then follow these steps:

1. **Decide how much time you want to fill with soundtrack music.**

   If you want the soundtrack to span your entire movie, make a note of the movie's length.

2. On the Timeline, choose Audio Tools⇨SmartSound.

3. Review and accept the SmartSound license agreement that appears, and then complete the registration information as requested.

4. In the SmartSound Quicktracks window that appears, click the Click Here to Select Music! option.

5. In the SmartSound Maestro window that appears, shown in Figure 8-7, choose a music style and review the music choices listed in that style.

   You can also filter the results by intensity.

6. Click a song in the list to review details about it on the right of the dialog box, as shown in Figure 8-7.

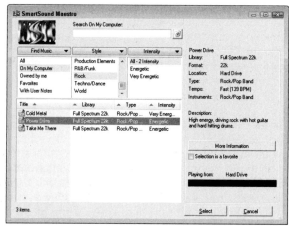

Figure 8-7:
SmartSound offers a wide variety of music styles.

7. Click the Select button in the lower right to select the song.

8. In the SmartSound dialog box (see Figure 8-8), enter the desired duration of the song in the Length field.

   The final song duration may not match exactly, but it should be close. The song may start to sound a little repetitive during long plays.

9. Click Play to preview the song.

10. Choose an option in the Variations menu to hear a slightly different variation of the song.

   If your soundtrack will be more than a few minutes long, try creating separate shorter versions of the song — but with different variations — to use in different parts of your movie.

11. **When you're happy with the song, click OK, and then name and save the new soundtrack file.**

    The new soundtrack song appears in the Soundtrack track of the Timeline. Click-and-drag the song left or right to move it to a new location in your movie.

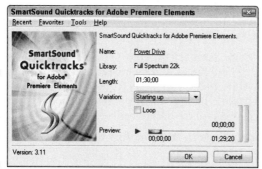

Figure 8-8:
Adjust the length of the soundtrack song.

Detecting audio beats

Dancers carefully choreograph their moves to synchronize with music beats. Video producers also often synchronize video edits to music beats, and Premiere Elements has a cool feature that automatically detects music beats to create "snap-to" markers in the Timeline. You can then use these markers to make Timeline edits in perfect time to the beat.

You can use beat detection with SmartSound soundtrack music, or with your own songs that you import into Premiere Elements. Follow these steps:

1. **Click an audio clip in the Timeline to select it.**

   The clip should contain the musical beats you want to detect.

2. **Choose Audio Tools⇨Detect Beats on the Timeline.**

3. **In the Beat Detection Settings dialog box that appears, adjust these settings:**

   • **Minimum time between beats:** The default time is two seconds. This is a pretty good default because two seconds may be about right for some short clips.

   • **Difference:** Premiere Elements detects beats by measuring differences in volume. Increasing the Difference setting means Premiere Elements looks for greater differences before creating markers.

- **Window:** Premiere looks at volume differences over a specific period of time. The default time is 100ms (milliseconds), which is one-tenth of a second. Increase the Window setting to make Premiere Elements analyze music over longer time periods.

Usually, it's best to just accept the default beat-detection settings. However, if you find that Premiere Elements creates too many markers to be useful, try increasing the Difference and Window settings so that Premiere Elements is more selective about what it thinks is a beat.

4. **Click OK to close the settings dialog box and begin detecting beats.**

When the detection process is complete, a bunch of musical notes appear along your Timeline, as shown in Figure 8-9. These notes are the beat markers. If there are too many (or not enough) beat markers, repeat Steps 2 and 3 and change the detection settings. When you redetect beats, previous beat markers are replaced.

5. **Click-and-drag edit points in the Timeline to match the beats.**

When you get close to a beat marker, the edit point snaps to the beat marker, as shown in Figure 8-9.

To get rid of an unwanted beat marker, right-click the offending marker and choose Clear Beat Marker from the menu that appears. You can also choose Clear All Beat Markers if you decide you don't want any beat markers.

Detected beats

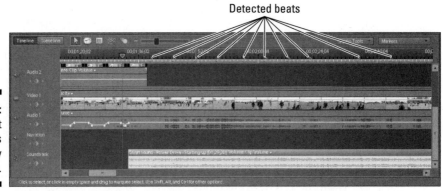

Figure 8-9:
Detect music beats to simplify your edits.

Using Audio Effects and Transitions

Adobe Premiere Elements comes with a valuable selection of audio effects and transitions. To access the list of audio effects, click the Edit tab and then click Effects. Video effects are shown by default (see Chapter 12 for more on working with video effects), so click the down arrow next to Video Effects and choose Audio Effects from the menu that appears. To view audio transitions, click Transitions on the Edit pane, click the arrow next to Video Transitions, and choose Video Transitions. (I show you how to use video transitions in Chapter 9.) The following sections describe audio effects and transitions available in Premiere Elements. I also show how to use the Dynamics effect.

Reviewing Premiere Elements audio effects

Premiere Elements comes with a good selection of audio effects that help you improve and modify audio clips. Some of these effects can make audio seem distorted or surreal; other effects help you repair audio problems. Audio effects offered in Premiere Elements include

- **Balance:** Controls balance between the left and right channels in a stereo clip.

- **Bass:** Provides control over bass response in the clip. Bass sounds are the deeper, low frequency sounds in an audio clip.

- **Channel Volume:** Allows you to control the volume of stereo channels independently.

- **Delay:** Echoes the clip. Echoes the clip.

- **DeNoiser:** Removes unwanted background noise during quiet parts of the clip. By removing audible pops and hisses, this effect works kind of like the Dolby noise reduction found on audio cassette tape players.

- **Dynamics:** A good one-stop tool for audio improvement. This effect helps reduce distortion and eliminate unwanted background noise. Use the AutoGate setting to set up a virtual gate that eliminates all sound below a specific volume, thus eliminating quiet background noise while keeping the louder sounds that you want to keep. I show how to use the Dynamics effect later in this chapter.

- **Fill Left:** Moves the audio completely to the left stereo channel.

- **Fill Right:** Moves the audio completely to the right stereo channel.

- **Highpass:** Removes lower frequencies from the audio clip.

- **Invert:** Inverts the audio phase (or delay) between the left and right audio channels in a stereo clip. For example, if the audio in the left channel is slightly delayed behind the right channel, the Invert effect inverts the phase so that the right channel (rather than the left) is delayed.

- ✔ **Lowpass:** Removes higher frequencies from the audio.

- ✔ **Notch:** Removes sound at a frequency you specify. Use this effect if the audio clip has a constant hum caused by a nearby power line or a flaw in the recording device.

- ✔ **PitchShifter:** Adjusts pitch in an audio clip. For example, if you speed up a clip and as a result the voices have an unnaturally high pitch, you can use this effect to make the voices sound more normal.

- ✔ **Reverb:** Makes the audio clip sound as if it's being played in a large hall or room.

- ✔ **Swap Channels:** Swaps the left and right stereo channels, if for some reason you decide that the sound in the right channel should be on the left, and vice versa.

- ✔ **Treble:** Provides control over treble (the higher frequency sounds) in the clip.

- ✔ **Volume:** Allows you to adjust volume with an effect rather than the Audio Mixer or the volume rubberbands.

A complete course on how to use each effect would take up nearly another whole book (each effect differs considerably from the others). Some general instructions are in order, however: To apply an audio effect to a clip, simply drag it from the Effects window and drop it onto your audio clip in the Timeline. Depending on which effect you chose, you can manipulate audio effect settings by using the Effect Controls window (right-click the clip in the Timeline and choose Show Properties from the menu that appears); you can also adjust the effect dynamically by using keyframes (see Chapter 12 for more on working with effect keyframes). Make sure a clip is selected in the Timeline if you want to view its controls in the Effect Controls window.

Using audio transitions

One of the most common reasons for adjusting volume on a clip (at least, in my experience) is to fade a clip in as it begins and fade it out as it ends. When done well, fading sound in and out is barely perceptible to the viewer. This fading — called *cross-fading* — takes a distinct "edge" off the transition as a loud noise gradually starts or stops. I like to apply audio transitions to fade between virtually all audio clips in a project, even though I usually don't use video transitions between every video clip.

The idea behind audio transitions is to make the audible transition between clips virtually imperceptible, and audio transitions can do that.

The process of fading in or out between clips has never been easier. Premiere Elements provides two audio transitions that you can apply to audio clips to quickly fade them in or out. If two clips are adjacent, the transition cross-fades the two clips. There are two Cross Fade transition effects available in Premiere Elements:

- ✔ **Constant Gain:** Audio fades in or out at a constant, linear level.
- ✔ **Constant Power:** Audio fades in a manner that sounds linear to the human ear, although from a purely mathematical standpoint, it is not linear.

I use the Constant Power transition most often, but you may want to experiment to get the best results for your projects. To apply a transition, simply drag and drop it from the Edit pane to the edge of a clip or a spot between clips. As you can see in Figure 8-10, audio transitions appear in the Timeline much like video transitions.

Video transition

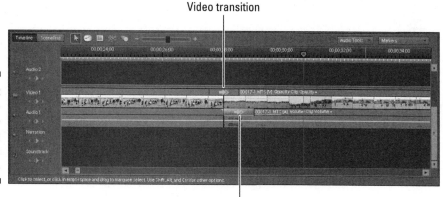

Figure 8-10:
Audio transitions make cross-fading audio a snap.

Audio transition

Fine-tuning audio dynamics

Your camcorder usually records audio along with video. This audio will be important to most of your movie projects, but unfortunately, you often don't have much control over ambient noise and other things that affect sound quality. For example, recently I shot video of my kids playing soccer. I want to keep the sounds of the game — kids kicking the ball, cheers from the crowd, whistles from the referee — but I want to eliminate the dull background noise coming from a nearby highway.

Dynamics effect to the rescue! The ambient sound I want to eliminate is relatively constant but quiet. The Dynamics effect helps eliminate unwanted noise while enhancing the quality of the audio that remains. To use the Dynamics effect, follow these steps:

1. **Open the Effects window if it isn't already open (click Effects on the Edit pane, and then choose Audio Effects).**

2. **Click-and-drag the Dynamics effect from the Effects window and drop it on the audio clip in the Timeline that you want to adjust.**

3. **Right-click the clip in the Timeline to select it, and then choose Show Properties in the menu that appears.**

4. **In the clip properties that appear on the Edit pane, click the arrow next to Dynamics to expand the controls for the Dynamics effect, and then click the arrow next to Custom Setup.**

5. **Use the Monitor to play the clip and listen for audio problems that you want to fix.**

   Use the J, K, and L keys on your keyboard to control playback. The J key plays the Timeline in reverse, K pauses playback, and L plays forward.

6. **To eliminate quieter background noise, place a check mark next to AutoGate (as shown in Figure 8-11) and fine-tune AutoGate settings.**

   Click-and-drag left or right on the adjuster knobs to modify the AutoGate settings. Constantly play the clip backward and forward as you make adjustments to see how your adjustments affect the sound.

7. **Use the Compressor to increase quieter sounds and/or decrease louder sounds.**

   The Compressor is sort of the opposite of the AutoGate, so you'll usually use one or the other. Again, experiment to get the desired sound.

8. **Use the Expander to increase the difference between soft and loud sounds.**

   The Expander is sort of like the AutoGate, but it softens rather than eliminates quiet background noises. Use the Expander if you find that AutoGate is too harsh.

9. **Use the Limiter to get rid of distortion or soften loud noises.**

   Really loud noises may become distorted (or just plain annoying). The Limiter limits the maximum volume of a clip, so it softens the loudest noises without affecting quieter sounds. In my soccer game video, I used the Limiter to soften the cheers of spectators who were close to the camera, while maintaining game sounds at their regular level.

10. **Click Done when you're finished fine-tuning your clip's audio dynamics.**

Figure 8-11:
Use the
Dynamics
effect to
fine-tune
your audio.

Part III
Special Touches and Advanced Techniques

The 5th Wave   By Rich Tennant

"Mary-Jo, come here quick! Look at this special effect I learned with the new Premiere Elements software."

In this part . . .

Virtually all affordable video-editing programs can do the things described in Part II of *Premiere Elements 8 For Dummies*. Most programs can easily capture video and edit them into a basic movie. (Of course, Premiere Elements does all that with a lot more finesse than the other programs. . . .)

Part III explores the features of Adobe Premiere Elements that *truly* set this program apart from other programs. In this part, I show how to improve the light and color in your video images, add special effects, perform advanced animation and video image compositing, and add titles.

Chapter 9

Using Video Transitions

Anyone with a DVD recorder and a cable can dub desirable bits of video from a camcorder to disc. This is movie editing at its most basic; it's also inefficient and crude. By using a program like Adobe Premiere Elements, you can fine-tune your edits frame by frame, apply your own musical soundtrack, dub in narration, and add special effects.

In previous chapters I show you how to capture video onto your computer's hard drive, sort through clips, pick out the parts you want to use, and assemble those clips in the Timeline. If you've done those things, you're ready for the next step in your video-editing adventure: dressing up your project with transitions between scenes. You can use Premiere Elements to add transitions that fade in or out, pull open like a stage curtain, spiral down into a vortex, and more. Transitions provide visual breaks between scenes that help the viewer understand changes in the movie's setting or mood. This chapter shows you how to choose, apply, and customize transitions.

Checking Out the Transitions Library

One of the trickiest aspects of movie editing (for me, anyway) is making clean transitions between clips. Sometimes the best transition is no transition at all, but a simple, straight cut from one clip to the next. Other times you need a fancy transition, say, one that rotates the old clip into a vortex — spinning, spinning toward the center until it's a tiny black dot in the middle of the screen — and then it disappears entirely. Most of your transitions probably fall somewhere in between.

Adobe Premiere Elements comes with more than 100 unique video transitions that you can use in your projects. These transitions are subdivided into 16 categories and range from simple dissolves to complex 3D motion effects. The following sections describe the transitions in each category. To find these categories, click the Edit tab, and then click Transitions (or choose Window➪Transitions). Use the category menu (see Figure 9-1) to view a category of transitions, or choose Show All and scroll down the list to see all the available transitions. The transition categories include

✔ **3D Motion:** This category consists of ten transitions that apply various kinds of three-dimensional motion to one clip as it disappears to reveal the next one. Most of the transitions here involve getting the exiting clip to swing like a door or spin in a spiral. Figure 9-1 shows the Doors transition, where the incoming clip appears to close in from either side like a pair of doors.

Choose Show All or a category

Figure 9-1: Premiere Elements offers more than 100 video transitions.

Mouse over a transition to preview

✔ **Dissolves:** My favorite transition, the Cross Dissolve, can be found in the Dissolve category. It's my favorite not because it is fancy but because it's *not*. The Cross Dissolve is subtle; one clip blends smoothly into the next. It's softer than a straight cut — and if I want the program to be about what's in the clips (and not about fancy transitions), this is the one I choose. You'll notice that Cross Dissolve is also the most common transition used in professional video products as well. Cross Dissolve is just one of seven Dissolve transitions available with Premiere Elements.

✔ **GPU Transitions:** If your computer has a powerful dedicated video card as I recommend in Chapter 2, you can use the five GPU transitions offered by Premiere Elements. These transitions leverage the graphics processing unit (GPU) in your video card to display advanced visual effects. Figure 9-2 shows the Sphere GPU transition, which wraps the outgoing clip around a 3D sphere that then rolls off the screen.

✔ **Iris:** The seven Iris transitions are all variations on a theme of one clip starting as a point in the middle and growing to fill the screen. Different Iris patterns include circles, squares, stars, diamonds (I know, it's starting to sound like a breakfast cereal!), and more. Like many transitions, Iris transitions can be customized by changing the shape and quantity of irises in the transition.

✔ **Map:** The Channel and Luminance Map transitions can be customized to use colors from incoming and outgoing clips to create interesting blended images. The Map transitions work best when you heavily customize their settings. (I show how to customize transitions later in this chapter.)

Figure 9-2: Sphere is an advanced GPU transition.

✔ **NewBlue transitions:** The four NewBlue categories contain a total of 29 snazzy transitions from NewBlueFX, a third-party developer of transitions and plug-ins for Premiere Elements and other editing programs. If you want a highly individualized movie, check out some of the NewBlue transitions such as Magic Carpet, Bouncing Cubes, or Wave.

✔ **Page Peels:** The five Page Peel transitions simulate the turning of a page or opening of a book. Use these to make the transition from your "Once upon a time . . . " screen to the story!

✔ **Picture Wipes:** This category contains three specialized transitions called Stars, Travel, and Wedding. These transitions incorporate themed graphics.

✔ **Slides:** The Slide category is a descriptively named group that contains 12 transitions. All the transitions in this group are variations on sliding a clip one way or the other. These subtle transitions are also among my favorites. Slide transitions are similar to Wipe transitions, which I describe later.

✔ **Special Effects:** The Special Effects category contains six advanced and varied transitions that apply various combinations of color masks and distortions while moving from one clip to the next.

✔ **Stretches:** The five transitions found in the Stretch category are pretty cool, even though technically some of them *squeeze* rather than stretch the clip image during transition. In Figure 9-3, the outgoing image is squeezed down a funnel, using the Funnel transition.

✔ **Wipes:** Wipe style transitions have been around for a while: One clip appears from the edge of the screen and appears to wipe over the preceding clip like a squeegee. Wipe transitions differ from Slide transitions, because in a wipe the outgoing image remains static while the incoming image wipes over it. In Slide transitions, the incoming image slides in while the outgoing image slides out. Premiere Elements includes no less than 17 Wipe transitions.

Figure 9-3:
The Funnel transition squeezes the outgoing image down a funnel.

✔ **Zooms:** There are four Zoom transitions, and as you would imagine, they all simulate different camera zooms. An outgoing transition can zoom out into the distance where it disappears, or the camera may appear to zoom in on the incoming clip.

When automakers choose paint color names, they tend to go crazy. What you and I might call *Pink* becomes *Moulin Rouge* or *Indian Ceramic* in car brochures. Fortunately, Adobe Elements keeps things simple by assigning descriptive names to video transitions. *Slides* slide, *wipes* wipe, and *zooms* … well, you get the idea. Still, if you aren't exactly sure what *Iris Diamond* does, hold your mouse pointer over the transition. The transition's icon plays a small preview of the transition so you can easily see what it does.

Using Transitions Effectively

With so many unique transitions to choose from, selecting just the right one can be challenging. When you consider that most transitions can also be fine-tuned and customized, the endless possibilities may have already started your head spinning. So how do you choose? Because video production is such a creative and personal endeavor, I couldn't possibly recommend a perfect transition for every situation. I do, however, have a few basic transition rules to follow as you develop your own editing style:

✔ **Use transitions sparingly.** You don't need to apply a transition between every single clip in your Timeline. That's too much. I try to save transitions for changes of scene. Simple changes to the camera angle or position in the same scene (for example) usually don't warrant a transition. Watch a typical feature-length movie and you'll probably see just a small handful of simple transitions, even though the movie may be a couple of hours long.

✔ **Keep 'em short.** Later in this chapter, I show you how to control the length of a transition. Most transitions should be short in duration, usually one second or less.

✔ **It's all about the pictures.** Editing can help shape the mood and flow of a movie, but ultimately the focus of your project is the video content. The desire to show off your editing skills with fancy transitions can be tempting — but generally speaking, transitions should complement and enhance the video images, *not* overpower them.

Thinking of the mood you want to set may help you narrow down your transition choices. For example, you want to avoid transmogrifying the scene with a high-tech Distortion transition if you're editing a movie that celebrates your grandparents' golden wedding anniversary. Remember, ultimately the movie is about your grandparents, not your incredible movie-editing abilities.

> ✔ **Follow your inspiration.** You should be familiar with the various transition styles that are available in Premiere Elements, even the ones you seldom, if ever, use. In a moment of late-night, caffeine-induced inspiration, it might come to you: "*This* is the spot for that fancy, spinning, 3D transition!"

Premiere Elements also offers a couple of audio transitions. In this chapter, I talk mainly about video transitions, so for more on working with audio transitions, slide, peel, or dissolve your way over to Chapter 8.

Incorporating Transitions into Your Movies

The tricky part of adding transitions to a movie project in Adobe Premiere Elements, in my opinion, is choosing a transition that looks good without detracting from the overall flow of the project. In the preceding section, I talk about choosing an effective transition. In this section, I show you how to actually put some transitions to use.

Finding transitions to use

If you're new to video, you may be surprised by how many different transitions are possible between two clips. As I mention previously in this chapter, Adobe Premiere Elements comes with more than 100 built-in transitions, and you can add even more through third-party plug-ins.

Premiere Elements stores all its transitions under the Edit tab of the Task pane. Click the Edit tab, and then click Transitions, or choose Window⇨Transitions. A list of transitions appears (refer to Figure 9-1). Transitions are divvied up into 16 subcategories, which I describe earlier in this chapter.

Applying a transition

The software designers at Adobe must really like drag-and-drop because, as with so many other editing actions in Premiere Elements, drag-and-drop is the best way to apply a transition. Simply choose a transition and drag it from the Edit pane to the desired spot on the Timeline, as shown in Figure 9-4.

Drag transition from here . . .

Drop transition here.

Figure 9-4:
Drop
transitions
between
video clips
in the
Timeline.

When you add a transition to the Timeline, the In and Out points of adjacent clips are automatically extended to facilitate the transition. Thus, each clip needs some unused frames that were trimmed off when you edited the clip into the Timeline. For example, if a transition lasts one second, the preceding clip must have at least a half-second of trailing material, and the following clip must have a half-second of leading material. Keep this in mind when you set In and Out points as you edit clips into the Timeline (see Chapter 6 for more on setting In and Out points).

If the clips lack sufficient leading or trailing material, you are somewhat limited in how you can position the transition. The default method in Premiere Elements is to drop it so that the transition evenly overlaps both adjacent clips, as shown in Figure 9-5. In the figure, the transition is 30 frames long, which means that 15 frames are added onto the end of the outgoing clip and 15 frames are added to the beginning of the incoming clip.

Transition

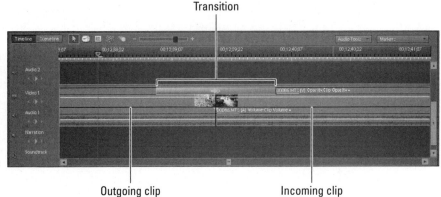

Figure 9-5:
Transitions
usually
overlap both
adjacent
clips.

Outgoing clip   Incoming clip

If neither clip has enough material, Premiere Elements won't let you drop the transition right on the edit line — your Timeline won't look neat and pretty like Figures 9-4 and 9-5. Instead, Premiere Elements may only allow you to drop the transition entirely on one clip or the other. You may even see a warning message advising you that some frames will be repeated.

If you find yourself in a situation in which you have too little media to accommodate a transition, you have a couple of options:

✔ **Skip using a transition at this point in your movie.** Maybe this problem is a sign that you don't really need a transition.

✔ **Shorten the length of the transition.** If the clips have *some* leading and trailing material, but not quite enough for the current transition length, you might be able to make the transition work if you make it shorter. I show you how to adjust transition duration later in this chapter.

✔ **Shorten the length of the clip(s).** Choose the Selection tool in the Timeline (see Chapter 7 for more on ripple edits) and drag the edges of the leading and trailing clips until you've trimmed about half a second from each clip. Because a ripple edit basically trims material off the clip and changes the In and Out points, this should create enough leading and trailing time to facilitate the transition.

If you want to apply a transition between two clips, those clips must be in the same Timeline track. Fortunately, Adobe Premiere Elements allows you to use transitions in any video track. Many other consumer-oriented video-editing programs allow you to use transitions in only one track.

Fine-tuning transitions

More often than not, you just plop a transition down on the Timeline and use it as it sits. Sometimes, however, you may want to fine-tune the transition.

You can change the length of a transition by clicking-and-dragging on either side of the transition. For example, you can shorten the duration of a transition to speed it up, or lengthen the transition if you want it to occur more gradually. To change the duration of a transition, first click the Selection tool in the upper-left corner of the Timeline (the Selection tool looks like a single large arrow), and then click-and-drag one side of a transition to lengthen or shorten it.

You can also modify the duration of a clip by using the Edit tab. After you apply a transition, double-click the transition in the Timeline to open transition controls, as shown in Figure 9-6. You can also open the transition controls by clicking the transition once to select it, and then choosing Window⇔Properties.

The default duration for most clips is one second, but you can make the transition as short or long as your source clips and common sense allow. To adjust the duration of a transition using the Edit tab, enter a new number in the Duration field. You can also click-and-drag left or right on the Duration field to adjust the time. In Figure 9-7, I have changed the duration of the transition to 25 frames, which is a little less than one second in NTSC video.

Transition duration   Show Timeline

Figure 9-6:
Use the Edit tab to fine-tune your transitions.

Select transition to edit.

Outgoing clip

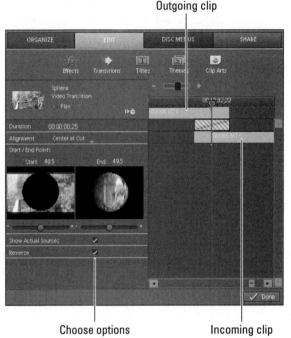

Figure 9-7:
Transition
controls
vary
depending
on the type
of transition.

Choose options   Incoming clip

Figure 9-7 shows a number of different controls in the Effect Controls window. Some key settings and features include

- ✔ **Split-track Timeline:** Click the Show Timeline button in the Edit pane (refer to Figure 9-6) to reveal a small Timeline window showing just the current transition. If you've used older versions of Adobe Premiere, you may notice that this looks similar to the split-track Timeline that was used in the old A/B Editing workspace, found in Adobe Premiere 6.5 and earlier.

  The split-track Timeline shown in Figure 9-7 is useful because it shows how much leading and trailing material is available for each clip. You can roll-edit the transition in this Timeline by dragging it back and forth.

- ✔ **Alignment:** Use the Alignment menu under the Duration field to control alignment of the transition. By default, a transition uses the Center at Cut setting, but you can also make the transition start or end at the location of the original cut between clips if you want to change the starting or ending frames of the transition.

- ✔ **Preview window:** Click the Play button above the preview window in the upper-left corner to see a visual representation of the transition. Some transitions, such as slides or wipes, allow you to change direction — simply click the arrows around the edges of the preview window to change the transition's direction. Some transitions have arrows around the preview window because they are directional transitions. Click an arrow to change the transition's direction.

✔ **Start/End controls:** The Start and End boxes represent the outgoing clip (Start) and the incoming clip (End). Use the slider controls underneath these boxes to change where the transition starts or ends.

✔ **Show Actual Sources:** If the Start and End boxes aren't clear enough for accurate editing, deselect this option to replace the clip thumbnails with a giant "A" (for the outgoing clip) and "B" (for the incoming clip).

✔ **Reverse:** Enabling the Reverse option can reverse the direction of many transitions.

✔ **Other options:** Some transitions have additional options which will be listed under Reverse. Some common options include borders and edge smoothing (called *anti-aliasing*). Experiment with other options to customize the appearance and function of your transitions.

More than 100 transitions come with Premiere Elements, all with different settings to adjust, so your Effect Controls window may not look exactly like Figures 9-6 or 9-7. Play around a bit to find the transitions and combinations of settings that work best for you!

Some transition options allow you to specify a color for transition elements (such as borders). To choose a color, click the color swatch to open the Color Picker window. When you choose a color in the Color Picker, watch out for a yellow triangle with an exclamation point in the upper-right corner of the window. If you see the warning icon, it means that the color you chose won't appear properly on video equipment in your area (NTSC or PAL). In that case, your best option is to choose a different color.

Changing the default transition

Premiere Elements knows that a lot of people have one type of transition that they use most of the time. It just so happens that the transition I use most often — the Cross Dissolve — is also the default transition in Premiere Elements. But if you want to set yourself apart from the crowd, you may want to change the default transition in Premiere Elements.

Setting the default transition comes in handy when you use Premiere Elements to create slideshows from still photos. (I describe how to create a slideshow in Chapter 17.) If the Cross Dissolve is not your favorite transition, I won't hold it against you. In fact, I'm even willing to show you how to change the default to *your* favorite transition. To set a new default transition, follow these steps:

1. **Open the Edit tab, and then click Transitions.**

   Alternatively, choose Window⇨Transitions. The list of transitions appears. The current default transition has a gray border around it.

2. **Locate the transition that you want to use as your default transition.**

3. **Right-click the transition and then choose Set Selected as Default Transition in the menu that appears, as shown in Figure 9-8.**

   Your new default transition should now have a gray border around it.

You can also change the default duration for transitions. Choose Edit⇨Preferences⇨General. Enter a new value next to Video Transition Default Duration. The default duration for video transitions is one second (30 frames for NTSC video, 25 frames for PAL), but you can change it to any length you want. This default duration applies to all transitions, not just the default transition.

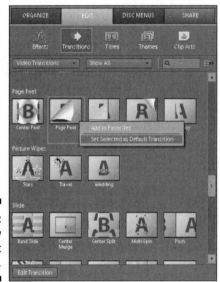

Figure 9-8:
Set a new default transition.

Chapter 10

Improving and Repairing Video Images

Anyone who has used a camera — be it a still camera or a camcorder — has probably learned some hard lessons about light and color. A scene that looks brilliant to human eyes often turns out dull and imperfect when it's photographed. You've probably experienced this before; pictures you take are too dark, colors look weird, or brilliant colors get washed out by bright sunlight. Managing light and color is one of the trickiest aspects of photography and videography.

When you shoot video, you can take advantage of the available light and color by using tips and techniques that I suggest in Chapters 3 and 18. But no matter how hard you try to follow the rules of photography and videography, you're going to wind up with video clips that appear less than perfect when you view them on a TV screen or computer. Don't feel bad — it happens to the best of us. Even when I shoot professional video with broadcast-quality cameras under controlled studio lighting, I still spend a fair amount of time post-processing my videos. *Post-processing* is just a fancy way of saying that I use special tools in Adobe Premiere (Pro or Elements) to clean up the final appearance of colors and light in my movies. This chapter shows you how to use the color-correction tools in Premiere Elements to improve the quality of your video images. I also show you how to stabilize shaky video footage by using the Stabilizer effect.

Understanding How Video Color Works

Remember back in the old days when many personal computers used regular televisions for monitors? In the early 1980s I had a Commodore 64 hooked up to a 13-inch color television set. As PC monitor technology improved, the notion of connecting computers to TVs fell out of vogue. Modern computer monitors offer incredibly high resolution and color accuracy compared to most televisions, even digital high-def TVs.

After decades of high-quality PC monitors, people are once again connecting their computers to TVs. Many new HDTVs have VGA and DVI inputs, allowing easy PC connections. This makes sense for media center PCs used for playing photos, music, and Internet media on a home theater, but for video editing and other traditional PC tasks, it isn't a good idea. Even the most expensive 1080p TVs deliver inferior resolution, brightness, and color accuracy compared to modern computer monitors. This means that you shouldn't use a TV as your computer's primary monitor. But it's also why using a TV as a second preview monitor is important for movies destined for TV viewing; images that look great on your PC monitor may have color issues on a TV.

Another big difference between computer monitors and TVs is the way they render color. Computer monitors utilize what is called the *RGB color space.* RGB stands for *red-green-blue,* meaning that all the colors you see on a computer monitor are combined by blending those three colors. Digital TVs, on the other hand, use the *YCbCr color space.* YCbCr stands for *luminance, chrominance (blue), and chrominance (red).* Analog TVs use the YUV *(luminance-chrominance)* color space. This tells you two things:

- ✔ Y = luminance? Whoever's in charge of video acronyms can't spell.
- ✔ Brightness in video displays is treated as a separate component from color. *Luminance* is basically just a fancy word for *brightness,* and *chrominance* means *color* in non-techie speak.

I could go on for pages describing the technicalities of the YCbCr color space, but there are really two important things you need to know about color:

- ✔ **Some RGB colors may not show up properly on TVs.** This is an issue mainly when you try to use JPEGs or other computer-generated graphics in a video project, or when you adjust the colors of a video image by using effects and color settings in your video-editing program. The RGB and YCbCr color spaces are fairly similar, but some RGB colors definitely won't appear properly on YUV monitors. RGB colors that don't translate perfectly to YUV are often said to be *illegal* or *out of gamut.* You won't get arrested for trying to use them, but they will not look right.

Generally speaking, illegal colors are ones with RGB values below 20 or above 230. Graphics programs can usually tell you RGB values for the colors in your images. Some graphics programs (including Adobe Photoshop and Photoshop Elements) even have special filters that help you filter out "illegal" TV colors from your images. In Photoshop Elements, open your image and choose Filter➪Video➪NTSC Colors to remove out-of-gamut colors from the image.

✔ **Video colors won't look exactly right when you view them on a computer monitor.** Because you'll probably do most of your video editing while looking at a computer monitor, you won't necessarily see the same colors that appear when the video is viewed on a TV. In other words, as you use the video filters in Premiere Elements to adjust colors, keep in mind that the changes you see on your computer screen don't necessarily reflect how the video will look when you output it to DVD. If possible, connect an external video monitor to your computer, as I describe in Chapter 19. Using an external video monitor allows you to more properly preview the final colors of your video.

Correcting Video Color

Correcting and changing colors in video is much more of an art than a science. Every video camera has unique characteristics, every scene is lit differently, and every project has special color needs. I guess this is my way of saying that you won't find a magic formula here to help you make each and every video clip look perfect. When you want to adjust video colors, trial-and-error is an inevitable part of the process. But the following sections can help you start using the color and lighting effects available in Adobe Premiere Elements.

Surveying color and light effects in Premiere Elements

Most consumer-oriented video-editing programs now enable you to adjust color and lighting in video clips. Usually such a tool chest consists of a few slider or dial controls that mimic the adjustment knobs on old TVs, with controls for color, tint, brightness, and contrast. Adobe Premiere Elements goes above and beyond with a collection of advanced color and lighting effects that give you capabilities formerly found only in expensive, professional-grade programs.

To view the selection of effects that Premiere Elements offers up, choose Window➪Effects, or click the Effects button under the Edit tab. Video Effects are divided into 19 categories, and you can scroll down the list of effects on the Edit pane to view the entire selection. You can find the effects that come in handy for fixing light and color in the Adjust and Image Control categories. The Adjust effects that will help your video images include

- ✔ **Auto Color:** This effect quickly adjusts color and contrast by limiting the range of blacks and whites in the image based upon its midtones. Use this effect to quickly improve color in high-contrast images.

- ✔ **Auto Contrast:** This effect adjusts contrast without changing the overall color cast of the image. If you don't like what Auto Color does to the colors in your video image, try Auto Contrast instead.

- ✔ **Auto Levels:** This effect adjusts all color levels to soften shadows and highlights, but it can change the overall color cast of the image. This is my favorite effect for making subtle color and light corrections to my video images.

- ✔ **Brightness and Contrast:** This effect does exactly what the name implies. If you just want to adjust the brightness or contrast of a clip, this effect can do the job.

Before you choose the Brightness and Contrast effect, you may want to experiment with the Auto Levels, Shadow/Highlight, and Color Balance (HLS) effects. Those effects can also fix brightness and contrast problems, often with more favorable results.

- ✔ **Channel Mixer:** This effect dynamically mixes color channels in the image, and is most useful when converting an image to a black-and-white or sepia-tone look. In Chapter 17, I show how to make new video look like old-fashioned film using the Channel Mixer effect.

- ✔ **Image Control:** You can manually adjust the brightness, contrast, hue, and saturation of any video clip in Premiere Elements, but the Image Control effect makes these adjustments automatically. This is a good catchall effect to use if you want to improve video images in a hurry.

- ✔ **Shadow/Highlight:** Use this effect to improve the appearance of heavily shadowed subjects, or to soften extreme highlights in the image. Use this effect if you find that the Auto Levels effect unfavorably changes the color cast in the image.

The Adjust category also includes two gimmicky effects: Lighting Effects and Posterize. These two effects stylize the appearance of video images, but ignore those for now because they don't do true image correction.

In the Image Control category, check out these effects:

- ✔ **Black & White:** This effect removes color from your video image and turns it to grayscale. Technically you could call this effect gimmicky, but it is useful for dream or flashback sequences. Alternatively, you may want to try desaturating the colors by using the Channel Mixer effect.

- ✔ **Color Balance (HSL):** This effect allows you to adjust hue, saturation, and lightness in the image. It is similar to the Hue/Saturation controls in Adobe Photoshop and Photoshop Elements.

- ✔ **Color Balance (RGB):** You can make direct changes to the levels of red, green, and blue in the image by using this effect.

- ✔ **Color Match:** This is one of the most powerful effects in Premiere Elements, and can match colors between video clips. I show how to use the Color Match effect later in this chapter.

- ✔ **Color Pass:** This effect removes all but one color from a video image. Use this effect to place special emphasis on a particular object by making everything except that object grayscale. The Color Pass effect works best if the object contrasts strongly with the background. Say you have footage of a red balloon against a blue wall: Turn everything else grayscale to make the red balloon burst with color.

- ✔ **Color Replace:** Use this effect to replace one color in a video image with another.

- ✔ **Gamma Correction:** This effect adjusts the brightness of midtones in an image without affecting shadows or highlights. I show how to use the Gamma Correction effect in the following section.

- ✔ **Tint:** This effect modifies only the color tint of the image. Use this to change the overall color cast of the image.

Making color adjustments

In the preceding section I list the various effects you can use in Premiere Elements to fix and repair color and lighting in your video images. In all, you will find at least 15 different effects to use, each with varying degrees of utility. Instead of explaining how to use them all, this section focuses on two effects that, in my opinion, are most likely to yield good results with the least amount of fiddling. You might experiment with other effects and find that they work quite well for you. But if you are new to color correction, the following two sections will help you get started.

As you correct colors and light, keep in mind that sometimes less is more. I don't mean less light, but rather less *editing*. Color correction should be done sparingly, or else colors can start to look artificial and cartoonish. Fortunately, Premiere Elements encourages creative experimentation because color corrections and other edits don't make permanent changes to your video clips. If you don't like your changes, simply delete the offending color effect from the clip, or use the Premiere Elements History palette (Window⇨History) to step back in time and undo your edits.

The following sections show how to apply color and light changes to an entire video clip. However, you can also apply changes to only portions of a clip, or have your changes vary as the clip plays. If you don't want to apply your adjustments to the whole video, you must use *effect keyframes*. I show how to use effect keyframes in Chapter 12.

Improving color and light with Auto Levels

When people are new to color correction, a common mistake is to assume that dull, lifeless images need more color saturation or adjustments to specific color channels. More often than not, a hazy or muddy-looking video image can be brought to life by simply tweaking the *levels* of the image.

When talking about images — be they video or still — the term *levels* refers to the amounts of blacks, whites, and midtones in the image. This is called the *tonal range* of the image. The best-looking pictures have a balanced tonal range that includes both true blacks and true whites.

Many video images lack proper tonal range. The problem can be subtle, and is often imperceptible to the untrained eye. But once levels are tweaked and the tonal range is improved, almost anyone can see an immediate improvement. To fine-tune the levels of your video images, follow these steps:

1. **Locate a clip you want to improve, and place the CTI on a representative frame so that it's displayed in the Monitor.**

2. **On the Task pane, click the Edit tab and then choose Effects.**

3. **Under Adjust, click-and-drag the Auto Levels effect and drop it on the clip in the Timeline that you want to adjust.**

   After you drop the effect, the clip is selected in the Timeline. Auto Levels automatically evaluates the clip and applies subtle levels adjustments. You may decide that you like the automatic adjustments, in which case, you can stop right here. But if you want to make your own fine adjustments, proceed with the following steps.

4. **At the bottom of the Edit pane, click the Edit Effects button.**

   Alternatively, choose Window⇨Properties. Clip properties and controls appear in the Edit pane.

5. **Locate Auto Levels in the list of clip controls, and then click the arrow to the left of Auto Levels.**

   The Auto Levels controls expand, as shown in Figure 10-1.

6. **Click-and-drag the Black Clip and White Clip sliders left and right to make adjustments.**

   Note how your changes affect the video image in the Monitor. Be subtle! Remember that video images may look different when they're viewed on a TV or compressed for Internet viewing. Images that look richly colored on your PC monitor may be too dark when viewed elsewhere.

7. **Preview the entire clip in the Monitor window.**

   Do your changes look okay across the entire clip? In some cases, automatic level corrections can fluctuate wildly throughout a clip, causing an unpleasant color-strobing appearance. If you see rapid fluctuations, increase the Blend With Original setting until the strobing is eliminated.

8. **Choose Done at the bottom of the Edit tab when you finish making changes.**

   Remember, err on the side of making only minor, subtle levels adjustments.

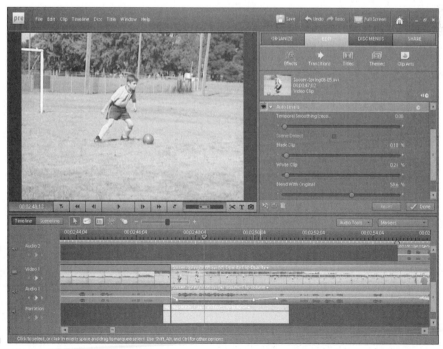

Figure 10-1: Adjust levels to improve tonal range.

Reading histograms

Ask anyone who has ever made a PowerPoint presentation: Graphs are cool. If "Sales are up" sounds like good news, it looks like even better news when you say it with a graph.

Recently, some genius realized that even photos and video images can be represented by graphs. An *image histogram* charts the tonal range of the image. The *tonal range* describes the relative levels of blacks, whites, and midtones in the picture. The figure below shows what a histogram looks like in Photoshop. Advanced digital still cameras — and even some video cameras — can also display histograms.

Histograms can be displayed in Photoshop and Premiere Pro. Premiere Elements doesn't display histograms, but it's still good to understand what histograms illustrate. Darker light values are represented toward the left of the histogram, and lighter values are toward the right. Midtones are shown in the middle.

The histogram shown here is for an image with a relatively even tonal distribution, but notice the lack of values near the black end of the scale. An image that looks hazy and dull often lacks true black values, like this one, and increasing the Black Clip level in Premiere Elements can reduce the hazy appearance and improve the overall quality of the image.

Levels adjustments are tricky if you can't view a histogram. If you need to make more precise levels adjustments of your video, you'll need to step up to a more advanced video-editing program like Premiere Pro.

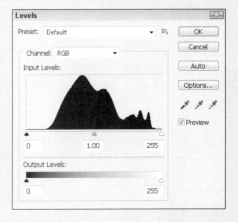

The Auto Levels effect won't fix images that are badly over- or under-exposed, but it can improve most clips that fall somewhere in between. I perform levels adjustments on almost every video clip I shoot because they're easy to make and provide obvious results.

Effects can be copied from one clip to another. This is handy with the Auto Levels effect because it helps you maintain an even light and color appearance across the entire project. When you're done making adjustments, click the effect's name in the clip properties window and press Ctrl+C to copy the effect. Select another clip in the Timeline, and then press Ctrl+V to paste the effect to the other clip. Repeat for other clips as needed.

Fixing poor exposure with Gamma Correction

In the preceding section, I explain how the Auto Levels effect can improve the tonal range of any image. For images with basically good exposure — not too dark, not too bright — Auto Levels is the best effect to use. But if you have more problematic images, you may want to try Gamma Correction instead.

Consider the image in Figure 10-2, where the subject has just stepped out of a dark cave into sunlight. When the subject steps into the sun, his face becomes too bright and detail washes out of the image. This is not an example of exceptional videography, but it is the kind of thing that inevitably happens when you shoot your own video, especially outside, where you have almost no control over lighting.

Figure 10-2:
This clip presents a tough lighting situation.

To improve the detail and appearance of the dark cave walls in the background, you could simply increase brightness of the whole video clip, but then the subject's face will turn into even more of a washed-out white blob than it already is. Instead, you should brighten the midtones — in my example, the cave walls — without affecting the highlights — the subject's face — or shadows.

Gamma Correction to the rescue! Find the Gamma Correction effect in the Image Control category. As with other effects, simply click-and-drag the effect from the Edit pane and drop it on the clip you want to adjust. Then use clip properties to adjust the Gamma Correction settings.

The baseline setting for the Gamma Correction effect is 10, but in Figure 10-3, I have adjusted the control to 7. This adjustment has dramatically improved the appearance of the cave in the background, without exacerbating the already too bright face of the subject in the foreground.

The Gamma Correction effect is especially useful for adjusting light when the image looks okay on your computer screen but is too dark or too light when viewed on a TV.

Figure 10-3:
Gamma
Correction
brightens
the back-
ground
without
destroying
the bright
subject in
the fore-
ground.

Matching Colors with the Color Match Effect

Another helpful image enhancement tool provided with Adobe Premiere Elements is the Color Match effect. This effect helps you match the colors in one video clip with the colors in another video clip. This effect is helpful when you have two scenes that were shot with different lighting conditions (or even different cameras) and you want to maintain a common look for both clips.

The Color Match effect uses two clips. The *sample clip* is the clip that has the colors or lighting that you like. The *target clip* is the clip you want to make look more like the sample clip. To use the Color Match effect, follow these steps:

1. **Click Effects on the Edit tab, or choose Window⇨Effects.**

2. **Drag-and-drop the Color Match filter from the Image Control category to the target clip.**

3. **Make sure that the target clip is selected, and click Edit Effects under the Edit tab.**

4. **Click the arrow next to Color Match to expand the Color Match options on the Edit pane.**

5. **In the Timeline, place the CTI (Current Time Indicator) somewhere in the sample clip.**

   Ideally the CTI should be stopped on a frame of video that shows representative colors that you want to match, as shown in Figure 10-4.

You can use the left- and right-arrow keys on the keyboard to move frame-by-frame through a clip. Make sure that the target clip remains highlighted in the Timeline, however, so that the Color Match controls are still visible under the Edit tab.

6. **On the Edit pane, choose a method from the Method menu under Color Match.**

   HSL (hue, saturation, lightness) is the most common method used for color matching, but you can also choose RGB (red, green, blue) or Curves if you want.

7. **Choose what you want to match using the check boxes at the bottom of the Color Match settings.**

   If you're using the HSL matching method, you can choose whether you want to match hue, saturation, or lightness individually. For example, you may find that each clip is adequately lit, but that one has better color hue or saturation than the other. In this case, disable the Match Lightness option. If you're using the RGB or Curves matching methods, you can choose whether to match red, green, or blue individually.

Choose a sample color.

Figure 10-4:
Use the eyedroppers to choose sample colors from the sample clip.

Target clip   CTI   Sample clip

8. **Click the eyedropper next to Master Sample, and then move the mouse pointer over a representative area of the sample clip.**

   A color is selected when you release the mouse button.

9. **In the Timeline, move the CTI so that it is now in the target clip.**

10. **Click the eyedropper next to Master Target, and choose a target color from the target clip.**

    Choose a color from a sample point in the target clip. For example, in Figures 10-4 and 10-5, I picked spots on a soccer player's uniform that should be about the same color in each clip.

11. **Click Done when you finish color matching.**

As with many other color-correction tasks, the Color Match filter requires a great deal of trial-and-error to achieve the right look.

Choose a target color.

Figure 10-5:
Use the
eyedroppers
to choose
a sample
point in the
target clip.

CTI   Target clip   Sample clip

Stabilizing Shaky Footage

The best way to fix shaky footage is to not shoot shaky footage in the first place. As I recommend in Chapters 3 and 18, use tripods, keep the camera level with the horizon, and avoid fire hosing (for example, panning back and forth wildly across a scene).

Wouldn't it be nice if you could always use perfect videographic technique! Perfection is, of course, impossible. Everyone who has ever wielded a video camera has ended up with some shots that were a little shaky. Modern camcorders have built-in image stabilization, but that feature can only do so much. If you have shaky footage that you'd like to fix, Premiere Elements can help. The Stabilizer effect helps you correct minor shakes in your video. Here's how to use it:

1. **Click Effects on the Edit pane, or choose Window⇨Effects.**

2. **Near the bottom of the list of effects, click-and-drag the Stabilizer effect and drop it on a shaky video clip in the Timeline.**

3. **Click Edit Effects on the bottom of the Edit pane to open effect controls.**

4. **Play the clip in the Monitor to preview it, and watch for problems such as the black bands shown in Figure 10-6.**

   The Stabilizer effect works by zooming in slightly on the image, and then panning back and forth across the remaining image to make it appear smooth and stable on-screen. But if it pans too much, you see black bands on the sides, top, or bottom of the image, as shown in Figure 10-6.

5. **If you see large black bands during playback, place a check mark next to Limit To Zoom.**

   Stabilization is reduced when you enable the Limit To Zoom option, but in most cases the black bars are more objectionable than a little bit of camera shake.

6. **Click Done when you finish adjusting the Stabilizer effect.**

Watch for black bands.　　　　　Limit to Zoom

Chapter 11

Compositing and Animating Video Clips

*Y*ou can hardly watch a movie or TV show today without seeing impossible scenes. These scenes may involve superheroes flying among skyscrapers in a major metropolis, giant monsters chasing hapless humans through a jungle, or even a TV weatherman hovering in outer space as he describes the swirling weather patterns down on planet Earth (just off the coast and poised to ruin your weekend, of course). Scenes like these are created using a bit of movie magic called *compositing*.

Guess what? You don't have to be a Hollywood movie mogul with a multi-million-dollar budget to use compositing. With some simple videography tricks and Adobe Premiere Elements, you can create composite scenes with the best of 'em. In this chapter, I show you how. This chapter also shows you how to use the powerful animation features that come with Premiere Elements; these features allow you to move video scenes, titles, and other graphics across the screen. The last section in this chapter shows you how to use Motion Tracking mode in Premiere Elements. This mode tracks moving objects in video images, and then lets you apply effects, clip art, or mattes to those objects.

Compositing Video Clips

Modern movie viewers have come to expect sophisticated visual illusions — starships flying into a space battle, lovers standing on the bow of a long-gone ocean liner, or a weatherman standing in front of a moving weather-satellite graphic. *Compositing* is a tool to make such scenes possible.

Fundamental to the process of compositing is the careful layering of images. A subject is filmed in front of a solid-colored background — usually a blue or green screen — and then the image of the subject is superimposed over a different background. Premiere Elements includes all the tools you need to make your own compositing effects, and thanks to the new Videomerge effect, compositing is now easier than ever.

Shooting source footage

Compositing works best if you start with good source footage. In my professional video studio at work, we use a fabric blue screen illuminated by expensive lights designed specifically for pro video. But you don't need a pro-caliber budget to do compositing; in the examples shown in this book, I used a roll of cheap vinyl picnic table covering from a local party store.

Shooting a subject against a solid-colored background is easier said than done. The backdrop needs to be as smooth and evenly lit as possible. Here are some techniques you might use:

✔ **Use the sky as your backdrop.** Position the camera low and shoot upwards at your subject. Unless there are clouds, you can be sure that the sky is evenly lit, and your subject isn't going to cast shadows on it.

When you use the sky as a background, make sure that backlighting doesn't cause your subject to be too dark. As described in Chapter 3, you can compensate for backlighting by putting additional light on the foreground subject.

✔ **Shoot against a solid-colored wall.** An interior wall in your home might work, so long as that wall doesn't have fancy wallpaper or trim.

✔ **Use a solid-color background material.** The color should contrast with the subject. In Figure 11-1, I've shot my cat in front of a blue tablecloth.

Figure 11-1:
Shoot your
subject in
front of a
solid back-
ground.

Merging clips with Videomerge

Adobe knows that sometimes you don't care about the technical complexi-
ties of moviemaking. You know what edits you want to make, and you want to
make them fast. Videomerge is a new feature in Premiere Elements that helps
you do compositing quickly. Videomerge is pretty easy to use:

1. **Put a background clip in the Video 1 track of your Timeline.**

   The background clip is what you want to appear behind your subject.
   The background might show the beach, outer space, or a soccer game.

2. **In the Timeline, position the CTI (Current Time Indicator) where you
   want the compositing effect to begin.**

   The background clip should appear in the Monitor.

3. **In the Task pane, find the clip you want to use as the overlay clip.**

   The overlay clip contains the subject that you want to superimpose over
   the background.

4. **Click-and-drag the overlay clip and drop it on the video image in the
   Monitor.**

5. **Choose Yes in the Videomerge dialog box.**

   Videomerge identifies the predominant background color in the overlay
   clip and makes it transparent. The overlay clip is inserted into the Video
   2 track in the Timeline, as shown in Figure 11-2.

Watch out for Catzilla! Color eyedropper Adjust Videomerge tolerance.

Figure 11-2:
Fine-tune
the color
tolerance in
Videomerge
settings.

Background clip Overlay clip

6. **Make sure the overlay clip is selected in the Timeline, and then choose Window⇨Properties.**

   Properties for the overlay clip appear on the Edit tab.

7. **Click the arrow next to Videomerge to expand Videomerge settings.**

8. **If parts of the background aren't as transparent as you would like, place a check mark next to Select Color.**

   When you enable Select Color, the overlay clip's background appears.

9. **Click the eyedropper tool to select it, and then click somewhere on the overlay clip's background.**

   If the background color is uneven, choose a color that is near the middle of the range of background colors. You may need to try clicking in a few different areas before you find a Videomerge color that works best.

10. **Choose Soft, Normal, or Detailed in the Presets menu.**

Soft makes Videomerge more forgiving of uneven background color. Use Detailed if Videomerge is causing some subject detail to disappear. In all other cases, choose the default setting of Normal.

11. **Adjust the Tolerance slider to fine-tune the Videomerge sensitivity.**

    Watch the video image in the Monitor as you make adjustments, to see how the image is affected.

12. **Click Done at the bottom of the Edit tab when you finish adjusting Videomerge.**

The traditional way to do video compositing is to use effects called *keys*. A key identifies a specific color (or range of colors) in a video image, and then makes that color transparent. Underlying video clips show through in the transparent areas. Keys provide more advanced control over compositing than Videomerge. If you find that Videomerge doesn't work quite as well as you hoped, try using keys as described in the next section.

Using keys for precise compositing

Videomerge makes compositing easy, but it's pretty basic. If you want more precise control over compositing, you can use one of the pro-quality keys that comes with Premiere Elements. To view a list of the keys, choose Window⇨Effects, or click Effects on the Edit tab. Premiere Elements' keys are

- ✔ **Alpha Adjust:** This key works a lot like the opacity controls (described later in this chapter); it's for still graphics that have an alpha channel. Use this key to adjust opacity of the whole graphic, or to ignore, invert, or mask the picture's alpha channel.

- ✔ **Blue Screen:** Use this key when you've shot video with the subject in front of a blue screen. The blue screen must be well lit and brilliant for this key to be effective. Shadows reduce the effectiveness of this key.

- ✔ **Chroma:** *Chroma* is just a fancy word for color. This key enables you to *key out* (for example, remove) a specific color or range of color. With some fine-tuning, you can use this key with almost any clip.

- ✔ **Mattes:** Use matte keys (such as Garbage Matte) to manually remove undesired objects from video images. An easier way to do this is to use Motion Tracking mode, which I describe later in this chapter.

- ✔ **Green Screen:** This key works just like the Blue Screen matte except it uses (surprise) green rather than blue.

- ✔ **Luma:** The Luma key is sort of like the Chroma key, except that instead of keying out a specific color, it keys out a specific brightness.

✔ **Non-Red:** This key works like the Blue Screen and Green Screen keys, but it keys out both blue and green screens. Try this key if you get rough edges (called *stair-stepping*) with the Blue or Green Screen keys.

✔ **RGB Difference:** The RGB Difference key is basically a less-powerful chroma key. Videomerge (described earlier in this chapter) is basically an RGB Difference key.

Applying a key to a clip is pretty easy. Follow these steps:

1. **Place an overlay clip in track Video 2 or higher.**

   Video 2 and higher-numbered tracks are all *superimpose tracks* because that's where you superimpose images over the background.

2. **Click the overlay clip to select it, and put the CTI on the clip.**

3. **Choose Window➪Effects to open the list of Effects.**

4. **Drag-and-drop a key from the Edit tab to the overlay clip.**

5. **Choose Window➪Properties to open the clip properties.**

   The key you applied in Step 4 appears in the properties list.

6. **Click the arrow next to the key to expand its controls.**

   If the key uses color information — like the Chroma key, for example — you may need to choose a base transparency color. If you don't need to choose a base color, skip to Step 8.

7. **Click the eyedropper next to Color in the key controls, and then click a color in the Monitor that you want to key out.**

8. **Adjust any other settings that may be available.**

   Each key is different, so experiment with the settings to achieve the best result. In Figure 11-3, I adjusted the Similarity and Blend settings.

Here's how keys work: The key recognizes certain colors, such as the special shades often used in blue or green screens. Anything in the video that matches this shade — including that wacky blue tie your subject is wearing — is made transparent by the key. Everything else is placed on a virtual "glass slide" and superimposed over the background. Pretty slick, eh?

Figure 11-3:
The Chroma
key is a
good all-
purpose
key.

Adjusting clip transparency

Compositing usually means making portions of a video clip transparent by
using Videomerge or a key. But you can also make an entire video clip more
transparent. Another way of saying *more transparent* is *less opaque*. If you
can see through a clip, it's transparent. If you can't see through the clip, it's
opaque. In the jargon of Premiere Elements, you adjust *opacity* rather than
transparency. To adjust the opacity of a clip, follow these steps:

1. **Add a clip to the Video 1 track in the Timeline.**

   Video 1 is the background layer that shows through when you make
   superimposed clips transparent.

2. **Add a clip to a superimpose track, as shown in Figure 11-4.**

   Video 2 and higher tracks are all considered superimpose tracks.

3. **Click the clip that you want to adjust, and position the CTI over it.**

   The clip is selected, and its image appears in the Monitor.

4. **Make sure that the words** `Opacity:Clip Opacity` **appear next to the clip's name in the Timeline.**

   If you see the word `Motion` instead, click `Motion` and choose Opacity⇨Clip Opacity from the drop-down menu that appears. A black line appears across the clip. This is the Opacity rubberband.

5. **To make the clip transparent, drag the Opacity rubberband down.**

   As you drag the rubberband down, the clip becomes more transparent. As you drag it up, it becomes more opaque.

You can adjust opacity over time using keyframes. See Chapter 12 for more on controlling opacity, keys, and other effects by using keyframes.

Superimpose track   CTI

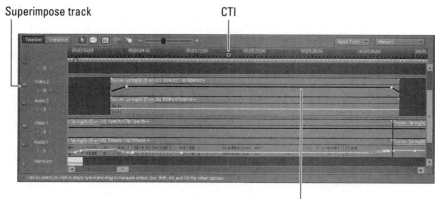

Figure 11-4:
Adjust transparency using the opacity rubberband.

Click and drag to adjust

Animating Video Clips

I know what you're thinking — *Why do I need to animate a video clip in which the subjects are already moving?* You may not need to animate the actual *subjects* in the video, but you can move the video image across the screen. For example, a small picture-in-picture image could sail across the screen to give a hint of action that will happen later in the movie. But wait — there's more. You can move a clip across the screen along a fixed path or a zigzag pattern, rotate clips, and distort clips. To begin animating a clip, follow these steps:

1. **Click the clip in the Timeline that you want to animate to select it, and make sure that the CTI is somewhere over the clip.**

   Just about any clip that you animate should be in a superimpose track — that is, the clip should occupy any track above Video 1.

2. **Choose Window⇨Properties to open the properties window for the selected clip.**

3. **Click the right-pointing arrow next to the Motion heading to expand the Motion controls.**

Now you're ready to start animating the video clip. The next couple of sections show you how to use the clip Motion controls in Premiere Elements. You can use the Motion controls to move or resize video clips.

Resizing a clip with Motion controls

Motion controls give you command over the size and position of clips. To adjust basic Motion controls, click a clip's image in the Monitor, and then click-and-drag corners of the video image to resize it (see Figure 11-5). To move the clip, click-and-drag the circle in the middle of the clip. For more precise control, use these controls under Motion in the clip properties:

✔ **Position:** The position of the clip is expressed in pixels along an X (horizontal) and Y (vertical) axis. Zero for the X axis is the left edge of the screen, and zero for the Y axis is the top of the screen. The default position for any clip is right in the middle.

✔ **Scale:** The default scale for any clip is 100, which means it takes up the whole screen. Reduce the scale to shrink the image size.

✔ **Scale Width:** If you remove the check mark next to Constrain Proportions, you can adjust height and width independently. With Constrain Proportions unchecked, the Scale control adjusts height, and the Scale Width control adjusts width. Just keep in mind that adjusting height and width independently distorts the video image.

✔ **Rotation:** Use this control to rotate the clip. Click-and-drag left or right on the clock-style rotation control to spin the image on its axis.

✔ **Anchor Point:** All the other controls work off the clip's *anchor point,* which is usually in the center of the clip. Adjust this control to move the anchor point to the corner or any other part of the clip.

✔ **Anti-flicker Filter:** If you notice flickering lines at the top or bottom of a resized image, adjust the Anti-flicker Filter slider to correct the problem.

Moving clips across the screen

As you play with the Motion controls, you'll quickly see how easy it is to change the on-screen position, size, and orientation of a clip. But what if you want the clip to move across the screen after you've shrunk it? To do this, you must use *effect keyframes*. Effect keyframes are reference points used by Premiere Elements to define the starting and ending points for effects and other changes. I explain keyframes in greater detail in Chapter 12, but to control motion with keyframes, follow these steps:

1. **Click the clip you want to animate in the Timeline to select it.**

2. **Move the CTI to the beginning of the selected clip.**

   The easiest way to do this is to first position the CTI somewhere over the clip, and then press Page Up on your keyboard.

3. **Choose Window⇨Properties to reveal the clip properties, if they aren't open already.**

4. **Click the Show/Hide Keyframes button (see Figure 11-5) to reveal a mini-timeline for the clip.**

5. **In the Motion controls for the selected clip, click the Toggle Animation button next to the control you want to animate.**

   For example, Figure 11-5 shows the Position and Scale controls being animated.

6. **Adjust the Scale, Position, and any other Motion controls you want to change.**

   These settings represent what the clip looks like and where it's positioned at the start of the animation.

7. **Click the Timeline window to make it active, and press Page Down to move the CTI to the end of the clip.**

8. **Adjust the Scale, Position, and any other Motion controls for the clip.**

   These settings represent what the clip looks like and where it's positioned at the end of the animation.

   Premiere Elements automatically creates keyframes at the beginning and end of the clip and automatically calculates how the clip should move and change to steadily go from one keyframe to the next.

In Figure 11-5, the animation in the clip begins on-screen in the lower-right corner, and the clip then expands to full size to fill the screen. You can add additional keyframes along the clip's path to make more dynamic changes.

Click and drag corners to resize. Show/Hide Keyframes

Toggle
Animation

Figure 11-5:
Video clips
can move
across the
screen as
they play.

Click and drag circle to move the clip. Add/Remove Keyframes

Tracking Moving Objects

You're watching a video clip and realize, "The only thing that would make this scene better is a silly hat." You could reshoot the scene and make your subject wear a silly hat, but that's a lot of work and silly hats are expensive.

An easier solution is to use Motion Tracking mode in Premiere Elements. Motion Tracking mode identifies moving objects in video images. You can then apply effects or clip art images that move with those objects across the screen. To use Motion Tracking mode, follow these steps:

1. **Position the CTI over a clip containing objects you want to track, and click the clip to select it.**

   Motion Tracking mode works only on analyzed clips. See Chapter 5 for more on auto analyzing clips.

2. **Click the Motion Tracking mode button on the Timeline.**

   Yellow boxes appear around moving objects in the video image, as shown in Figure 11-6.

3. **Click the box around the object you want to track.**

   The box turns blue, and a list of clip art appears in the Task pane.

  4. **Find a piece of clip art you want to use, and drag and drop it onto the blue box in the Monitor.**

  5. **Use the handles to move and resize the clip art.**

  6. **Click Add Object above the Monitor.**

  7. **Play the Timeline to preview the motion tracking effect.**

If you aren't happy with the result, select the clip art clip in the Timeline and fine-tune its size and position by using Motion controls and keyframes, as described earlier in this chapter. Motion Tracking mode can also be used to apply effects to certain areas of a video image. For example, if your Old West scene is spoiled by an airplane flying in the background, use Motion Tracking mode to apply a garbage matte that hides the airplane.

Select an object to track.   Use handles to resize.   Choose clip art.

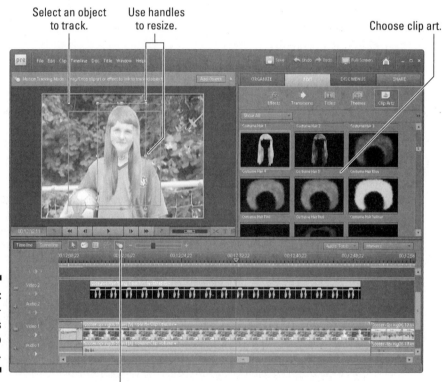

Figure 11-6: Track moving objects and add clip art to them.

Motion Tracking mode

Chapter 12

Adding Special Effects to Your Movies

A dobe Premiere was first released in 1993, making it one of the first video-editing programs for desktop computers. Many competitors have come onto the market over the years — Adobe Premiere Elements now shares the stage with other affordable moviemaking programs like Pinnacle Studio, Microsoft Windows Movie Maker, and others.

Not all video-editing programs are created equal, however. Many programs offer special effects, but few offer the quality and variety available with Adobe Premiere Elements — over 90 professional-grade effects. And you can add even more effects available from third-party vendors. What's more, each effect in Premiere Elements is fully customizable, giving you full creative control over the intensity and timing of each effect.

Effects can help you improve video quality or add special touches that amaze and astound your audience. Effects can be added to any video clip, and the changes they make aren't permanent so you can remove them if you change your mind. Although this book can't cover all 90 effects in detail, this chapter does show you the basics of using effects — including the brass-tacks specifics of using several common effects.

Surveying Effects

Adobe Premiere Elements comes with more than 90 effects. Some effects may not seem immediately useful, but you may be surprised someday to find that a seemingly obscure effect suddenly comes in handy. You can get a look at all the effects Premiere Elements serves up by choosing Window⇨Effects, or clicking the Edit tab in the Task pane and then clicking Effects. Video effects are organized into 19 categories. (See Chapter 8 for information about audio effects.) The following sections provide an overview of the effects available to you in Premiere Elements.

Just like transitions and other edits, video effects are meant to enhance the content of your movie, not showcase your editing skills. Choose and use effects carefully — and only when they serve your editing style.

Adjust

The ten effects in the Adjust category let you tweak levels of color and light. They can be useful for fixing color- and light-related problems in your video clips. I describe most of the Adjust effects in Chapter 10. One effect that I don't cover in Chapter 10 — the Extract effect — removes all trace of color from a clip, as shown in Figure 12-1. This effect can be used to create an interesting background for a title screen.

Figure 12-1:
The Extract effect removes all color from a clip.

Blur & Sharpen

You find five effects in the Blur & Sharpen effects category, including the following:

✔ **Antialias:** This effect blends edges together through an *anti-aliasing* process. Anti-aliasing blends colors in adjacent pixels to reduce the "stairstep" appearance that sometimes happens to curves in digital images. Sometimes anti-aliasing smoothes the appearance of the image; other times it just makes the whole image look blurry.

✔ **Fast Blur:** Use this effect to soften outlines to simulate disorientation, or to suggest speed by "unfocusing" parts of the video image.

A blur effect can be used like a transition to make it appear that the camera starts out blurry and then focuses in on the clip. This technique can be effective when simulating the view of a person who is waking up from a slumber or coma. Use keyframes (described later in this chapter) to make the image start out blurry and then gradually come into focus.

✔ **Gaussian Blur:** This effect is similar to Fast Blur, but it also removes *noise* (specs or visual "static") from the image. Gaussian Blur can't blur an image quite as much as the Fast Blur effect.

✔ **Ghosting:** This effect creates ghost images of moving objects on-screen, and can often be used to place increased emphasis on the path of motion.

✔ **Sharpen:** This effect sharpens images that appear too soft or slightly out-of-focus. Be careful when using this effect on clips with a lot of motion — moving objects may appear to have blocky edges.

Channel

The Channel category contains only the Invert effect. This effect inverts colors in a clip so that the image looks like a photographic negative. Use this effect to add a psychedelic or "sci-fi" look to a video image.

Distort

The Distort category contains ten effects that bend, twist, exaggerate, or otherwise distort your video images so that they look like they are being viewed through a fun-house mirror. The Distort effects include

✔ **Bend:** The video image is bent both horizontally and vertically in a series of waves. The waves move as the clip plays, giving viewers the impression that they are viewing the scene from underwater.

✔ **Corner Pin:** The video image is pinned to a corner, hence the name. Use Corner pin to make the video image appear to be on a different plane from the viewing screen.

✔ **Lens Distortion:** This effect distorts the image to look like it is being viewed through the bottom of a soda-pop bottle or another distorted lens.

- ✔ **Mirror:** Give the appearance that part of your video image rests on a mirror or reflecting pool with this effect. You can adjust the angle and center point of the reflection.

- ✔ **Polar Coordinates:** If the Bend or Lens Distortion effects don't provide quite enough distortion for your tastes, try this effect. Pixels are adjusted to give the appearance of extreme image distortion, like portions of the video image are being pulled like taffy.

- ✔ **Ripple:** Similar to the Bend effect, this effect adds ripples to the video image, like ripples in water.

- ✔ **Spherize:** This effect makes it appear as though you are viewing the video through a thickly curved lens.

- ✔ **Transform:** Use this effect to turn or skew the image in the two-dimensional plane.

- ✔ **Twirl:** Twirl the video image into a vortex.

- ✔ **Wave Warp:** This effect warps and waves the video image as it plays.

Generate

When the Sun or a bright light reflects on a camera lens, it causes a bright spot called a lens flare. Usually, photographers and videographers try to avoid lens flares, but if you want to add a simulated lens flare to your video — flares can enhance the feeling of being in a hot desert, for example — use the Lens Flare effect found in the Generate category.

GPU effects

The graphics processing units (GPUs) in most modern video cards allow advanced visual effects. The three GPU effects in Premiere Elements take advantage of the power in modern GPUs to display visually complex effects like water ripples, page curls, or lens refraction.

Image Control

The eight effects in the Image Control category change the way color is viewed in your clips. They can remove a color (or range of colors) from a clip, convert a color image to black-and-white, or adjust the overall tint of the image (which you will find useful if, for example, you want to transform an ordinary outdoor scene into an alien landscape). Chapter 10 shows you how to use the Image Control effects in greater detail.

Keying

The effects in the Keying effects category allow you to control transparency in clips and perform compositing effects such as blue screening. (See Chapter 11 for more on using keys in your video projects.)

NewBlue effects

NewBlue is a third-party video content and effects developer that provides 12 snazzy effects for use with Premiere Elements. Divided into three categories, the NewBlue effects make otherwise complex edits easy. The Old Film effect, for example, simulates the look of old movies, complete with monochrome colors and fake film scratches (thin vertical lines that show up in the film image).

Perspective

The four effects you find in the Perspective category add a three-dimensional feel to your clips. They include

- ✔ **Basic 3D:** This effect turns and tilts your image on a plane. You can move the corners of the video image to give the appearance that the image is on a plane that is not parallel with the viewing screen.
- ✔ **Bevel Alpha:** If an image doesn't fill the entire screen, use this effect to smoothly bevel the edges of the image.
- ✔ **Bevel Edges:** This is similar to Bevel Alpha effect, except that the edge bevels are rectangular rather than softly rounded.
- ✔ **Drop Shadow:** A drop shadow sometimes comes in handy behind titles or picture-in-picture windows.

Pixelate

The Pixelate category contains only the Facet effect, which modifies the pixels in your video image to create a textured appearance.

Render

The two Render effects allow you to simulate the look and feel of real light. The Render effects are

- **Lightning:** The Lightning effect is kind of cool because it creates realistic lightning on-screen. Simulated lightning created by this effect is much safer to work with than the real thing.

- **Ramp:** This effect creates a color gradient on the screen. Adjust the Blend With Original setting to make the original video image show through the gradient. This effect is of limited use, though you may find it helpful when you want to put titles on the screen and want to slightly soften or darken the background image without totally hiding it.

Stylize

The ten effects in the Stylize effect category create a variety of image modifications:

- **Alpha Glow:** If your image includes a masked alpha channel (usually a still graphic from Adobe Photoshop Elements with a transparent layer), this effect creates a glow around the alpha channel.

- **Color Emboss:** This effect creates an embossed appearance to the clip without changing any of the clip's original colors. This usually gives the video image a cartoonish appearance.

- **Emboss:** The image is given an embossed appearance, and most color information is removed.

- **Find Edges:** Major edges in the image are identified and replaced with black lines, and the rest of the image information is discarded. This effect works well for creating backgrounds for title screens.

- **Mosaic:** The image is blurred in a block pattern for a pixelated appearance.

- **Noise:** Do not attempt to adjust the transmission! This effect adds artificial video noise to the image, as if the viewer has poor antenna reception.

- **Replicate:** Duplicate a single video image, as shown in Figure 12-2.

- **Solarize:** This effect blends the image with its negative. It is similar to the Invert effect, except that you can adjust the blend along a scale from zero (normal) to 100 (full negative).

✔ **Strobe Light:** Flash your video image on and off, using this effect. Just be careful not to give your audience members seizures!

✔ **Texturize:** This effect applies the apparent texture from one clip to another clip.

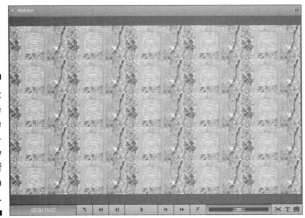

Figure 12-2:
The Replicate effect creates many copies of our video image.

Time

In the Time category, you can find two effects. The Echo effect creates visual echoes (or a double-image) of a picture. Look here also for the Posterize Time effect, which modifies the apparent frame rate of a clip. Use this effect to make it look like you are a cable news channel correspondent broadcasting via video phone from the other side of the world.

Transform

The nine effects in the Transform category transform the view of your clip in a variety of interesting and sometimes humorous ways:

✔ **Camera View:** Use this to simulate various camera angles and views.

✔ **Clip:** This basic effect trims off portions of the video image. This may come in handy if you want to create a black bar on the side of the screen to insert some bulleted points.

✔ **Crop:** This effect is similar to the Clip effect, but it adds the zoom feature, which appears to zoom the image off the edge of the screen.

- ✔ **Edge Feather:** Use this effect to create a feathered frame around the edge of your video image.

- ✔ **Horizontal Flip:** The image is flipped horizontally.

- ✔ **Horizontal Hold:** This effect simulates TV horizontal-hold problems.

- ✔ **Roll:** The image appears to roll horizontally across the screen.

- ✔ **Vertical Flip:** The image is flipped vertically.

- ✔ **Vertical Hold:** Use this effect to simulate TV vertical-hold problems. (Just imagine your friends banging on their old TVs trying to figure out why the vertical hold is messed up!)

Video Stabilizer

If the video you recorded is shaky and jittery and you aren't going for an earthquake look, you can use the Stabilizer effect to smooth out some of the video shakes. I show how to use the Stabilizer in Chapter 10.

Videomerge

Videomerge is basically an RGB (red-green-blue) difference key that helps you easily do compositing effects like the ones I describe in Chapter 11. Usually Videomerge is applied automatically when you perform certain kinds of edits. Chapter 11 shows you what those certain kinds of edits are.

Taking Control of Visual Effects

To apply an effect to a clip, drag the effect from the Task pane and drop it on a clip in the Timeline. (Choose Window⇨Effects to open the list of effects.) You can also adjust attributes of an effect by using the Task pane. To reveal effect controls, click the clip in the Timeline to select it and then choose Window⇨Properties. The effect controls appear, as shown in Figure 12-3. Key features of the effect controls include

- ✔ On the left side of the effect controls, next to each effect's title, is a tiny eye. To disable an effect, click the eye to remove it. You can see the eye displayed in Figure 12-3 next to the Camera View effect.

- ✔ Each effect has its own unique controls. Click the right-pointing arrow next to an effect control to view more specific controls. The Camera View effect, for example, enables you to adjust longitude, latitude, and more.

✔ To enable keyframing so that the effect can change over the duration of a clip, click the Toggle Animation button, as shown in Figure 12-3. I show you how to use keyframes in the next section.

✔ The effect controls window can display a keyframe viewer, which, as you can see in Figure 12-3, looks like a miniature Timeline, complete with its own CTI (Current Time Indicator). To reveal the keyframe viewer, click the Show/Hide Keyframes button, as shown in Figure 12-3.

✔ To add a keyframe for a control at the current location of the CTI, click the Add/Remove Keyframe button. Use the arrows on either side of any Add/Remove Keyframe button to move the CTI to the next (or previous) keyframe.

✔ Some effects have Color Pickers. For example, if you're using the Camera View effect, shown in Figure 12-3, you use the Color Picker to choose a fill color for the background after the camera view has been modified. In Figure 12-3, the current background color is white.

Some Color Pickers have eyedroppers next to them. Eyedroppers are used to choose a color from the video image in the Monitor. To use an eyedropper, click the eyedropper icon, move the mouse pointer over the desired color in the video image, and then click on the color. Your desired color is selected when the mouse button is released.

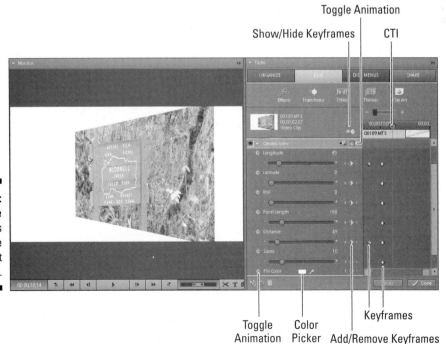

Figure 12-3: Fine-tune your effects using the effect controls.

Using Keyframes

Effects can have a variety of, er, *effects* on clips in Premiere Elements. You can blur, recolor, distort, and more. You can apply an effect so that it changes the clip uniformly across its entire duration, or you can customize the effect so that it changes over time. To make an effect change as it plays, you need to tell Premiere Elements what those changes will be and when they should happen. You do this by using reference points called *keyframes.* Premiere Elements automatically extrapolates changes from one keyframe to the next.

The types of keyframes I talk about in this chapter are *effect keyframes.* Video codecs (the compression/decompression schemes used to shrink video file sizes) use *compression key frames.* Although the names sound familiar, the two terms refer to very different things. (See Chapter 15 for a more detailed explanation of compression key frames.)

After you have applied an effect to a clip, you can adjust that effect using keyframes. To set keyframes, follow these steps:

1. **In the Timeline, locate the clip you want to modify.**

2. **Select the clip, and then open the effect controls for the clip (Window⇨Properties) if they aren't already open.**

3. **Click the Show/Hide Keyframes button to open the keyframes viewer.**

4. **Click the Toggle Animation button next to the name of the effect.**

   The Toggle Animation button enables the use of keyframes for the effect. If Toggle Animation is disabled, the effect is applied evenly across the entire clip.

5. **Move the CTI in the keyframes viewer to the exact frame where you want to set a keyframe.**

   You can move the CTI using the playback controls in the Monitor window, or you can use the J, K, and L keys on your keyboard. Use the left- and right-arrow keys to move a single frame at a time.

6. **Click the Add/Remove Keyframe button next to an effect control.**

   You need to add a keyframe for each control that you want to change. For example, if you apply the Camera View effect (refer to Figure 12-3), and you only want the camera view to change after the clip has played for a few seconds, set all the controls to their defaults at the first keyframe. At the second keyframe, adjust the Longitude, Focal Length, Distance, and Zoom controls to the desired settings. These changes cause the clip to play normally from the beginning until it reaches the first keyframe. At that point, the camera angle starts to morph until it gets to the settings you specify at the second keyframe.

7. **Set additional keyframes as desired.**

Don't forget to use those Previous and Next Keyframe buttons. They provide an easy way to move from keyframe to keyframe. If you want to remove a keyframe, simply move to the keyframe and click the Add/ Delete Keyframe button to remove the check mark.

If you apply multiple effects to a clip, each effect gets its own keyframes. Thus, if you set a keyframe for one effect, don't assume that it applies to the other effects on that clip as well. To view the keyframes for an effect, click that effect in the clip properties to select it.

Removing Effects

You'll probably change your mind about some of the effects you apply to your clips. Don't worry; this is perfectly natural. A lot of video editing involves good ol' trial-and-error. You'll try an effect, you won't like it, and then you'll try something else. To get rid of an effect, click the clip in the Timeline to select it, and then choose Window➪Properties to reveal the effect controls. You have two options for removing effects from a clip:

- ✔ **Temporary disability:** You can temporarily disable an effect by click-ing the little eye next to the effect's listing in the effect controls. This is a handy option because your effect settings are preserved. Disabled effects are not applied when the movie is rendered or output.

- ✔ **Permanent leave:** To delete an effect from a clip, click its title in the effect controls and then click the Trash can button at the bottom of the Task pane. Don't worry! The effect is not deleted from Premiere Elements; you're only removing it from the current clip.

Working with Effect Presets

When Adobe decided to create an "Elements" version of Premiere, the goal was to create a program that is easier to use than Premiere Pro. This included the effects editing process, because let's face it: Adjusting multiple effect controls and setting keyframes can be complex and time consuming.

To make it easier to use and modify video effects, Premiere Elements comes with a collection of effect presets. Presets are preprogrammed effect set-tings that perform common tasks like panning across still images or creating picture-in-picture (PiP) effects. Instead of spending minutes or even hours fine-tuning motion controls, keyframes, and other settings, you just drop a predesigned preset onto the clip. Presets are timesaving tools that even vet-eran video professionals appreciate.

Using a preset is easy. Just drag and drop a preset from the Effects window to a video clip, just like any other effect. Preset settings are applied automatically, but you can still fine-tune those settings if you want.

Surveying effect presets

You can find Effect presets in the Effects window under the Task pane's Edit tab (Window⇨Effects). In the menu in the upper-left corner of the list of effects (by default it says Video Effects), choose Presets. Like standard video effects, effect presets are organized into several categories. They are

- **Bevel Edges:** The two presets in this category quickly bevel the edges of the video image, providing a beveled picture frame appearance.

- **Blurs:** The Fast Blur In preset causes the clip to begin extremely blurry. The picture quickly comes into focus and the clip plays normally to the end. Fast Blur Out is similar, but the image blurs at the end of the clip.

- **Color Effects:** These 13 presets quickly apply color changes to a clip. For example, if you want to quickly give a radically red tint to the clip, apply the Hyper Tint Red preset. The Increase Saturation preset quickly increases color saturation to improve clips that are sun washed or otherwise lack color depth.

- **Drop Shadows:** Drop shadows can be used behind picture-in-picture windows, still graphics, titles, and other things. Premiere Elements includes eight drop-shadow presets.

- **Horizontal Image Pans:** If you've used Apple's iMovie (available only for Macs), you may be familiar with the Ken Burns effects that come with that program. The Horizontal Image Pan presets in Premiere Elements are similar to Apple's Ken Burns effects. They help you pan across still images that would otherwise sit static and lifeless on the screen. Movies by renowned documentarian Ken Burns often use this technique. The historical subject matter of Burns's films usually requires many still images, and panning slowly across those images restores a sense of dynamic motion that viewers expect from video.

- **Horizontal Image Zooms:** Similar to the image pan presets, the Horizontal Image Zoom presets zoom in or out on an image. I especially like to use these presets on titles. Titles that zoom in or out of view are very cool when they aren't overdone.

- **Mosaics:** These two presets are much like the Blur presets, but the image "mosaics" in or out rather than blurs.

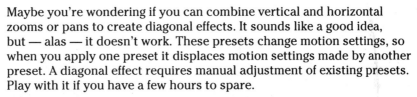

- ✔ **PiPs:** PiP stands for picture-in-picture, and these are my favorite presets. I show you how to use PiP presets later in this chapter.

- ✔ **Solarizes:** As I mention earlier in this chapter, the Solarize effect blends an image with its negative. The two Solarize presets make a clip "solarize" in or out as it plays.

- ✔ **Twirls:** Do you want a video image to twirl into view or twirl out in a vortex? Apply one of the Twirl presets to quickly create this effect.

- ✔ **Vertical Image Pans:** These presets are just like the Horizontal Image Pans, but they pan vertically rather than horizontally.

  Maybe you're wondering if you can combine vertical and horizontal zooms or pans to create diagonal effects. It sounds like a good idea, but — alas — it doesn't work. These presets change motion settings, so when you apply one preset it displaces motion settings made by another preset. A diagonal effect requires manual adjustment of existing presets. Play with it if you have a few hours to spare.

- ✔ **Vertical Image Zooms:** Yep, you guessed it. Vertical Image Zooms are just up-and-down versions of the left-and-right Horizontal Image Zooms.

Saving your own presets

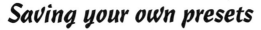

If you have your own custom effect settings that you like to use on a regular basis, you can save those settings in a preset of your own. For example, if you apply a horizontal image pan preset to an image and then fine-tune the Motion settings so that the image actually pans diagonally, you may want to save your own "diagonal pan" preset. To save a preset, follow these steps:

1. **Adjust your effect settings the way you like them.**

2. **In the effect controls, right-click the name of the effect you want to save and choose Save Preset from the menu that appears.**

3. **In the Save Preset dialog box that appears, enter a descriptive name for the preset in the Name field.**

4. **Choose a Type setting for the preset.**

   Your options are Scale, Anchor to In Point, and Anchor to Out Point. Anchor to In Point means that the effect will begin at the clip's In point. Anchor to Out Point means the preset will be applied to the end of the clip. Scale simply scales the effect to encompass the entire clip.

5. Enter a description for the preset in the Description field.

This information is important because several months from now you may forget exactly what this preset does — even if you have given it an exciting and descriptive name.

6. Click OK to save the preset and close the dialog box.

When you save your own preset, the preset is added to the Effects window on the Task pane. Choose Window⇨Effects, and then choose My Presets in the menu in the upper-left corner of the effects list. Drag-and-drop presets to clips to apply them, just like any other effect or preset.

Using Some Common Video Effects

Lots of effects are available with Premiere Elements, and unfortunately I don't have room to describe them all in detail. What I *can* do is provide detailed instructions on how to apply a few common video effects. You can adapt the techniques described here when using many other effects.

Stylizing video images

I like to think of each movie project as a delicious recipe. Every recipe starts with a main ingredient, which in the case of a movie is your video footage. Like a salmon filet, video footage may be pretty good all by itself, but it can be enhanced with some creative seasoning. Video effects are like seasonings; you don't eat fresh dill or ground pepper alone, but add just the right seasonings to your source footage, plus a liberal splash of creative juices — butter and lemon juice for salmon — and the finished product will be delectable!

If you're hungry now, go grab dinner or a snack. When you're done, consider the cinematic spice rack in Premiere Elements, which holds almost 100 video effects. But like ketchup and salmon, some things don't go well together. Choose effects that contribute to the desired feel of your movie. Remember, you're trying to make a great movie, not show off your editing skills.

Many video effects help you stylize the video image. Consider the way color tints affect the look and feel of movies like *The Matrix* or *300*. Subtle color casts can give the film a dreary tone (as in *The Matrix*) or suggest the look of a graphic novel (as in *300*). You can stylize the color of your movies by using the Colorize effect, one of the NewBlue effects that comes with Premiere Elements. To use the Colorize effect, follow these steps:

1. **Open the Effects window by choosing Window➪Effects, and scroll down to the NewBlue Art Effects Elements category.**

2. **Click-and-drag the Colorize effect and drop it on a clip in the Timeline.**

3. **Make sure that the clip is selected in the Timeline, and then choose Window➪Properties.**

   The effect controls for the selected clip appear in the Task pane.

4. **Locate the Colorize effect in the list of clip properties, and click the right-pointing arrow next to Colorize to expand the list of controls, as shown in Figure 12-4.**

   If you don't see Colorize or other controls on the Task pane, click the clip in the Timeline to make sure that the clip is selected.

5. **Click the color swatch next to Color A, and then choose a color in the Color Picker that appears.**

   Color A will be the predominant color tint appearing in the video clip. After you choose a color, click OK to close the Color Picker.

   Alternatively, click the eyedropper next to the color swatch in the effect controls, and then select a color somewhere in the Monitor's video image.

6. **Click the color swatch next to Color B, and then choose a color in the Color Picker that appears.**

   Color B will be the secondary color used in the clip. All other color will be removed from the clip. In the example shown in Figure 12-4, I have selected red as Color A and blue as Color B, effectively eliminating green from the image. Considering that the original scene had a lot of green in the foliage and ground cover, this effect gives the image an almost other-worldly appearance while still seeming natural.

7. **Click-and-drag the Strength sliders for Color A and Color B to achieve the desired color intensity.**

   As with most video effects, this is where you'll spend a lot of time experimenting.

8. **Play the clip and watch for visual problems.**

   With the Colorize effect, one problem you may encounter is large areas that seem to have no color at all. Adjust the strength sliders or the Color A and Color B colors until the video image looks how you want it.

Click arrow to expand controls

Figure 12-4:
The Colorize effect changes a clip's color cast.

Slider controls   Color swatches

Disorienting your audience

Suppose a subject in a movie is sick or disoriented. What is the best way to communicate this to the audience? You could have someone in the movie say, "Hey, you don't look well. Are you sick?" Then the unwell person can stumble and fall down. That may be effective, but an even better way to convey a feeling of illness or confusion is to let your audience see through the subject's blurry and distorted eyes.

You can begin by shooting some footage from the subject's point of view. Hand-hold the camera and let it move slightly as you walk. You probably don't need to exaggerate the movement, but the camera shouldn't be tripod-stable either. As you shoot, pan across the scene — but not too quickly — as if the subject were looking around the room, confused by his surroundings. Occasionally you may want to dip the camera slightly left or right so the video image appears to tilt. A tilting video image has a strong disorienting effect on the viewer.

Now that you have footage to work with, you can perform the real magic in Premiere Elements. One effect that can provide a feeling of illness or disorientation is Fast Blur (found in the Blur & Sharpen category). Use keyframes to adjust camera blur throughout a clip, as if the subject's vision were moving in and out of focus. Another good one is Ghosting (also in the Blur & Sharpen category). Ghosting produces ghost images of moving objects. Similar to Ghosting is the Echo effect, found in the Time category, which is used in Figure 12-5. Echo gives you a bit more control over the number and timing of echoed images.

Figure 12-5:
The Echo effect can be used to disorient the viewer.

Flipping video

Do you ever wish you could produce a mirror image of a video clip, or maybe rotate and change its orientation on the screen? Such modifications are easy with Premiere Elements. Effects that you can use to flip video can be found in the Transform category of video effects. These effects include two classics:

- ✔ **Horizontal Flip:** This effect flips the video left to right, as shown in Figure 12-6.

- ✔ **Vertical Flip:** This effect flips the video top to bottom.

When flipping video, watch out for letters and numbers that appear in the frame. Backward or upside-down letters stick out like sore thumbs (or rude gestures) when your audience views the movie.

Figure 12-6:
The Horizontal Flip effect was applied to the clip on the left.

Creating a picture-in-picture effect

Your TV might have a *picture-in-picture* (PiP) feature that allows you to watch your favorite show in a small window while your significant other watches another show on the main screen. (See Figure 12-7.) Picture-in-picture effects can also be handy in your movies. For example, if you're interviewing a star soccer player, you may want to show the interviewee in a small window while the action of a soccer game appears in the main screen. Premiere Elements has presets that make picture-in-picture effects easy to accomplish.

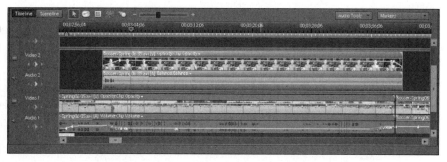

Figure 12-7:
The picture-in-picture clip should be placed in a superimpose track.

Before you can create a picture-in-picture effect, you must set up the video clips properly in your Timeline. Place the main background image in the Video 1 track. Then place another clip in Video 2 or a higher video track, as shown in Figure 12-7 (remember, tracks Video 2 and higher are also called *superimpose* tracks). After you have placed the picture-in-picture clip in a superimpose track, follow these steps:

1. **Open the Effects list in the Task pane by choosing Window⇨Effects.**

2. **Choose Presets in the menu in the upper-left corner of the Effects list, and then scroll down to the PiP categories.**

3. **Scroll to a 25% or 40% PiP category, as appropriate.**

   The 25% PiP presets create picture-in-picture clips that are 25% of their original height and width, and the 40% PiP presets create images that are 40% of their original height and width.

   Presets are also divided into LL (lower-left), LR (lower-right), Motion (these move from one orientation to another), UL (upper-left), and UR (upper-right) categories.

4. **Find the preset that best matches the effect you want to create, and click-and-drag it to the clip in the superimpose track.**

In Figure 12-8, I am using the preset PiP 25% LR Scale Out. The image's height and width will be reduced to 25%, and the image will be positioned in the lower-right corner of the screen. At the end of the clip it will scale down to a point and disappear.

Picture-in-picture effects are cool, but always consider how your audience will view the movie. Will most of your audience view it on YouTube or an iPod? If so, the smaller viewing screen may turn picture-in-picture windows into tiny little postage stamps, especially 25% PiPs. Picture-in-picture works best when the audience will view the final movie on a large TV.

Choose Presets

Figure 12-8: Picture-in-picture effects are categorized by size, position, and motion.

PiP clip   Background clip   Select a PiP preset

Chapter 13

Adding Titles to Your Movies

· ·

· ·

*I*n a rush to get to the pictures, folks who are new to video editing often overlook the importance of good audio (see Chapter 8). The same could also be said of titles — the subject of this chapter. Titles are the words that sometimes appear on-screen to tell your audience things such as the name of your movie, who made it, who starred in it, who paid for it, who made the titles, and who baked cookies for the cast. Titles can also clue the audience in to vital details — where the story takes place, in what time period, and even what time of day or year — with minimum fuss. And, of course, subtitles can reveal what the characters are saying if they're speaking a different language.

Adobe Premiere Elements includes powerful tools to help you add titles to your movies. Few affordable video-editing programs offer the creative control and power over on-screen text that you get with Premiere Elements. In this chapter, I show you how to create attractive and functional titles with Premiere Elements, as well as show you how to integrate those titles into your projects.

Creating Basic Titles

Sure, you can think of titles as just words on the screen. But think of the effects, both forceful and subtle, that well-designed titles can have. Consider the *Star Wars* movies, which all begin with a black screen and the sentence, "A long time ago, in a galaxy far, far away . . ." This simple title screen quickly and effectively sets the tone and tells the audience that the story is beginning.

Before you start adding titles to your movies, you should know some important *Do's* and *Don'ts* about working with titles. The next section lists rules to follow when creating titles. Subsequent sections show you how to configure Premiere Elements for title editing, and I show you how to create titles and modify their appearance.

Important title formatting rules

If you've ever worked in print or Web design, you've probably spent some time changing the size, color, style, and font of text. You may know the general rules for text on the Web or in print: Use dark text on light backgrounds; use serif typefaces for large bodies of text; don't use too many different typefaces on a page.

Video has text rules too, although they differ considerably from print. One of the things you must take into consideration when creating text for video is the effects that interlacing can have on text. Interlacing (explained in greater detail in Chapter 3) is found on NTSC and PAL standard-definition TV screens, as well as on 1080i high-def displays. Interlacing causes thin lines to flicker or crawl on-screen. To prevent this headache (literally), make sure that you follow these important guidelines:

- ✔ **Do make sure that all the lines in your text are thicker than 1 pixel.** Lines that are only 1 pixel thick will flicker on interlaced TV displays.

- ✔ **Don't use serif typefaces in video, especially for smaller text.** Serif typefaces — such as Times New Roman — have those extra little strokes at the ends of characters, while sans serif typefaces — like Arial — do not. Those little strokes in serif typefaces are often thin enough to cause interlacing flicker. The text you're reading right now uses a *serif face,* while the text in the caption for Figure 13-1 uses a *sans serif face.* To be on the safe side, always carefully preview your titles on an external video monitor and check for flickering or other appearance problems.

- ✔ **Do not assume that dark text is better.** In print and on the Web, dark text over a light background usually looks best because it provides good contrast. Although adequate contrast is important in video, light text on a dark background usually works better.

    The best possible combination for video is white text on a dark background.

- ✔ **Do experiment with shadows and graphics.** Simpler isn't always better. If the background of the video clip is light or has mixed color, you can use shadows or graphics to create a dark background just for your titles.

- ✔ **Do stay within the boundaries.** *Always* keep your titles inside the Title Safe Margin. Not only does this prevent text from running off the screen on TVs that overscan the image, but it also means that your text isn't running right up against the edge of the screen.

Revealing the safe margins

One of the first things you should do before creating titles is make sure that the safe margins are visible. To do so, choose Window⇨Show Docking Headers. In the docking header for the Monitor window, click the header menu (see Figure 13-1) and choose Safe Margins from the menu that appears. Two margins appear on the Monitor display, as shown in Figure 13-1. They are

- ✔ **Title Safe Margin:** The inner margin is the Title Safe Margin. All your titles should stay inside the Title Safe Margin.

- ✔ **Action Safe Margin:** The larger outer margin is the Action Safe Margin. Important action in the scene should be inside the Action Safe Margin.

The Safe Title and Safe Action Margins are especially important if you're producing a movie that will be viewed on TV screens. Most TVs *overscan* images (they allow some of the video image to be cut off at the edges of the screen). Overscan is most prevalent on older analog TVs, but overscan is encountered on digital displays as well. Keeping your text inside the Safe Title Margin ensures that words won't be cut off by overscan. It also improves readability, the same reason that margins are used when printing text on paper.

Action Safe Margin

Title Safe Margin

Click to open header menu.

Figure 13-1:
Make sure your titles stay inside the Safe Title Margin.

Inserting default titles

After you have edited together video clips and revealed the safe margins, you can start adding titles. To add a basic title, move the Timeline CTI (Current Time Indicator) to a location where you want to add a title, and then choose Title⇨New Title⇨Default Still. (You can also choose Default Roll or Default Crawl. I show you how to create rolling and crawling titles later in this chapter.) Then start typing.

When you're done typing, click the Selection Tool (it looks like an arrow) and click-and-drag the finished title to a new location, as shown in Figure 13-2. Move the title to a place where it doesn't cover important elements of the video image, but remember to keep the title inside the Safe Title Margin. Don't get too picky at this point; you'll probably move the text again later after you adjust the text attributes. Click Done if you're happy with the title, or go to the next section if you'd like to improve the title's appearance.

Selection tool

Figure 13-2: Arrghh! Text can be hard to read when you first type it.

Click-and-drag title

If you want long lines of text to automatically wrap to a new line when space runs out, right-click the text and choose Word Wrap from the menu that appears.

Setting text properties

You can adjust the attributes of the text in your titles to make them more to your liking. For example, you can pick a font that's consistent with the project's style (and is easy to read), pick a color that contrasts adequately with the background, adjust the size and scaling of the text, and more.

To adjust text properties, activate the title Selection tool (refer to Figure 13-2) and click the text object once to select it. Then adjust the text attributes by using the menus and controls shown in Figure 13-3. The options include

✔ **Font menus:** Choose a different font in the Font menu, and then specify whether you want to use boldface, italic, or other styles in the Formatting menu.

✔ **Text size:** Click-and-drag left or right on the number to change the text size.

✔ **Leading:** *Leading* is the vertical space between lines of text. It's called leading because printing press operators used to place strips of lead between text lines. Click-and-drag left or right on the leading number to increase or decrease the vertical space between multiple lines of text.

✔ **Kerning:** Kerning controls the horizontal space between characters. Click-and-drag on the kerning number to increase or decrease spacing.

✔ **Alignment:** Click one of the alignment buttons to align the text left, right, or centered.

If you spend a lot of time tweaking text appearance, click Save Style, enter a name for your new text style, and click OK. You can then easily apply the style to other titles, which helps you maintain a consistent appearance throughout your movie.

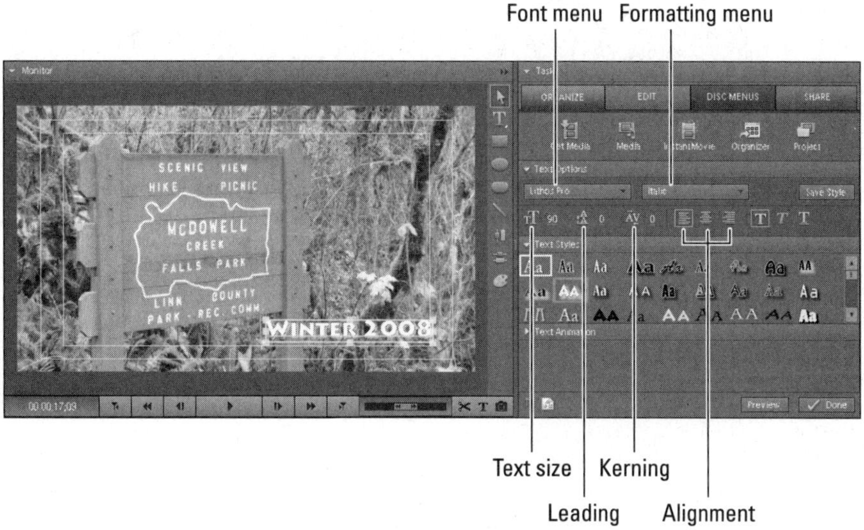

Font menu   Formatting menu

Figure 13-3:
Fine-tune
the appear-
ance of
your text.

Text size | Kerning

Leading   Alignment

Coloring and shadowing text

If you want to apply a different color and perhaps a drop-shadow to some text, Premiere Elements provides a great deal of control, although the tools aren't easy to find. To change the color of text or apply a drop-shadow, right-click the title text in the Monitor and choose Color Properties from the menu that appears. A Color Properties dialog box like the one shown in Figure 13-4 appears. With this dialog box, you can control several important text attributes:

- ✔ **Color:** Use the Color Picker at the top of the Color Properties dialog box to select colors for text fill and stroke.

- ✔ **Stroke:** Stroke is an outline around text characters. A thin stroke often greatly enhances the appearance of text. Click the Stroke Color button (next to the Fill color) to pick a color for the stroke, and then adjust the Stroke Weight to change the thickness.

- ✔ **Gradient:** In addition to solid-color text, you can also make text that is a color gradient. Choose a gradient style from the Gradient menu and pick colors for the gradient in the controls that appear. Depending on the type of gradient you choose, you can usually adjust the angle of the gradient as well.

Figure 13-4:
Fine-tune the appearance of your text.

- ✔ **Drop Shadow:** Place a check mark next to this option if you want your text to have a drop-shadow. You can then modify the drop-shadow's appearance as follows:

- **Angle:** Adjust this setting from 0 to 359 degrees to precisely set the angle of the drop-shadow.

- **Distance:** The distance should be greater than 0, but it shouldn't be so great that the shadow makes the text appear blurry and difficult to read.

- **Softness:** Use this setting to soften the shadow's appearance.

Click OK to close the Color Properties dialog box and apply your changes.

A shadow can help offset text from the video image somewhat, especially if the title appears over a light-color or busy background.

Using styles

If a title template seems too fancy and manually adjusting title attributes is too time consuming, try using one of the predesigned styles available in Premiere Elements. Various styles are available in the Text Styles area when you edit titles (refer to Figure 13-3). To apply a style to text that you have already typed, simply click the text object to select it, and then click a style in the Text Styles list. The style is automatically applied to the text.

Styles can be thought of as starting points. Even if one of the styles doesn't exactly match what you need, choosing one that is close can still save you a lot of time. After you've applied the style, you can always fine-tune attributes such as color, size, and shadows.

Making a rolling or crawling title

Titles are often animated in video productions. Text can fly onto the screen, crawl along the bottom like a stock ticker, or scroll from bottom to top as you roll the credits at the end of your movie. You can animate text using one of two methods:

- ✔ Animate the title clip in the Timeline by using the animation tools that come with Premiere Elements. (For more on animating titles and other clips in the Timeline, see Chapter 11.)

- ✔ Use the title animation tools built into Premiere Elements.

The second method is the less complex of the two, so it's a good general choice. To create animated titles, follow these steps:

1. **In Premiere Elements, choose Title⇨New Title⇨Default Roll or Default Crawl.**

   Rolling titles roll vertically (often from bottom to top), while crawling titles crawl horizontally (usually from right to left).

2. **Type the text for your rolling or crawling title, and format the text as described in the preceding section.**

   Don't worry if your text runs off the screen in the Monitor. It'll roll or crawl into view when the movie plays.

3. **Select the title that will roll or crawl, and then choose Title⇨ Roll/Crawl Options.**

   The Roll/Crawl Options dialog box appears, as shown in Figure 13-5.

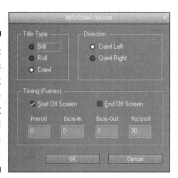

Figure 13-5: Use this dialog box to create titles that roll or crawl across the screen.

4. **If you want the rolling or crawling title to begin off-screen, select the Start Off Screen option. If you want the title to end out of view, choose the End Off Screen option.**

   In Figure 13-5, I've selected the Start Off Screen option, which means the titles will appear from the right and crawl left into view. I've left the End Off Screen option unchecked, however, which means that the titles will stop scrolling when the end of the text appears.

5. **If you want the title to remain static for a while before it starts to roll or crawl, enter a time in frames in the Preroll field.**

   If you enter 15 in the Preroll field, the title appears on-screen for 15 frames before it starts to roll or crawl off the screen. This field is not available if you choose the Start Off Screen option.

6. **If you want the title to roll or crawl on-screen and then stop, enter a time in the Postroll field.**

   Like Preroll, Postroll is measured in frames. In Figure 13-5, I've entered a Postroll value of 30 frames, which means the titles will roll up the screen and then stop, staying in view for 30 frames, which is about one second.

7. **If you want the title to gradually increase speed as it starts to move or gradually decrease as it stops, enter times in the Ease-In and Ease-Out fields.**

   Like Preroll and Postroll, Ease-In and Ease-Out are expressed in frames. If you enter an Ease-In time of 15 frames, the title starts moving slowly and gradually builds up to full speed within 15 frames.

8. **If you are creating a crawling title, choose whether you want the title to crawl Left to Right or Right to Left.**

9. **Click OK when you're done.**

   The Roll/Crawl Options dialog box closes.

You can scroll in the Monitor to see all the contents of your titles. To preview the actual roll or crawl, simply click Play in the Monitor. Premiere Elements dynamically adjusts the speed of the roll or crawl based on the length of the clip in the Timeline. The entire title rolls or crawls past, whether you have the title set to play for five seconds or five minutes in the Timeline. Obviously, the more time you give the title to play, the slower it rolls by. To quickly increase the amount of time that a title plays in the Timeline, choose the Time Stretch Tool in the Timeline and then click-and-drag an edge of the title to change its duration. (See Chapter 7 for more on using the Time Stretch Tool.)

Using Title Templates

One simple way to start creating titles is to use one of the built-in title templates. Premiere Elements comes with dozens of predesigned templates that can save you oodles of time when you're creating complete titles. To use a title template, follow these steps:

1. **Click the Edit tab to bring it to the front, and then click Titles.**

   A list of title templates appears in the Edit pane.

2. **Choose a template category from the category menu, as shown in Figure 13-6.**

   You can further refine the display to templates from a specific design by using the subcategory menu, if you want.

3. **Scroll through the list and find a template that you like.**

   The template icons are sort of small, so if you want to see a bigger preview of a template simply double-click it. The template opens in a larger preview window.

4. **To use a template, click-and-drag it from the Edit pane to a video track on your Timeline.**

In Figure 13-6, I have dropped a title template from the "Topo" subcategory onto my Video 2 track. See Chapter 7 for more on working with video tracks.

5. **If you are asked if you want to apply Videomerge to the title, click Yes or No.**

Some titles have solid or semitransparent backgrounds. If you enable Videomerge, the background is made partially transparent. This makes the title blend in better with the video, but it also makes some title design elements harder to see.

6. **Edit title text, as shown in Figure 13-6.**

Choose a category.   Sub-categories

Figure 13-6: Create cool titles using templates.

Drop title in a video track.   Edit text.

Adding Graphics to Titles

In addition to inserting text into your movies, you can also draw some basic graphics and shapes in your titles. The drawing tools can serve a variety of useful purposes, including

✔ Drawing a line under text, thus making the text stand out a bit more on the screen. This is often done when identifying a speaker or subject on-screen.

Drawing a line with Premiere Elements title-drawing tools gives you more control over the size and appearance of the line than simply using the Underline text formatting option.

✔ Adding a solid-colored box behind the text to create adequate contrast between words and the background image.

When you're editing titles, you can find the drawing tools along the right side of the Monitor window. Their functions are pretty self-explanatory; simply click a tool and then click-and-drag the shape on-screen. Use the Color Properties button to adjust colors and other attributes of the objects you draw. In Figure 13-7, for example, I've drawn a line underneath a row of text using the Line tool, and created an oval using the Rounded Rectangle tool to provide a contrasting background for the title.

Figure 13-7:
Subtle graphics can make your text much more readable.

You may want to adjust several other attributes of your graphics as well. When you select a graphic object using the Selection tool, the Title menu (located on the main Premiere Elements menu bar) provides access to a couple of important options:

✔ **Arrange:** If you want objects in a title to overlap with other objects (say, for example, you want text to appear over a background graphic), you need control over which objects are arranged on top of others. To move an item forward or back relative to other objects in the title, select that item and choose Title➪Arrange. Then select an option from the submenu that appears. In Figure 13-7, I created a black, rounded, rectangular background graphic for the text and chose Send to Back from the Arrange menu to ensure that the graphic was behind the words.

✔ **Opacity:** By default, all graphics you create in a title are opaque, which means you can't see through them. You can reduce the opacity of graphic objects, thereby making them more transparent. To adjust opacity, select a graphic object and choose Title➪Transform➪Opacity. Enter a percentage less than 100 to make the object less opaque. In Figure 13-7, I placed a black oval behind the text. An opaque black oval looked like a heavy black blob — but with its opacity reduced to 60 percent, the background oval gained some subtlety. Now it still helps the text stand out, but it doesn't completely blot out the action going on in the video image.

Adjusting Titles in the Timeline

When you add a title to a movie project, the title is usually added to an overlay track, which is Video 2 or higher. This is because titles usually appear over other video. The default length for titles in Premiere Elements is five seconds, but in some cases you may want to change how long the title appears. You can also make titles fade in and out, or change other aspects. Some things you can do with titles in the Timeline include

✔ **Change the duration of your title.** Click-and-drag the edge of the title clip to increase or decrease its duration. See Chapter 7 for details on changing the duration of clips in the Timeline.

✔ **Fade a title in or out.** Double-click a clip in the Timeline, and then scroll down to "Fades" under Text Animation options in the Edit tab, as shown in Figure 13-8. Premiere Elements offers various fading options for titles; click a fade to preview it. When you find a fade option you want, click it once to select it and then click Apply.

Figure 13-8:
You can
fade your
titles in
and out.

Part IV
Finishing and Sharing Your Movies

The 5th Wave · By Rich Tennant

"It's a site devoted to the 'Limp Korn Chilies' rock group. It has videos of all their performances in concert halls, hotel rooms and airport terminals."

In this part . . .

The ultimate goal of video editing is to make movies that other people will enjoy. The chapters in Part IV of *Premiere Elements 8 For Dummies* show you how to prepare and share your movies. I show you how to make sure your movie is ready for "prime time," and then I show you how to share your movies on the Internet, YouTube, DVD, or Blu-Ray.

Chapter 14

Wrapping Up Your Movies

. . . .

In This Chapter

▶ Casting a critical eye on your finished movies

▶ Exporting audio files and still images

▶ Saving high-quality AVI files

▶ Creating movies for iPods, PSPs, and videotape

. . . .

As you work on more movie projects, you may find that you have a really hard time finishing a movie project. Some clip always lasts a few frames too long, or an effect keyframe isn't in exactly the right spot, or a title font doesn't look exactly right. There's always *something* — no matter how miniscule — that could be improved upon. Moviemaking is like that. But at some point, you have to give up tweaking your masterpiece and decide that it is "good enough."

Before you can actually stick a fork in your movie and call it done, you have a few tasks to perform to finalize the movie and get it ready for output. You should sit back and preview the whole thing, of course. You need to make sure that the project is rendered and ready for output. This chapter helps you put the finishing touches on your project and shows you how to export audio or still images from Premiere Elements. I also show you how to export movies for certain video devices like iPods, PSPs (PlayStation Portables), and tape-based camcorders.

Previewing Your Movie

I could start and end this section by simply telling you to click Play in the Monitor window to preview the current project. As an "oh-by-the-way," I could also mention that the effects and edits should be *rendered* before you export them. Rendering is the process of building preview files that incorporate your edits.

Thanks to the powerful real-time capabilities of Adobe Premiere Elements, rendering usually isn't necessary for simply previewing your edits. But rendering should be done before you export your movie to tape, DVD, or the Internet.

Any portion of a movie that needs to be rendered — but isn't yet — shows a red line under the Work Area bar, as shown in Figure 14-1. A green line means that you have already rendered a section that needed it. To render the unrendered portions of the Timeline, choose Timeline⇨Render Work Area (or just press the Enter key on your keyboard).

Work Area bar   Red bars indicate areas that need to be rendered

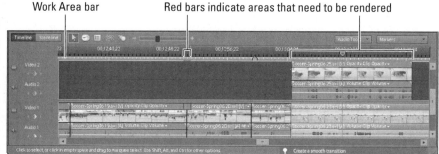

Figure 14-1:
The Work Area bar shows portions of your project that should be rendered.

Of course, there's more to previewing your project than simply rendering the Timeline and clicking Play. Consider carefully what you are actually previewing when you play a movie. Here are some ways to get the most out of previewing your project:

- ✔ **Watch the whole program from start to finish.** You may be tempted to periodically stop playback, make a few tweaks, and then click Play again. This is fine, but to get a really good sense of the flow of the project, watch the whole thing from start to finish — just as your audience will. Keep a notepad handy and jot down notes if you must.

- ✔ **Watch the program on an external television monitor.** If you plan to export your movie to tape or DVD, previewing on an external monitor helps you ensure the best color and image reproduction.

Whatever export format you use for your movie — whether it's a high-quality Blu-Ray disc or a highly compressed file for the Internet — make sure you preview the exported movie before you share it with others. Export settings can be tricky, and you may find that the audio output or other aspects of the final file are unacceptable. And of course, always preview the file on the target hardware. Video files for iPods, for example, often don't play correctly on PCs even though they look great when played on an iPod.

Making final additions to your video

Movies and videos often have some elements that you may take for granted (or never consider at all). Broadcast engineers use special video elements to help adjust video equipment. These include counting leaders and color bars and tone. A third element seems like nothing at all: black video. Do you need these elements? Not necessarily. Unless you're producing video for a local public-access cable TV channel or other broadcast outlet, you probably don't *need* bars and tone or a counting leader. But they can sometimes come in handy, and when used creatively they can lend a cool Hollywood feel to your movies. Black video is more commonly useful, because it can come in handy for short visual breaks in your project.

To create black video, bars and tone, or a counting leader, click the Organize tab in the Task pane, and then click Project. Click the New Item button in the upper-right corner of the Project screen to reveal a menu of choices. Select an item in the menu, such as Black Video. A five-second black video clip appears in the list of clips, and you can then click-and-drag the clip to the Timeline to use it.

The best way to figure out how to use the other things in the New Item menu is to just play with them. Create color bars or a counting leader, and add them to your projects as desired. The Universal Counting Leader is mainly useful for lending a retro film look to your movie, but the Bars and Tone element can be used to calibrate audio speakers and TV monitors.

✔ **Have trusted third parties review the project.** Moviemakers and writers are often too close to their creations to be totally objective; an outside point of view is helpful. I worked hard to write this book (for example), but my work was reviewed by various editors who provided invaluable feedback. Movie projects benefit from similar reviews.

Exporting Audio Only

Many people think of Adobe Premiere Elements as a video-editing program, but you can also edit and export a plain old audio file with Premiere Elements, too. Formats you can export to include AAC, MP3, QuickTime, Windows Media Audio (WMA), Windows waveform (WAV), and others.

Exporting audio files from Premiere Elements is one way to create custom ringtones for your mobile phone. Check the documentation for your phone to find out if custom ringtones are supported, and if so, what format is used. Then use Premiere Elements to export an audio file in the necessary format.

If you want to export audio in QuickTime or WMA format, see the sections in Chapter 15 on exporting movies in those formats. When you export the movie, you can choose to export only audio if you want. If you just want to quickly export audio in AAC, MP3, or WAV format, follow these steps:

1. **Click the Share tab on the Task pane, and then click Personal Computer.**

   The Export Audio dialog box appears.

2. **Scroll down the list of formats and click Audio.**

3. **Choose a format in the Presets menu.**

   The Presets menu contains options for four basic formats:

   - **AAC:** This format is supported on iPods and a few other media players. The High Quality preset delivers better audio quality, while the Medium Preset reduces quality but cuts the file size in half. AAC offers a good balance of compression and quality, but it isn't as widely supported as MP3.

   - **AIFF:** This is a lossless audio format used to store CD-quality audio on Macintosh computers and many professional audio-editing applications. Unless you know that you need AIFF files, consider exporting Windows Waveform audio instead. AIFF files are large and not supported by most portable media players.

   - **MP3:** This ubiquitous format is supported by all modern computers and digital media players. There are three quality presets so you can choose between better quality or smaller file size.

   - **Windows Waveform:** This lossless format stores CD-quality audio on Windows computers. WAV files are compatible with most Windows applications, but the files are big and not supported by most portable media players.

4. **Enter a name in the File Name field.**

5. **Click Browse and choose a location in which to save the file.**

6. **Place a check mark next to Share Work Area Bar Only if you want to share only part of the Timeline.**

   You can export the entire Timeline or just the range covered by the Work Area bar. See Chapter 7 for more on using the Work Area bar.

7. **Click Advanced to open the Export Settings dialog box.**

   Options in the Export Settings dialog box vary, depending on the format you chose in Step 3. Figure 14-2 shows options for MP3 files.

8. **Choose Stereo or Mono next to Channels.**

   Stereo improves audio quality but inflates file sizes.

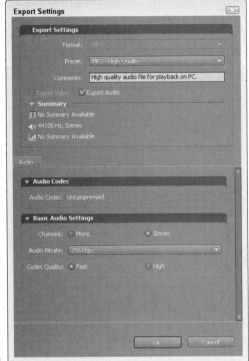

Figure 14-2:
Choose
audio export
settings
here.

9. **Choose an Audio Bitrate.**

   Higher bitrates mean better audio quality and (surprise!) bigger file sizes. For MP3 and AAC files, even the most casual listener will notice the reduced audio quality found in bitrates below 128 Kbps.

10. **Click OK to close the Export Settings dialog box.**

11. **Back in the Task pane, click Save to export the audio file.**

Capturing Still Images from Your Movie

Premiere Elements lets you export still images from your movies, which comes in handy for a variety of reasons. For example, you may want to display stills from the movie on a Web page, or use stills as background images in DVD menus. Just keep in mind that stills extracted from video are usually of lower quality than stills shot with a conventional still-photo camera. Even frames extracted from high-def video have less than two megapixels of resolution. To export a still image from Premiere Elements, follow these steps:

1. **Move the CTI in the Timeline to the exact frame that you want to export.**

   You can use the J, K, and L keys on your keyboard to control playback. Press K to pause playback, and then use the left- and right-arrow keys to step forward or back a single frame at a time.

2. **In the Task pane, click the Share tab and then click Personal Computer.**

3. **In the list of sharing options that appears, click Image.**

4. **Choose an export format from the Presets menu.**

   The available export formats for still frames are GIF, JPEG, Targa, and TIFF. TIFF provides the highest quality, but JPEG and GIF are more Web-friendly. If you have an image-editing program like Photoshop or Photoshop Elements, I recommend that you export in TIFF format. Otherwise, export to JPEG if you plan to use the image directly on the Web. Targa is an older image format still in some video-editing applications, but it has inferior color bit depth compared to TIFF or JPEG.

5. **Enter a filename in the File Name field, and click Browse next to Save In to choose a location in which to save the file.**

6. **Click Save.**

7. **Choose a location and name the file, and then click Save.**

   The still image is saved. The still image also shows up in your media lists on the Organize tab of the Task pane.

You may need to edit still images exported from video, especially if the image comes from interlaced video. Fast-moving objects in the image may show *combing.* This is a term that describes the horrid horizontal distortions that occur in an image that has been interlaced. Also, if the video comes from a rectangular-pixel video image, it may appear stretched or squeezed on computer screens. Adobe Photoshop Elements and other photo-editing programs usually have de-interlacing filters to help you remove combing.

If you want poster-quality promotional shots of your movie, bring a high-quality still camera along with you during a video shoot and use it to take pictures of the scenes or subjects in the movie.

Saving AVI Files

Besides making movie editing easy, Premiere Elements also makes it easy to record your movies to DVD, YouTube, or various other viewing modes. You can also export your movies directly to an AVI format file.

AVI is short for Audio-Video Interleave and is also sometimes called Video for Windows. It has been a common Windows multimedia format for many years. When you capture standard-def video from a tape-based camcorder, the captured video footage is stored on your hard drive in AVI format. High-def video and video captured from flash, disc, or hard-drive–based camcorders is captured in the camera's native MPEG format.

AVI files are usually too big to share online. (See Chapter 15 for Web-friendly sharing formats.) But AVIs are useful as full-quality archive copies, and they can be used by other video programs. To export your movie in AVI format, follow these steps:

1. **Click the Share tab, and then click AVI.**

2. **Choose a preset in the Presets menu.**

   The Presets menu contains four DV presets offering choices of NTSC or PAL, and standard (4:3) or widescreen (16:9) aspect ratios (see Chapter 3 for more on aspect ratios). In addition to DV, there are presets called Microsoft AVI and Uncompressed AVI. Which one you choose depends on a couple of factors:

   - **DV presets:** Choose NTSC or PAL depending on your local broadcast standard, and choose standard or widescreen depending on the aspect ratio of your movie. All the DV presets output video in standard definition, and widescreen presets letterbox the video image to fit in a 4:3 video image. The DV presets are best if you ultimately plan to view the movie on a TV.

   - **Microsoft AVI:** This is a good preset to use for general archiving purposes. The output is similar to the DV presets, but you can customize the pixel aspect ratio and other settings.

   - **Uncompressed Microsoft AVI:** This preset is also intended for archiving. By default, it uses square pixels and progressive scanning. Use this preset if you feel that you have unlimited storage space; otherwise, the Microsoft AVI preset is adequate.

   If small file size is a priority, I recommend that you use the QuickTime, Flash, or Windows Media formats described in Chapter 15.

3. **Enter a filename, and click Browse to choose a location in which to save the file.**

4. **Click Advanced.**

   The Export Settings dialog box appears. Depending on which preset you use, you may be able to change the frame size, frame rate, color depth, and other settings to yield a smaller file size.

   Keyframe Options (under Advanced Settings) are available only if you are exporting in Microsoft AVI format. Rendering keyframes control how Premiere Elements compresses video. The default setting of 15 frames is usually adequate, but if your video images don't contain a lot of movement, you may want to increase it to 30 frames. If your video contains many fast-moving images, setting keyframes every 10 frames offers better video quality — and larger file sizes.

5. **Click OK to close the Export Settings dialog box.**

6. **Click Save.**

The movie is rendered and exported. Depending on the size of the movie, rendering and output may take awhile.

Exporting to Digital Devices

Decades ago, visions of the future predicted hover cars, vacations in space, and wristwatch TVs. Well here we are in the 21st century and we're still waiting for our hover cars, and outer space tourism is reserved for those who can afford to pay more than $20 million for a rare flight on a Russian Soyuz rocket. Although I don't see a lot of wristwatch televisions, modern media players and mobile phones are making handheld portable video a reality.

Whether you're bored at work or stranded at the spaceport, if you have a portable phone or device that can play video, Premiere Elements can probably export video for your device. Supported formats include

- ✔ **Apple iPods and iPhones:** Video-capable devices from Apple use a unique video format based on the H.264 codec (a video compression scheme). Options include a 640 x 480 high-quality format (best for larger devices like the iPhone or iPod Touch) or a 320 x 240 medium-quality format (best for smaller iPod devices). Premiere Elements can also output audio-only Podcast files.

- ✔ **Creative Zen:** This format option exports a good-quality 320 x 240 Windows Media file. Even if you don't have a Zen, this format is a good choice for many different brands of digital media players that can handle Windows Media Video.

- ✔ **Microsoft Zune:** Microsoft's Zune players play Windows Media Audio and Video. This format option in Premiere Elements is similar to the Creative Zen option, except for slightly better audio quality and superior compression for smaller file sizes.

- ✔ **Pocket PC:** The term "Pocket PC" is rather ambiguous, because this option simply outputs a small (240 x 176) video image in a highly compressed format. It can be played on Pocket PCs, yes, but these videos can also be played on many WMV-capable media players. For that matter, most Pocket PCs running a modern version of the Windows Mobile operating system can play videos output for the Creative Zen, too.

- **Smartphone:** Smartphones are like Pocket PCs that also happen to be phones. The Smartphone output option in Premiere Elements produces a tiny 224 x 128 video image in Windows Media format.

- **Sony PSP:** PlayStation Portable (PSP) devices from Sony use a special H.264-based video format that is similar to (but not exactly like) the formats used by Apple iPods and iPhones. PSP video files have a good-quality 320 x 240 image size, and the files even have the same .MP4 file-name extension as iPod files. But iPod and PSP files are not compatible, so make sure you output the correct format for your target audience.

- **Mobile Phone:** Smartphones aren't the only mobile phones that can play video. Many non-smartphones (dumb phones?) can play video. Mobile phone video uses the .3GP filename extension and provides a teensy little 176 x 144 video image. Be sure to send your audience magnifying glasses so they can actually see the movie.

The next couple of sections show you how to export movies for iPods, iPhones, and personal media players such as the Creative Zen. I don't need to show you how to export videos for each format, because the process is almost the same for each format. The process for making iPod and iPhone movies is similar to the process for Sony PSP and mobile phone videos, while the steps for personal media player files work equally well for Creative Zens, Microsoft Zunes, Pocket PCs, and smartphones.

Making iPod and iPhone movies

If you want to have the coolest portable media player, you need to get an iPod or iPhone. The only problem is that everyone else has an iPod, too. So how do you outcool the cool people? When everyone else is just listening to iMusic, you can be watching your own personal iVideos!

Apple iPods and iPhones use a special H.264 video codec that provides excellent playback quality and small file sizes. The file extension is MP4. In theory, videos that you export from Premiere Elements using the iPod output format should play on any device that can play MP4 videos; however, I have found that iPod videos often will only play properly on an iPod or iPhone.

The steps for exporting smartphone and PSP videos are very similar to the process for producing iPod videos. iPhones and iPods use exactly the same format, of course. To export an iPod video, follow these steps:

1. **Click the Share tab, and then click Mobile Phones and Players.**

2. **Choose Apple iPod and iPhone in the list of devices that appears.**

   If you're outputting a movie for PSPs or mobile phones, choose one of those options instead.

3. **Choose an iPod/iPhone preset in the Presets menu.**

   The high-quality preset creates a movie with a 640 x 480 image size. This preset is best for devices with larger screens, such as the iPhone and iPod Touch. The medium-quality preset gives an image size of 320 x 240, which is better for smaller-screened iPod devices.

   The high-quality preset produces file sizes that are about 30 percent to 40 percent larger than medium-quality movies. In the example shown in Figure 14-3, my 18-minute movie will be about 146MB at high quality or 111MB at medium quality. Both presets offer CD-quality audio.

4. **Give your movie a name in the File Name field.**

   In Figure 14-3, I have named my movie "McDowellCreekFalls."

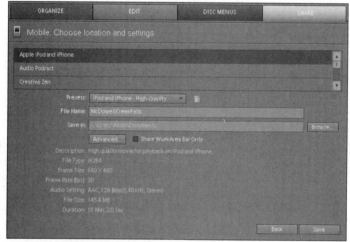

Figure 14-3: Choose an iPod preset and name your movie.

5. **Click Browse and choose a location in which to save the movie.**

   Strictly speaking, choosing a location for your movie is optional. But I recommend that you manually choose a location so that you'll easily be able to find the movie later.

6. **If you want to fine-tune output settings, click Advanced.**

   The Export Settings dialog box appears, as shown in Figure 14-4. It's usually best to just accept the default settings with the high- or medium-quality presets. However, if you're trying to reduce file sizes, there are a couple of settings you can adjust:

   • **Frame Rate:** On the Video tab, reduce the frame rate to 15 frames per second (fps). This will drastically reduce the playback quality, but if you need a smaller file size and the video doesn't contain a lot of fast action, you may find that a reduced frame rate is a reasonable sacrifice.

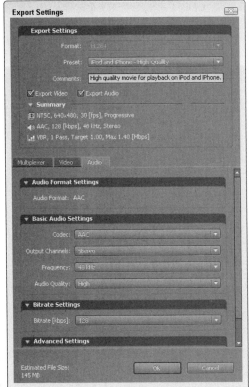

- **Video Bitrate Settings:** Scroll down on the Video tab to reveal bitrate settings. Choose VBR, 2 Pass in the Bitrate Encoding menu to make the compression more efficient (this will also cause the export to take a longer amount of time). Slide the Target and Maximum Bitrate sliders left to reduce the overall video bitrate (and thus image quality).

- **Basic Audio Settings:** If your movie's audio quality is less critical, click the Audio tab. Change the Output Channels menu to Mono, reduce the Frequency to 32 kHz, and choose Low or Medium in the Audio Quality menu.

- **Audio Bitrate Settings:** Scroll down the Audio tab and click-and-drag the Bitrate slider left to reduce the audio bitrate.

Don't change anything on the Multiplexer tab. If you change settings on that tab, the video format will be incorrect and your movie won't play properly on iPods. Click OK to close the Export Settings dialog box.

7. **Review the output settings and estimated file size shown on the Share tab, and then click Save to begin exporting your movie.**

   Premiere Elements renders and exports the movie. This may take awhile depending on the length of your movie and the complexity of your edits.

8. **When the movie is done exporting, open iTunes, choose File⇨ Add File to Library, and then browse to your exported MP4 file.**

   Use iTunes to copy the movie to your iPod or iPhone. Visit Chapter 15 if you want to share your iPod-format movies on the Internet.

Creating videos for personal media players

A lot of portable media players and devices can play video. Every device is different, and I can't cover every brand and variation here. But many smartphones and media players support video playback using some variation of the Windows Media Video (WMV) codec. The Creative Zen, Microsoft Zune, Pocket PC, and Smartphone output options in Premiere Elements all output Windows Media in a variety of quality and size settings. To output video in one of these formats, follow these steps:

1. **Click the Share tab, and then click Mobile Phones and Players.**

2. **Choose a format that most closely matches the target device.**

   In the example here, I am exporting a movie for Pocket PCs.

3. **Choose an output preset in the Presets menu.**

   Some formats — such as the Zen and Zune players — let you choose your local broadcast standard (NTSC or PAL; see Chapter 3 for more on broadcast standards). The Smartphone format lets you choose between portrait or landscape picture orientations. Videos are usually landscape, but many smartphones have portrait-shaped video screens.

4. **Give your movie a name in the File Name field.**

5. **Click Browse and choose a location in which to save the movie.**

   You can just accept the default location, but I recommend that you manually choose a location so you can easily find the movie later.

6. **If you want to fine-tune output settings, click Advanced.**

   The Export Settings dialog box appears, as shown in Figure 14-5. Here you can adjust settings to balance between movie quality and file size:

   • **Video Bitrate Settings:** To improve compression efficiency, on the Video tab, choose two encoding passes and then select Variable Constrained in the Bitrate Mode menu, as shown in Figure 14-5.

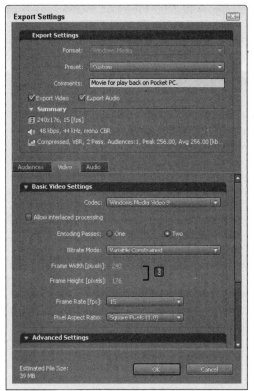

Figure 14-5:
Find the right balance of file size and quality.

- **Frame Rate:** On the Video tab, reduce the frame rate to 10 fps to reduce file size, or increase it to 25 or 30 to improve quality.

- **Audio Bitrate Settings:** To improve compression efficiency, choose two encoding passes, and then select Variable Constrained in the Bitrate Mode menu.

- **Basic Audio Settings:** Choose a lower-quality option in the Audio Format menu, and slide the Peak Audio Bitrate slider left to reduce quality and file size.

7. **Click OK to close the Export Settings dialog box.**

8. **Review the output settings and estimated file size shown on the Share tab, and then click Save to begin exporting your movie.**

   Premiere Elements renders and exports the movie. This may take awhile depending on the length of your movie and the complexity of your edits.

9. **When the movie is exported, use Windows Media Player or another program to sync the movie to your Pocket PC or media player.**

Recording Movies to Tape

Before you think that videotapes are old fashioned, consider that most pro-quality camcorders — including high-definition cams — still use tapes. Digital videotapes are cheap, reliable, and can be archived for many years. If you have a tape-based digital camcorder, you can output finished movies from Premiere Elements directly to tape. After the movie has been recorded to a tape in your camcorder, you can then archive the tape, use the camcorder to transfer the movie to a VHS tape, or connect the camcorder to a TV for playback. The following sections show you how to export finished movies to a tape-based camcorder.

If you want to export a movie directly to an analog VHS tape (remember those?), your options are somewhat limited. One option is to connect a VHS VCR to your computer with an analog video converter (see Chapter 19 for more on video converters). Follow the steps described in this chapter to export a movie to tape, and manually set the VCR to record the output from your computer.

Getting ready for tape output

Before you export your movie to tape, you should make sure that your movie is actually ready. Naturally, you should review the project and all of your edits. Because any movie you export to tape will be viewed primarily on broadcast-style TVs, you should also check the following:

✔ **Is the movie compatible with the appropriate broadcast standard?** See Chapter 3 for more on video standards. Review settings in the General Project Settings (Project➪Project Settings➪General).

✔ **Has the movie been rendered?** Effects, transitions, and other edits should be rendered before you record to tape. If you see any red lines at the top of the Timeline, click the Timeline to make it active and press Enter. Premiere Elements renders all your edits.

✔ **Is your computer optimized for export to tape?** Your computer must be able to play the movie flawlessly in real time. To make sure that your computer is ready, do the following:

- **Turn off extra programs.** Make sure all unnecessary programs are closed, including your e-mail program, MP3 jukebox, and Web browser. Every open program uses up memory and processor resources that should be devoted to video export.

- **Disable programs that run in the background.** Disable memory-resident programs such as antivirus programs and any programs that have icons in the Windows system tray (the area in the lower-right corner of the screen, next to the clock). You should be able to close or disable most of these items by right-clicking them and choosing Close, Disable, or Exit from their respective menus. (Just don't forget to turn that antivirus program back on when you're done exporting!)

- **Disable screen savers and power-management settings to ensure that they don't kick on in the middle of a long export operation.** If you're working on a laptop, make sure that it's plugged in to wall power so that it doesn't hibernate or run out of battery power in the middle of export.

- **Defragment your hard drive.** A recently defragmented drive ensures efficient operation during video capture and export.

✔ **Is your hardware connected?** Connect the camcorder to the computer's FireWire or USB 2.0 port, and turn the camera on to player mode.

✔ **Do you have a new, blank tape?** It's best to use a brand-new, blank tape for export. This prevents timecode breaks and other problems that may cause your movie to play poorly or not at all.

✔ **Have you previewed your project on a TV monitor yet?** Previewing your movie on a real TV monitor can help you identify problems such as weird colors or titles that get cut off at the edge of the screen.

Exporting your movie to tape

After you have prepared your movie, computer, and camcorder for export to tape, you're ready to begin the actual export process. If you are exporting to a device that has device control (such as a digital camcorder; see Chapter 2 for more on device control), follow these steps:

1. **Connect your recording device (your camcorder or DV deck) to your computer and turn it on.**

   Make sure that the camcorder is turned on to VTR (Player) mode, and not to Camera mode.

2. **Click the Share tab, and then click Tape.**

   The Export to Tape dialog box appears, as shown in Figure 14-6.

3. **Make sure that a check mark is placed next to the Activate Recording Device option.**

   The only time you would disable this option is if you're exporting video through a video converter connected to your computer's FireWire port. (I describe video converters in Chapter 19.)

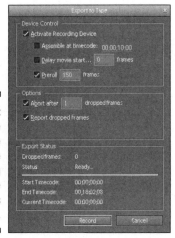

Figure 14-6:
Make sure
that the
Activate
Recording
Device
option is
selected.

4. **If the tape already has a timecode on it, select the Assemble at Timecode option and specify a timecode where you want recording to begin.**

   Start the recording at about the ten-second mark on your tape.

5. **Enter the number of frames, if any, that you want to delay before the movie starts playing.**

   Some devices need a delay between receiving the *record* command and the actual movie.

6. **Enter the number of frames that you want to preroll the tape in the Preroll field.**

   Preroll allows the reels in the tape deck to spin up to the correct speed before recording begins. I recommend at least five seconds (150 frames for NTSC video, 125 frames for PAL video) of preroll.

7. **Place a check mark next to Abort After.**

Of course, you can tell Premiere Elements to stop export after only 2 or 3 or 50 frames have been dropped, but even one dropped frame is an unacceptable quality problem. If you have trouble with dropped frames during capture, review the earlier sections of this chapter and Chapter 4 to make sure your computer is ready and that it meets the specs for running Premiere Elements.

8. Click Record.

Your movie is recorded on the tape. The camcorder will automatically stop when the recording process is complete.

Chapter 15

Sharing Your Movies Online

Making movies with Adobe Premiere Elements is so much fun that it's easy to forget the most important part: Sharing your movies with others. Entertaining and informing others is one of the main reasons for manipulating raw video clips into interesting and creative movies.

You can share your completed movies with the world in many different ways. This chapter shows you how to share your movie projects in the online world of the Internet. I help you identify some of the special problems involved with putting movies online, help you choose a player program for your movies, and show you how to export your movies in a variety of Web-friendly formats directly from Adobe Premiere Elements. I also show you how to upload your movies to YouTube.

Archiving Movies on Photoshop.com

I'll never forget the first time I left a vinyl record sitting next to a window in direct sunlight. I came back a few hours later and the record was warped beyond repair. Ruined! If only I had a backup!

Today most media is stored on computer hard drives rather than on vinyl LPs. Computers don't warp if you leave them out in the sun, but the digital age has made us no less vulnerable to data loss. An unexpected hard drive failure can mean that all your stored music, photos, and movies are gone forever. But if you have a Photoshop.com membership, you can use this service from Adobe to back up photos and videos online. Follow these steps:

1. **When you're done editing, click the Share tab on the Task pane.**

2. **Click Online, and then select Photoshop.com in the list of online sharing options.**

3. **Click Next and enter a title for your movie, as shown in Figure 15-1.**

4. **Choose how widely you want to share the movie:**

   • **Everyone:** Anyone on the Internet can view your movie.

   • **People I Invite:** This option lets you pick and choose who can view the movie, and it automatically generates invitation e-mails.

   • **Private:** Only you can access the movie through your Photoshop.com account.

5. **If you chose to invite specific people to view the movie, type a message in the Email Message box, and then place a check mark next to contacts who should receive the invitation.**

   Premiere Elements maintains a contacts list for movie invitations. To add contacts, click the Address Book button (it looks like a person and is at the upper-right corner of the contacts list). In the Address Book dialog box that appears, click Add Contact and then type a name and e-mail address for the person you want to add. Click Done to close the Address Book.

6. **Click Share to begin uploading your movie.**

The sharing process may take awhile, because the movie is encoded in the Photoshop.com video format before it is uploaded. When the upload is complete, a link appears to take you online to view your movie.

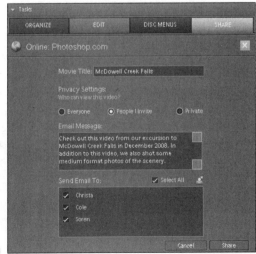

Figure 15-1:
Share your movies using Photoshop. com.

Uploading Your Movies to YouTube

Today, digital video and the Internet go together like Kirk and Spock. But back in the early days of digital video and the online world, the relationship was more like Spock and Dr. McCoy, which is to say challenging and complex. If you wanted to share movies online, you had to pay for dedicated Web server space, and you needed knowledge of how to build and maintain Web sites. Then in 2005 along came YouTube, and online video was revolutionized. YouTube introduced several important innovations:

- ✔ **Free Web server space:** There's no charge to upload videos to YouTube, and watching videos is free too.

- ✔ **Simple upload interface:** You don't need to be a trained Internet engineer to use YouTube. The upload page uses simple options to help you upload any video file from your computer.

- ✔ **Flash video conversion:** You can upload videos to YouTube in almost any common video format. YouTube automatically converts your videos to the Adobe Flash format. The Flash Player browser plug-in from Adobe is free, and it's installed on nearly all modern computers.

Because you have Adobe Premiere Elements, there's even more good news: Premiere Elements can upload your videos directly to YouTube. The only limitations — besides good taste and the YouTube terms of use — are that videos you upload can be no longer than ten minutes and no larger than 100MB.

YouTube is a tremendous information resource, but certain kinds of information can be controversial or even illegal in some countries. A few countries have blocked access to YouTube at various times, and certain kinds of videos may be blocked in some countries. Likewise, some corporate networks block YouTube videos. Keep in mind that in rare cases your intended audience won't be able to watch your YouTube videos.

Creating a YouTube account

Uploading videos to YouTube is free, but you must have a YouTube user account. You can create an account in Premiere Elements during the upload process, or you can visit the YouTube Web site directly and create an account at any time:

1. **Visit www.youtube.com, and click the Sign Up link in the upper-right corner of the Web page.**

   An account creation page appears.

2. **Enter a valid e-mail address, and provide a password.**

   Create a password that is at least eight characters long and includes numbers, uppercase letters, and lowercase letters. The e-mail address you enter must be valid because YouTube will send you a confirmation e-mail as part of the account creation process.

3. **Provide a unique user name.**

   Click the Check Availability link to see if your user name is available.

4. **Enter other requested information, and review the Terms of Use and Privacy Policy files.**

   YouTube asks for your general location, date of birth, and gender. Make sure that you review the Terms of Use and Privacy Policy links carefully.

5. **Click Create Account.**

6. **Open your e-mail account and click the Confirm your email address link in the YouTube confirmation e-mail.**

   If you don't receive a confirmation e-mail, check the anti-spam settings for your e-mail program or account to make sure that the confirmation e-mail isn't erroneously sent to spam prison.

Uploading the movie

You can upload virtually any video file on your computer to YouTube by visiting www.youtube.com, logging in to your account, and finding the Upload link on the YouTube Web page. But why go to all that hassle when you can easily upload YouTube videos right from within Premiere Elements? When you're done editing your movie in Premiere Elements, make sure your computer is connected to the Internet. Then follow these steps:

1. **Click the Share tab, and then click Online in the list of sharing options that appears.**

2. **Click YouTube in the list of online sharing choices.**

   Review the file size and duration of your movie on the Share tab. Premiere Elements limits YouTube file sizes to less than 100MB and durations to ten minutes or less. If your movie is longer than ten minutes, you either need to break it up into segments and upload each one separately, or do more editing to shorten the movie's duration. If you really need to share a longer movie, you may need to share the movie using another method, which I describe later in this chapter.

3. **Choose an option in the Presets menu.**

   If your movie has a 4:3 aspect ratio (see Chapter 3 for more on aspect ratios), choose Flash Video for YouTube. If your movie has a 16:9 aspect ratio, choose Flash Video for YouTube (Widescreen).

4. **Click Next, and enter your YouTube account name and password.**

   Place a check mark next to Remember Me to make logging in easier.

5. **Click Next again, and enter a title and other descriptive information about your movie, as shown in Figure 15-2.**

   This is the information that YouTube users will see when they watch your movie. It also helps the YouTube search engine find your movie.

Figure 15-2:
Enter a title
and descrip-
tion for your
movie.

6. **Decide whether you want to share your movie with the public.**

   If you choose Yes, anyone can find and view your video on YouTube. If you choose No, you can still share your video with select friends, but those friends must log in to a YouTube user account, and you have to manually allow them to view your video in your YouTube account control panel. Click the Account link at YouTube to manage your privacy settings.

7. **Click Share.**

   Premiere Elements renders your movie in the Flash format and then uploads it to YouTube. The rendering and upload process may take awhile, depending on the complexity and length of your movie.

When the movie finishes uploading, a screen appears with a link to your video at the YouTube Web site. You can e-mail that link to other people to share your video. If you go to YouTube and find that your movie isn't yet ready for playback, don't worry. The video needs to be processed by the YouTube server before it can play, which usually takes a few minutes.

Creating Web-Friendly Video Files

YouTube provides an easy way to share your movies online, and you can't beat the price (it's free). But YouTube isn't your only option, and Premiere Elements can output movies in the most popular Web-friendly video formats. These formats include Adobe Flash, Apple QuickTime, and Microsoft Windows Media Video.

Sharing video online presents technical challenges that you need to know about. The good folks who built the foundations of the online world many decades ago envisioned it as a staging ground for efficient global information exchange, but sharing full-motion video over the Internet wasn't part of the original plan. Video, and especially streaming video, is at odds with the fundamental design of the Internet for two key reasons:

- ✓ **Bandwidth:** High-speed broadband Internet connections have become far more commonplace in recent years, but the term "high speed" is relative. Large video files can still take awhile to download, and some of your audience members may not have the patience to sit around waiting for downloads to finish. Large movie files can also quickly eat up the monthly bandwidth allotment for your Web server space, especially if your movies become popular with other Internet users.

- ✓ **Packet delivery:** Data is transmitted over the Internet in packets rather than in steady streams. This makes data transfer over the Internet reliable, but not fast.

Data is broken into packets for transmission over the Internet. These packets travel many different pathways to the destination, where they are reassembled in the correct order to form a Web page, e-mail message, or any other file that is shared online. Contrast packet delivery to, say, a radio or television broadcast, which transmits data in a continuous wave. Packet delivery is reliable because it doesn't require an unbroken connection between the sender and receiver. Confused? Imagine you want to give your phone number to someone across a crowded room. You could try yelling across the room (a broadcast), but the receiver might miss a number or two because of the crowd noise. A more reliable method would be to write your number on a piece of paper and send it across the room via messenger. The paper method is slower, but at least you know the recipient will get the correct phone number.

Choosing player software

Distributing your movie digitally actually means distributing it as a file — so you have to make sure that your intended audience can open that file. With Premiere Elements, you have three basic choices: Flash, QuickTime, or Windows Media.

First, remove Adobe Flash from consideration. Although Flash is used by YouTube and other video-sharing Web sites, it isn't conducive to hosting videos on your own Web site. That leaves you with the Apple QuickTime and Microsoft Windows Media formats. Yes, that's right: Apple versus Microsoft. Which one is best?

Having worked extensively with both the QuickTime and Windows Media Video formats, I can tell you that neither format has a clear tech-

nical advantage. Both offer small file sizes and good quality. The most important consideration boils down to what software your audience has. QuickTime is preinstalled on all Macintosh PCs, and Apple offers a free QuickTime player for Windows. Likewise, Windows Media Player is installed on all Windows PCs. Microsoft doesn't directly offer Windows Media Player for Macs, but a free QuickTime plug-in called Flip4Mac (available on both Apple and Microsoft Web sites) lets Mac users watch Windows Media Video.

QuickTime or Windows Media? Go with your gut. Use the format that you like best. If your audience complains about the format you put on your Web site, that will also be a good indication of what they prefer.

So what's the point of all this technical discussion about bandwidth and packets? Video for the Web must be highly compressed, the frame size must be reduced, and you must accept some sacrifices in quality. Video can be distributed over the Internet in one of two ways:

- ✔ **Download:** Users download the entire movie file before it is played. Most current video player programs can start to play the movie before it is all downloaded. The program calculates when enough of the movie has been received so that playback can begin and continue without interruption. This is called *progressive playback* or *progressive download,* and it does a fair job of mimicking streaming video.

- ✔ **Stream:** The movie plays as it downloads to the user's machine. Some of the video is *buffered* (portions of the data are temporarily stored in computer memory) to provide uninterrupted playback. The predominant formats for streaming video are Apple QuickTime Streaming, RealMedia, and Windows Media Streaming Video. In each case, special server software is required to host streaming media.

Regardless of which distribution method you choose, the export process for the movie from Adobe Premiere Elements is still the same. You export the movie as a file that resides on your hard drive. Whether that file is later streamed is determined by whether you use streaming server software on your Web server. See Chapter 19 for more on choosing a Web server.

You may want to produce a lower-quality movie for people who are impatient or have slow dialup connections, and make a higher-quality movie for folks with fast broadband access. You may also want to offer versions for several different players. For example, you can offer both Apple QuickTime and Windows Media versions. Face it: Some people are very touchy about using software from certain companies.

Saving an Apple QuickTime movie

Apple QuickTime is popular for sharing movies online because it provides a good balance of file size and quality. Before you can export to QuickTime format, you must have QuickTime Player 6 or later installed on your computer. To download QuickTime, visit www.apple.com and click the Downloads link. Once QuickTime is installed, exporting a QuickTime movie is simple. When you're done editing your movie, follow these steps:

1. **Click the Share tab, and then choose the Personal Computer option.**

2. **Scroll down the menu at the top of PC sharing options and choose QuickTime, as shown in Figure 15-3.**

3. **Choose a preset from the Presets menu.**

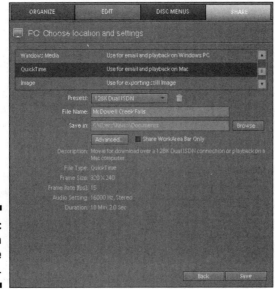

Figure 15-3:
Choose a
QuickTime
preset here.

When you choose a preset, a description of the preset appears at the bottom of the Share tab. The presets offer different combinations of frame size, frame rate, and audio frequency to suit a variety of bandwidth needs. The highest quality preset is the LAN preset, which has a frame size of 640 x 480, a frame rate of 29.97 fps (NTSC) or 25 fps (PAL), and an audio frequency of 44 kHz, which is roughly CD-quality. The 128K Dual ISDN preset shrinks the picture size to 320 x 240, cuts the frame rate to 15 fps, and reduces audio quality to 16 kHz. If neither of the presets matches your needs, click the Advanced button to customize export settings. I describe advanced QuickTime settings in the next section.

4. **Enter a filename for your movie in the File Name field.**

5. **Click Browse and choose a location in which to save the movie.**

6. **Click Save.**

When you click Save, Premiere Elements begins to render and save the movie. A Rendering progress bar appears to let you know the progress of the export. The progress bar also estimates the remaining time; saving the file might take awhile, especially if this is a long project.

Choosing advanced QuickTime settings

When you export a QuickTime movie, you may want to customize your export settings rather than use a preset. To customize the settings, click Advanced on the Share tab when you export a QuickTime movie (see the preceding section for the basic steps of saving a QuickTime movie). The Export Settings dialog box appears, as shown in Figure 15-4. Click the tabs in the Export Settings dialog box to access advanced Video and Audio settings.

When you're done adjusting settings in the Export Settings dialog box, click OK and continue saving your movie as described in the preceding section. The next few sections describe advanced QuickTime export settings in detail.

Adjusting QuickTime video settings

QuickTime videos are *videos,* so it makes sense that advanced video settings are the first thing you see when you open the Export Settings dialog box. The QuickTime video settings are pretty easy to sort through. Review these settings on the Video tab of the Export Settings dialog box:

✔ **Codec:** This is the compression/decompression scheme used to compress the movie to a smaller file size (see Chapter 3 for more on codecs). There are many choices in the Codec menu, but for online use, the H.264 codec is usually best. If people have a hard time playing your QuickTime movies — jerky playback is one common problem — try using one of the Sorenson codecs instead.

✔ **Quality:** This setting controls how the video image is compressed. It should come as no surprise that higher quality results in larger file sizes.

✔ **Frame Width/Height:** These boxes control the size of the video image. Try to maintain the aspect ratio of 4:3 to prevent distorting the video image (16:9 widescreen videos will be letterboxed in QuickTime Player). Chapter 3 explains aspect ratios. Larger video sizes mean larger files. (Is there an echo in here? Is there an echo in here?)

✔ **Frame Rate:** Broadcast-quality video usually has a frame rate of 25 or 29.97 frames per second (fps). You can save file size and bandwidth by using a frame rate of 12 or 15 fps. To ensure smooth playback, choose a frame rate that is one-half or one-third of the original frame rate.

✔ **Field Order:** For online movies, you usually choose None (Progressive). However, if you find that the movie you output has combing or other interlacing problems, choose Upper or Lower. Some experimentation may be necessary. I explain interlacing in Chapter 3.

✔ **Pixel Aspect Ratio:** Square Pixels is the most common choice here, but if your video image appears stretched or squeezed you may need to choose one of the rectangular pixel options. Choose the option that matches the format of your original source footage.

✔ **Set Bitrate:** Place a check mark next to Set Bitrate and adjust the Bitrate slider to change the video bitrate. A higher bitrate means higher video quality, and of course, larger file sizes.

✔ **Set Key Frame Distance:** Compression key frames help video compress more efficiently. A longer interval between key frames often reduces file size and quality. Enable the Set Key Frame Distance check box to change the interval between compression key frames.

✔ **Frame Reordering:** This option makes compression a lot more efficient, but it may also cause playback problems for some people, especially those who have older versions of QuickTime.

Despite the name similarity, compression key frames are entirely different from effect keyframes. A compression key frame is a picture of the entire video image. When video is compressed, a key frame might only occur once every one, five, or even ten seconds. All the frames between those key frames — the in-between frames are called *delta* frames — contain information only about things in the video image that have changed.

Adjusting QuickTime audio settings

Apple QuickTime's audio settings are simple. You can choose an audio codec from the Codec menu (the AAC codec works well), select mono or stereo output, and specify a frequency. A frequency of 44 kHz provides CD-quality audio, but keep in mind that high-quality audio can inflate file size in a big hurry.

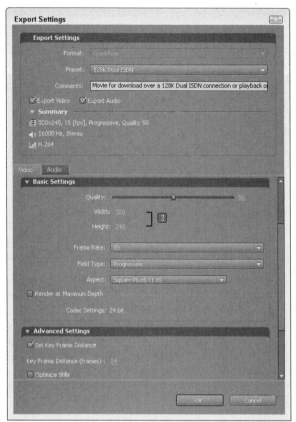

Figure 15-4:
Customize
the size and
quality of
the video
image.

If your exported files are too big, start here to whittle down the file size. A simple reduction of the audio frequency, as well as switching from Stereo to Mono, can make a big difference in the file size.

Exporting Windows Media

Another Web-friendly export option in Adobe Premiere Elements is Windows Media. This export option produces Windows Media Video (WMV), an efficient export format for online media. WMV-format video supports progressive download (also called *hinted download*), which means it starts to play as soon as a sufficient amount of data has been received to ensure continuous playback from start to finish. Windows Media Player is free and preinstalled on all Windows PCs, and a free program called Flip4Mac is available on the Apple and Microsoft Web sites to allow Macintosh users to view unprotected WMV files as well.

Exporting Windows Media video is a lot like exporting QuickTime movies. To export Windows Media video, follow these steps:

1. When you're done editing your movie, click the Share tab.

2. Choose the Personal Computer sharing option.

   Even though your ultimate plan might be to share it online, don't choose the Online option. The Online option gives you access only to Flash video formats.

3. Scroll down the menu at the top of PC sharing options and choose Windows Media, as shown in Figure 15-5.

4. Choose a preset from the Presets menu.

   When you choose a preset, a description of the preset appears at the bottom of the Share tab. The presets offer different combinations of frame size, frame rate, and audio frequency to suit a variety of bandwidth needs. The highest quality presets are the HD 1080i and 720p presets (available only if you're working with a high-def movie). These presets offer essentially broadcast quality playback, but the files sizes are usually way too big for online use. The highest quality Web-friendly preset is Local Area Network (LAN), which includes a frame size of 640 x 480, a frame rate of 30 fps (NTSC) or 25 fps (PAL), and an audio frequency of 44 kHz, which is roughly CD-quality. Contrast this with the lowest-quality preset, which is the DialUp 56K Modem preset. This preset has a frame size of 176 x 144, a frame rate of 10 fps, and 16 kHz audio. Obviously, the LAN preset gives much better playback quality, but it also yields a much bigger file size. In Figure 15-5, I have chosen the Cable Modem/DSL preset, which falls somewhere between the LAN and DialUp presets in terms of quality and file size.

   If none of the presets exactly match your needs, click the Advanced button to customize your export settings. I describe advanced Windows Media settings in the next section.

   As with QuickTime, presets that offer a higher frame rate, a larger frame size, or greater audio quality tend to produce larger movie files. To customize your Windows Media export settings, click Advanced. I describe advanced settings in the following section.

5. Enter a filename for your movie in the File Name field.

   If you plan to export your movie in several different sizes to accommodate a variety of online viewers, make sure that the filename reflects the preset used for this version. For example, if one version of a movie shot at a jazz festival uses the Cable Modem/DSL preset, you might name the file JazzFestDSL. A second version which uses the 56K Modem preset might be called JazzFest56K.

6. **Click Browse and choose a location in which to save the movie.**

7. **Click Save.**

   When you click Save, Premiere Elements begins to render and save the movie. A Rendering progress bar appears to let you know the progress of the export. The progress bar also estimates the remaining time; saving the file might take awhile, especially if this is a long project.

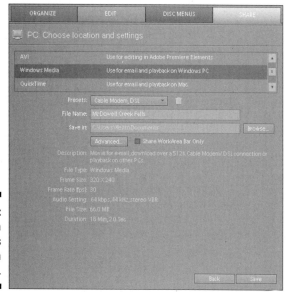

Figure 15-5:
Choose a
Windows
Media
preset.

Customizing Windows Media settings

The Windows Media export presets should cover most of your needs, but if you're the kind of person who likes to tinker, click Advanced on the Windows Media sharing screen. This gets you under the hood, which looks like Figure 15-6. The Export Settings dialog box has tabs for Video settings, Audio Settings, and Audiences. Try not to scrape your knuckles on these settings:

✔ **Video Codec:** Several Windows Media codecs are available on the Video tab. You can choose older versions of the Windows Media codec (such as 7 or 8) to make your movie compatible with older versions of Windows Media Player. If a user tries to view a Windows Media Video 9 movie with Windows Media Player 7 or 8, the movie may play improperly or not at all. Windows Media Player 9 has been available since 2003, so there's usually no reason to use an older codec.

- ✔ **Allow Interlaced Processing:** The Video settings also allow you to specify interlaced processing. Choose this if your exported videos have interlacing-related combing (see Chapter 3 for more on interlacing) or other interlacing-related problems.

- ✔ **Bitrate Settings:** Next to Encoding Passes, choose Two Encoding Passes. This choice increases the time it takes the movie to export, but it also helps the movie compress more efficiently. Choose One Encoding Pass only if you're in a hurry to export the movie. For the Bitrate Mode, the Variable Unconstrained option is your best bet for efficient compression and higher quality.

- ✔ **Frame Width/Height:** These boxes control the size of your video image. Try to maintain the aspect ratio of 4:3 (16:9 widescreen videos will be letterboxed in Windows Media Player) to prevent distortion of the video image. See Chapter 3 for more on aspect ratios. Remember, larger video sizes mean larger files.

- ✔ **Frame Rate:** Broadcast-quality video usually has a frame rate of 25 or 30 frames per second (fps). You can save file size and bandwidth by using a frame rate of 12 or 15 fps. To ensure smooth playback, choose a frame rate that is one-half or one-third of the original frame rate.

- ✔ **Pixel Aspect Ratio:** Square Pixels is the most common choice here; however, if your video image appears stretched or squeezed, you may need to choose one of the rectangular pixel options in this menu. Choose the option that matches the format of your original source footage.

- ✔ **Keyframe Interval:** Compression key frames help video compress more efficiently. A longer interval between key frames often reduces file size and quality. Adjust the Keyframe Interval to change the interval between compression key frames.

- ✔ **Average Video Bitrate:** Adjust this slider to change the average video bitrate. Surprise: Higher bitrates yield better quality and larger file sizes.

- ✔ **Audio settings:** As with video, you can choose a specific audio codec and bitrate settings on the Audio tab.

- ✔ **Audiences:** On the Audiences tab, you can choose whether the exported movie will be compressed or uncompressed.

You should always choose Compressed unless file size is absolutely not a concern. When is it *not* a concern?

When you're done reviewing and adjusting Windows Media export settings, click OK to close the Export Settings dialog box. Continue saving and exporting your Windows Media movie as described earlier in this chapter.

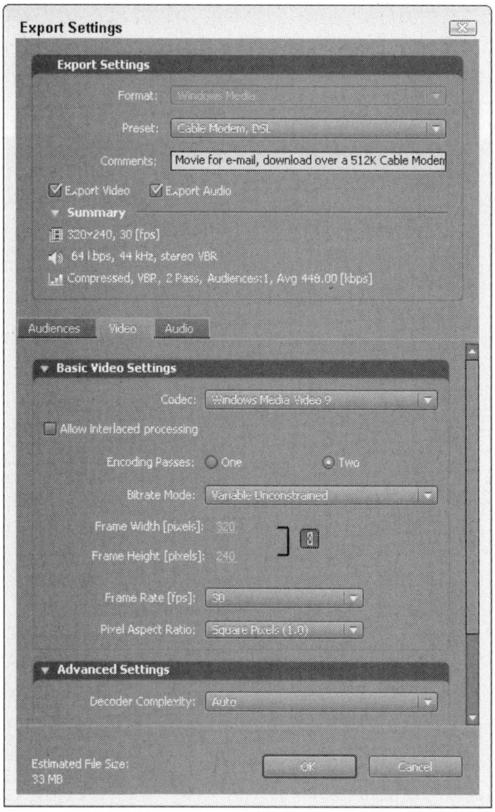

Figure 15-6:
Customize video settings for Windows Media export.

Chapter 16

Burning Your Movies to Disc

· ·

· ·

*I*n 1997, a new medium for distributing video came onto the market. That new medium was the *Digital Versatile Disc,* more commonly known as DVD. DVDs packed full-length, high-quality movies in digital format onto compact laser discs that were the same size as audio CDs and CD-ROMs. In 2003, DVDs surpassed VHS videotapes as the most common movie distribution method, and today DVDs are *the* world standard for video recording.

Standard DVDs support only standard-definition video. That brings us to the next step in video storage evolution: the high-definition DVD. You might remember the Great High Def Format War, which began in 2006 when the competing HD DVD and Blu-Ray formats were released to the public. Fortunately the only guns and explosions in this war were the ones in action movies recorded to HD DVD and Blu-Ray. HD DVD format was the casualty, and Blu-Ray the victor. Blu-Ray discs can store and play high-def movies. If you have a high-def camcorder, Blu-Ray discs allow you to easily share high-def movies with others. Blu-Ray players are increasingly affordable, and Blu-Ray disc burners are starting to appear in some PCs.

If your computer has a DVD or Blu-Ray burner, Adobe Premiere Elements is ready to put that burner to use. This chapter shows you how, with just a few mouse clicks, you can burn your Premiere Elements movie projects onto DVD or Blu-Ray, complete with navigation and scene menus. But first I introduce you to the fundamentals of DVD and Blu-Ray technologies.

Decrypting Video Disc Standards

One of the nice things about VHS tapes was that when you recorded a movie onto a tape, you could be sure that it would play in any VCR. It was also easy to understand the storage capacity of a tape. A tape labeled T-120, for example, held 120 minutes of NTSC video.

Alas, video discs are a little more complicated. Although most DVD players can play the discs you record yourself, some players are flaky and have trouble with homemade discs. And the storage capacity on a blank disc is usually listed computer-style (gigabytes) rather than human-style (minutes). If a blank DVD says it can hold 4.7GB, how many minutes of video is that, exactly? The next few sections answer common questions about video discs.

DVD and Blu-Ray discs are often called *optical* discs. No, they can't take the place of your reading glasses. They're called optical discs because data is read optically, using a laser beam. VHS tapes, MiniDV tapes, and computer hard drives store and read data magnetically rather than optically.

How much video can you cram on a DVD?

A standard recordable DVD has a theoretical capacity of 4.7GB (actually 4.38GB in practice), which works out to a little over two hours of high-quality MPEG-2 video (MPEG-2 is the codec used by DVD video). Two hours is an approximation; as I show later in this chapter, quality settings affect how much video will fit on a disc. If you're willing to sacrifice some quality, you can squeeze a lot more video onto a disc.

Some DVDs are double-sided or have multiple data layers, allowing them to hold more than 4.7GB. Table 16-1 lists the most common DVD capacities.

Table 16-1	DVD Capacities	
Type	*Capacity*	*Approximate Video Time*
Single-sided, single-layer	4.7GB	More than 2 hours
Single-sided, double-layer	8.5GB	4 hours
Double-sided, single-layer	9.4GB	4.5 hours
Double-sided, double-layer	16GB	More than 8 hours

You've probably seen double-sided DVDs before. They're often used to put the widescreen version of a movie on one side of the disc, and the full-screen "pan-and-scan" version on the other. Double-sided discs require special manufacturing processes, so (for now) you can't easily make double-sided DVDs in your home or office.

Double-layer discs also used to require a special manufacturing process. Early double-layer discs were actually glued together (I'm not making this up) with a special transparent glue applied in "clean rooms" by technicians clad in white lab coats. Double-layer DVD burners and discs became available in 2004, and most new computers now come with double-layer DVD burners — sometimes called DVD-R DL burners. So if you buy some recordable DVD-R DL discs, you can record discs that will hold 8.5GB. Wearing a white lab coat is optional. A double-layer disc can hold about 4 hours of video at the highest DVD quality, or about 16 hours of video if you ramp the quality back to about what you get on a VHS tape.

The capacities listed in Table 16-1 assume standard-size DVDs, which are about 12cm in diameter. Some companies offer miniature recordable DVDs, and of course, these smaller discs also have a smaller capacity. For example, Verbatim's 8cm miniature DVD-R discs hold about 1.4GB of material.

How much video can you cram onto a Blu-Ray disc?

Blu-Ray discs (BDs) have a lot in common with DVDs. Both types of discs are round, flat, and 120mm in diameter. They're both optical storage discs, and they can both have multiple layers. Most Blu-Ray players can also play standard DVDs (and audio CDs, too). Alas, BDs do *not* work in standard-def DVD players.

Blu-Ray discs and DVDs may look alike, but BDs are a generation ahead technologically. A single-layer BD-R can hold 25GB of data, which is almost three times as much as a double-layer DVD. A double-layer BD can hold 50GB of data. A variation of BDs is the 80mm BD-R Camcorder disc, which is used in special Blu-Ray disc camcorders. In Chapter 2, I generally recommend against disc-based camcorders. Table 16-2 lists the capacities for Blu-Ray discs.

Table 16-2	Blu-Ray Disc Capacities		
Type	*Diameter*	*Capacity*	*Approximate Video Time*
Single-layer BD (BD-R)	120mm	25GB	2–3 hours of HD video
Double-layer BD (BD-R DL)	120mm	50GB	4 hours of HD video
BD-R Camcorder	80mm	7.5GB	1 hour of HD video

Reading the DVD/BD alphabet soup

When it comes to buying a drive to record your own discs, you're going to see a lot of similar — yet slightly different — acronyms thrown around to describe the various formats that are available. The basic terms you'll encounter are

- ✔ **DVD-R (DVD-Recordable):** Like a CD-R, you can record onto this type of disc only once. DVD-Rs hold 4.7GB of data.

- ✔ **DVD-R DL (DVD-R Dual Layer):** These are also one-time-use discs, but dual-layer discs can hold 8.5GB of data.

- ✔ **DVD-RW (DVD-ReWritable):** You can record onto a DVD-RW disc, erase it later, and record something else onto it.

- ✔ **DVD-RAM (DVD-Random Access Memory):** These discs can also be erased and reused repeatedly. DVD-RAM discs are compatible only with DVD-RAM drives, which makes this format pretty useless for movies.

- ✔ **BD-R (BD-Recordable):** These 25GB discs can be recorded only once, and can be played only in Blu-Ray drives and players.

- ✔ **BD-R DL (BD-R Dual Layer):** Like BD-Rs, these can be recorded only once, but two recording layers yield a capacity of 50GB.

- ✔ **BD-RE (BD-R Erasable):** These BD discs can be erased and reused.

As you shop for DVD burners, notice that some drives say they record DVD-R, whereas others record DVD+R. The dash (-) and the plus (+) aren't simply a grammatical curiosity. The -R and +R formats are unique standards. If you have a DVD-R drive, make sure that you buy DVD-R blank discs. Likewise, if you have a DVD+R drive, you must buy DVD+R blank discs. Fortunately, most manufacturers now offer dual-format DVD burners that can handle both DVD-R and DVD+R discs. These drives are sometimes marked as DVD+/-R drives.

What are VCDs and SVCDs?

A few years ago, DVD burners and blank DVD-Rs were still sort of expensive, and not everyone had made the switch from VCRs to DVD players. An alternative was to record a VCD (Video CD) or SVCD (Super VCD) on 700MB CD-Rs. A VCD could hold about 60 minutes of lower-quality video, and an SVCD could hold about 20 minutes of DVD-quality video.

Premiere Elements can't record VCDs or SVCDs directly. Third-party programs like Nero Burning ROM can create such discs, but why bother? Your computer almost certainly has a DVD burner, and almost everyone in your audience now has a DVD player too. Furthermore, these days DVD-Rs are often *cheaper* than CD-Rs, so VCDs don't save you any money. You may still hear some people mention VCDs or SVCDs, but these formats are now just a historical footnote and really aren't worth your time.

Getting Your Movie Ready for Disc

A great feature of DVDs and BDs is consistent high-quality playback, whether the movie has been played once or a hundred times. Optical discs store data digitally, so they don't suffer from generational loss. (See Chapter 3 for a detailed explanation of generational loss.)

Viewers expect very high quality from DVD and Blu-Ray movies. They're more likely to buy high-quality TVs so that they can watch their movies on crisp, bright displays. Viewers also expect DVDs and BDs to be easy to use, with features like scene markers and navigation menus. This means you're going to have to make an extra effort to prepare your movies for disc:

- ✔ **Make image quality superb.** Spend time improving the colors and lighting in your video images. Chapter 10 shows you how to fix lighting problems, improve colors, stabilize shaky video, and more.

- ✔ **Use effective scene markers.** If you create scene markers in the Timeline when important new scenes begin, the movie will be easy to navigate in a DVD or Blu-Ray player. Viewers can click the Next Scene or Previous Scene button on their remotes to quickly jump between scenes. I show you how to add scene markers in Chapter 7.

Premiere Elements stores and edits your video at full quality. Both standard and high-def projects can be recorded to DVD. If you plan to record Blu-Ray discs, start with high-def footage from an HD camera.

Recording DVDs and Blu-Ray Discs

Until a few years ago, recording your own DVDs was complex and time consuming. Adobe wanted to eliminate most of that complexity from Premiere Elements, so the company created a special Disc Menu workspace to help you prep your movies for disc. To open this workspace, click the Disc Menus tab in the Task pane or choose Window⇨Disc Menus. The process for creating DVDs and Blu-Ray discs is the same; it just depends on what kind of burner you have in your computer. The following sections show you how to choose a menu template, customize your menus, and record your disc.

Choosing a menu template

If you've ever watched a movie on DVD — I'm probably not going out on a limb here — you're probably familiar with disc menus. Menus are graphical screens that appear on your TV. Using the remote control for your DVD or Blu-Ray player, you select a link in the main menu to play the movie, or you can go to submenus for scene selection or special features.

Creating menus from scratch can be time consuming, but not with Adobe Premiere Elements. Premiere Elements comes with a nice selection of menu templates to help you quickly and easily create attractive, easy-to-use menus. When you first open the Disc Menus workspace (Window⇨Disc Menus) you see a list of menu templates. The templates are divided into 16 categories with themes like Travel, Seasons, Happy Birthday, and Sports, which is shown in Figure 16-1.

You don't have to choose a template. Premiere Elements can also create an "auto-play" disc with no menus. An auto-play disc automatically starts playing your movie as soon as it is placed in the player. To create an auto-play disc, skip the Disc Menus tab and go right to the Share tab. Later in this chapter, I show how to burn discs using the Share tab.

To select a disc menu template, follow these steps:

1. **Click the Disc Menus tab to bring it to the front.**

2. **Choose a category from the Theme menu.**

   In Figure 16-1, I'm selecting a template from the "Sports" category.

Figure 16-1:
Premiere
Elements
comes
with many
built-in
menu
templates.

3. Scroll down the list of templates and click a template to select it.

In Figure 16-1, I have chosen a template named "Soccer Action." Previews of both the main menu and scene menu are displayed.

4. When you have chosen a menu, click Apply to apply the template to your project.

Alternatively, you can click-and-drag the template to the Monitor window. DVD menus are automatically generated for your project, and the menus appear in the Disc Menus box under the Monitor, as shown Figure 16-2.

After you customize your menus, you may decide that you don't like the template that you originally chose. Not a problem! Simply return to the Disc Menus tab and choose a new template.

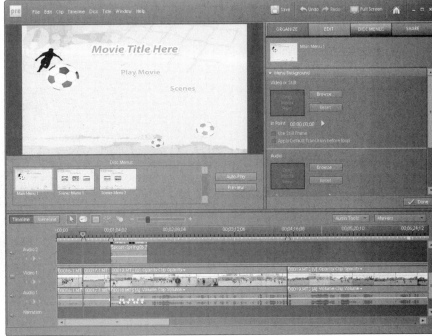

Figure 16-2:
Menus
are auto-
matically
generated
from the
Premiere
Elements
templates.

Customizing menus

When you create disc menus using a Premiere Elements template, the template inserts default text and links that you may want to edit. The default text is usually generic and may not be relevant to your project. For example, in Figure 16-2, the main menu has the title `Movie Title Here`. If that name is too ironic and edgy for you, you may want to change it. The following sections show you how to customize your disc menus.

Changing menu text

To change text in a menu, double-click it. A Change Text dialog box appears, as shown in Figure 16-3. Enter your new text and click OK. The new text appears in the menu, as shown in Figure 16-4.

Figure 16-3:
Enter new
text for disc
menus here.

Unfortunately, Premiere Elements doesn't allow you to change the size or alignment of text, so be careful not to enter too much text in the Change Text dialog box. If you enter too much text, the words will flow off the screen or possibly obscure other elements on the menu.

Figure 16-4: Personalize your menus with customized text.

Modifying scene selection menus

You should also take a look at your scene menus, which is where viewers can select specific scenes in the movie. The number of scene menus for your project depends on

- **How many scene markers are in your Timeline:** Premiere Elements considers each scene marker the beginning of a new scene.

- **How many scenes per page are supported by the template:** Different template designs allow different numbers of scenes on each page. The template in Figure 16-4 allows three scenes per page, so a second page accommodates the five scenes in my project.

Customizing your scene menus is an important part of the menu-creation process because link names may overlap, or a scene's thumbnail image may not be exactly what you want. To view your scene selection menus, click a scene's menu at the bottom of the Monitor window.

Moving and resizing links

If you don't like the arrangement of the links in your scene menus, you can easily move or resize them. Click a scene link once to select it, and then click-and-drag it to a new location. Click-and-drag a handle at the corners or sides of a link to resize it, as shown in Figure 16-5.

As you move and resize links, be careful to avoid links that overlap each other. Overlapping links can make the scene menu essentially unusable. Overlapping links are outlined in red. Move or resize links until all the red lines are gone.

Red lines indicate
overlapping links.

Click and drag handles
to resize a link.

Figure 16-5:
Overlapping
links must
be resolved
before you
burn your
disc.

Click a scene menu to change it.

Changing link thumbnails

You normally create scene markers (Chapter 7 describes them) at the beginning of scenes. By default, the thumbnail image on a scene link is the first video frame of that scene, but sometimes the first frame doesn't properly illustrate the scene's contents.

To change the thumbnail (also called the *poster frame*) for a scene marker, double-click the scene link in the Monitor. In the Menu Marker dialog box, click-and-drag left or right on the timecode under the Thumbnail Offset window. Keep dragging until you find a frame that would make a good thumbnail. In Figure 16-6, I have chosen a frame that is three seconds (00;00;03;00) ahead of the scene's first frame. Click OK to close the Menu Marker window when you have selected a good thumbnail.

Removing links

You may decide that some of your scene menu links are superfluous, especially if you created the markers a long time ago. Don't worry; removing scene links from your menus is easy. Just double-click the offending link in the Monitor window, and click Delete in the Menu Marker dialog box that appears. The scene is removed from your scene menus.

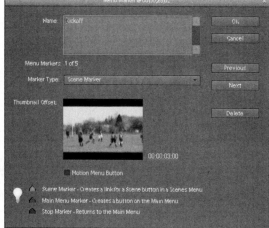

Figure 16-6:
Use the
Menu
Marker
dialog box
to choose
preferred
scene link
thumbnails.

Adding a stop marker

Have you thought about what will happen when your movie ends? When your movie is over, ideally the DVD's main menu appears. To make sure this happens automatically, insert a stop marker at the end of your movie if you haven't done so already. Adding a stop marker is easy. Follow these steps:

1. **Click somewhere in the Timeline window to make it active.**

2. **Press the End key on your keyboard.**

   This moves the CTI to the very end of your project.

3. **Choose Disc⇨Set Menu Marker.**

   The Menu Marker dialog box appears.

4. **Choose Stop Marker in the Marker Type menu.**

5. **Click OK to close the Menu Marker dialog box.**

Previewing your disc

When you have all your menus set up the way you want them, take a few moments to preview your disc. To generate a preview of your project, click Preview in the Monitor window. A Preview Disc window appears. This window is a fully functional mock-up of the final disc, complete with the same controls found on a typical DVD remote. When you preview your disc, the following things are important to check:

- ✔ Do the menus look as attractive as you'd hoped? If not, consider choosing a new template.

- ✔ Click every scene link in the scene's menu. Does each scene seem to start at the correct place? If some of the scene links don't link to the right places, you may need to move markers in your Timeline.

- ✔ Click Play Movie in the main menu, and then click the Next Scene button to jump to the next scene. Continue clicking Next Scene to review each scene marker. Are the scenes spaced at appropriate intervals? You may need to add or remove scene markers in the Timeline.

- ✔ Play the final scene in the movie until it ends. Does the movie return to the main menu when it ends? If not, make sure that you've placed a stop marker at the end of the movie, as described in the preceding section.

When you're done previewing your disc, click the Close (X) button in the upper-right corner of the Preview Disc window. If you make any more changes, make sure that you preview the revised project.

Burning your disc

When you have previewed your disc and you're certain that it's ready to go, you're ready to — drum roll, please — burn the disc. Don't worry; you don't need matches and a burning permit! The term *burn* is often used in place of "record" when you record stuff onto DVDs and Blu-Ray discs.

Before you start burning your disc, keep in mind that the encoding and burning process can take many hours. For this reason, I usually burn discs near the end of a workday. You can click Burn and let the disc burn overnight, when you don't need to use the computer for anything else. Encoding — which Premiere Elements does automatically before the actual disc is burned —

requires a lot of computer memory and processing resources, so make sure that you close noncritical programs before you start to burn.

To burn a disc in Premiere Elements, follow these steps:

1. **Choose Timeline⇨Render Work Area.**

   It's a good idea to make sure that transitions, effects, titles, and other edits in the Timeline are rendered before you burn a disc.

2. **When rendering is complete, click the Share tab and then click Disc.**

3. **Click DVD or Blu-Ray, depending on the type of disc you're burning.**

   You can only burn DVDs if your computer has a DVD-R drive. You'll need a BD-R drive to burn Blu-Ray discs.

4. **In the Burn To menu, choose whether you want to burn to a disc or to a folder.**

   Usually you burn a disc, but you can also create a disc image in a folder on your hard drive. That image can be recorded to a disc by using other software such as Roxio Easy CD Creator or Nero Burning ROM.

5. **Enter a name for the disc in the Disc Name field.**

   In Figure 16-7, I have named my disc SpringSoccer.

6. **If you have more than one burner on your computer, make sure that the correct burner is selected in the Burner Location menu.**

   If you have an external DVD burner connected to your computer's USB or FireWire port, but the burner doesn't show up in the Burner Location menu, make sure that the external burner is properly connected and the power is turned on. Wait several seconds, and then click the Rescan button.

7. **Choose how many copies you want to burn.**

   You may want to burn a single test disc first, and then burn multiple copies later when you know that the first disc burned just fine.

8. **Insert a blank recordable disc in your burner drive.**

   If you see a yellow asterisk icon and the words Media Not Present next to the Status indicator, make sure that you have inserted your blank disc and click Rescan. After several seconds, you should see Ready next to the Status indicator, as shown in Figure 16-7.

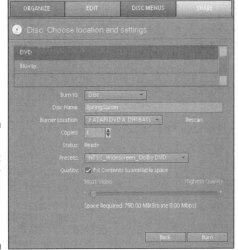

Figure 16-7:
Adjust
quality
settings
before
burning
your disc.

9. **Choose a Preset.**

If you're burning a standard-def DVD, you have to make two choices:

- **NTSC or PAL:** Choose a preset that matches your local TV standard. (See Chapter 3 for more on TV standards.)

- **Aspect ratio:** If your movie uses a 16:9 widescreen ratio, choose a
  widescreen preset. If you're recording high-def video to a standard-
  def DVD, choose a widescreen preset because HD video is almost
  always widescreen. Aspect ratios are covered in Chapter 3.

If you're burning a Blu-Ray disc, you have three choices to make:

- **NTSC or PAL:** Choose a preset that matches your local TV standard.

- **Resolution:** Choose a resolution that matches your source footage.
  If your footage is from an HDV camcorder, the resolution is probably 1440 x 1080. Many AVCHD camcorders record footage at 1920
  x 1080, which is the resolution of so-called "Full HD." See Chapter 2
  for more on camcorder formats.

- **Codec:** You can burn your Blu-Ray disc using either the H.264 or
  MPEG-2 codec. H.264 compresses video more efficiently, but if
  your H.264 discs don't play in some Blu-Ray players, try using the
  MPEG-2 codec instead.

10. **Choose a quality setting.**

Usually I recommend leaving the Fit Contents to Available Space option
checked. Premiere Elements automatically detects how much space is
available and burns your movie at the highest quality that will fit. You

can disable this option for DVDs and manually choose a quality level by using the Video Quality slider. Drag it left to cram more video on the disc, or drag it right to maximize the image quality. The quality slider isn't available when burning Blu-Ray discs.

Pay attention to what is listed next to the Space Required indicator. If you are burning to a folder, make sure that the amount of space shown in the Space Required indicator will fit on whatever kind of media you plan to use when you burn the movie onto a disc.

11. **When you are ready to burn the disc, click Burn.**

    The Burn Progress window appears. Remember — burning can take a long time. The longest part of the process is encoding, which is where the movie is converted into the format used by DVD and Blu-Ray players.

12. **When the burn process is complete, click Close to close the Burn Progress dialog box.**

    When the burn process is complete, make sure that you test your disc in as many players as possible.

Some players won't play certain DVDs or BDs. If you find that your discs often don't play properly, try a different brand of blank discs, or try burning the disc by using different software, such as Nero Burning ROM or Roxio Easy CD Creator.

Part V
The Part of Tens

The 5th Wave — By Rich Tennant

"Honey - remember that pool party last summer where you showed everyone how to do the limbo in just a sombrero and a dish towel? Well, look at what the MSN Daily Video Download is."

In this part . . .

Most people love top-ten lists. Most people have ten fingers. Coincidence? I don't think so. If you've ever read a *For Dummies* book, you know what this part is all about. The chapters in this part provide top-ten lists to help you find useful stuff by tens — ten advanced editing techniques in Premiere Elements, ten secrets of movie-making, and ten pieces of software and hardware you just won't want to do without.

At the end of this part is an appendix. Unlike the appendix that is part of the human anatomy, the appendix of *Premiere 8 Elements For Dummies* serves an important function. Throughout this book, and indeed through your entire adventure in video editing, you will encounter an entirely different language referring to video editing and technologies. You encounter new terms like *interlacing* or *pixel aspect ratio* and countless acronyms like NTSC and NLE. Thus, this glossary serves as a dictionary of videography lingo.

Chapter 17

Ten Advanced Premiere Elements Techniques

*A*dobe didn't design Premiere Elements for professional video editors. Premiere Elements is primarily aimed at video hobbyists, people who have digital camcorders and want to turn their raw video into fun, personalized movies. But Premiere Elements brings a level of pro-caliber video-editing capabilities heretofore unseen in affordable video-editing programs, and I think it's only natural that you'll want to use this better software to make better movies.

Moviemaking is an art, and as with any art there's no single formula or magic technique to guarantee a great movie. At least with Premiere Elements your creativity probably won't be limited by the software. Premiere Elements has so many features and capabilities that you'll probably come up with editing tricks and techniques all your own. But if you lack inspiration at the moment or just want to practice more advanced techniques, this chapter is for you. Here I've collected some (ten, to be precise) advanced editing techniques that didn't quite seem to fit anywhere else in the book.

Creating Cinematic Slideshows

Once upon a time — back before Flickr.com, before PowerPoint presentations, and way before digital cameras — the slideshow was a time-honored tradition for sharing vacation photos. You'd invite all your friends and family over, close the curtains, dim the lights, and fire up your slide projector. Your audience was enthralled (or bored) by your narrated photo presentation.

Most people don't shoot slides anymore, and the bulb in your slide projector probably burned out 15 years ago. But it's still possible to enthrall (or bore) your friends with personalized slideshows. Premiere Elements can help you create a slideshow that, when burned onto a DVD, can be viewed on any TV.

In Chapter 7, I show you how to put clips — both video and stills — into the Timeline. The most basic way to create a slideshow is to drop a series of still images in the Timeline, add some transitions (Chapter 9) and titles (Chapter 13), and burn the finished "movie" to a disc (Chapter 16). Creating a slideshow manually is time consuming, so I recommend that you instead use the SlideShow feature in the Adobe Organizer. Here's how:

1. **Launch Premiere Elements, and click Organize on the splash screen.**

2. **In the Organizer, choose File⇨Get Photos and Videos⇨From Files and Folders.**

3. **Browse to the still images you want to use in your slideshow, select the desired images, and click Get Media.**

   The still images are imported into the Adobe Organizer.

4. **In the Organizer, select the photos you want to use in the slideshow.**

   Ctrl+click or Shift+click to select multiple photos.

5. **Click the Create tab on the right side of the Organizer, and then click Slide Show.**

6. **Choose slideshow settings, and then click OK.**

   You can choose the length of time images play, the length and style of transitions, the background color, and more. Choose Apply Pan & Zoom to All Slides to add motion and visual appeal to the slideshow.

7. **In the Slide Show Editor that appears, as shown in Figure 17-1, click a slide in the slideshow Timeline to customize that slide.**

   Under Extras, click the Titles or Narration buttons to add those elements, or click-and-drag graphics to an image. In Figure 17-1, two animals and a frilly shirt have been added to the slide. You can also enable or disable Pan & Zoom for individual slides, or change the background color.

8. **Click a transition in the Timeline to open transition controls.**

   You can change the duration or style of each transition.

Add silly elements to your slides.

Titles   Narrative

Figure 17-1:
Add
finishing
touches and
fine-tune
your
slideshow.

Slide show timeline   Transition

9. **Click-and-drag slides left or right in the Timeline to change the play-back order.**

10. **Click Output, choose an output format and file size, and click OK.**

11. **Enter a filename for the slideshow and click Save.**

    It may take a few minutes to export the slideshow.

Bringing Still Photos to Life

When motion pictures first appeared in the 19th century, some people probably thought it meant the end of still photography. But still photos have stubbornly refused to go away, and you may find that you sometimes want to use photos in your movie projects.

The problem with still photos is that they're just so, well, still. To help still photos fit in better with your movies, I recommend adding some subtle pan-and-zoom effects. Slowly zooming or panning across an image makes that image come alive and feel more natural in your movie. To pan or zoom, click the Edit tab on the Task pane and then click Effects. In the categories menu, choose Presets, and then choose one of the following categories from the subcategories menu. The pan and zoom subcategories are

- ✔ **Horizontal Image Pans:** These presets pan horizontally left-to-right or right-to-left across the image.

- ✔ **Horizontal Image Zooms:** These zoom in or out on the image along a horizontal plane.

- ✔ **Vertical Image Pans:** These presets pan vertically up or down the image.

- ✔ **Vertical Image Zooms:** These zoom in or out on the image along a vertical plane.

Drag and drop an image pan or zoom preset to a still image in the Timeline, just like any other effect. These presets modify the image's Motion settings. As with most effects, you may have to experiment to get just the desired effect. And of course, preview your edits carefully.

Making Stop-Motion Video

If you love to make movie magic, stop-motion video should definitely be in your spell book. Stop-motion video is one of the oldest special effects techniques in all of moviemaking, and it's used to create a variety of visual illusions. Remember those claymation shows like *Gumby* and *Frosty the Snowman* you used to watch when you were a kid? Stop-motion animation was used to make the clay figures in those shows appear to move on their own. Stop-motion video can also be used to speed up something that would otherwise happen very slowly, such as the blooming of a flower.

Premiere Elements makes it easy for you to create your own stop-motion video. To make your stop-motion idea successful, follow these steps:

1. **Plan the video shoot carefully.**

   You may be tempted to try to shoot a series of still photos, but I recommend that you just use your video camera and record video instead. You can then select individual frames later in Premiere Elements. Important elements for a successful stop-motion video shoot include:

   • **Use a tripod.** This is absolutely mandatory for successful stop-motion video capture. When you shoot, be extremely careful not to bump the tripod or move the camera. Tiny camera movements will be jarringly obvious in the final stop-motion video. See Chapter 19 for tips on choosing a tripod.

   • **Maintain constant lighting.** If you're shooting a blooming flower outside, you probably don't have any control over the sun. But watch out for shadows or other lighting changes because they will appear as flashes in your stop-motion video.

- **Let the camera roll.** Don't try to stop recording between each "frame" of stop-motion video. Just record video as normal. This saves time and minimizes the risk of bumping the camera. If you need to stop and restart recording, use the camera's remote control.

- **Clear your schedule.** Even if you use five frames from every minute of video (an ambitious goal), one hour of recorded video will yield only about ten seconds of stop-motion video.

2. **Open the video capture window, as described in Chapter 5.**

3. **At the top of the Capture window, choose Stop Motion, and then click Create New Stop Motion in the Capture window.**

4. **Place a check mark next to Time Lapse, click Set Time, and then choose an interval for capturing frames.**

   Time lapse capture works well if you want to capture frames automatically at regular intervals.

5. **Click Play to start playing the video, and click the Grab Frame button whenever you want to grab a frame.**

   I recommend that you leave the Onion Skinning option enabled. This option overlays a ghost image of the preceding frame over the video as it plays. Onion skinning helps you maintain continuity and proper smooth motion as you capture your stop-motion video.

6. **Click Stop, and close the Capture window when you're done capturing frames.**

7. **Click Yes when you are prompted to save the images as a video file, and then enter a name for the file.**

Premiere Elements creates an AVI video file of the frames you captured, and it appears as a video clip in the Organizer. You can then drop it into the Timeline and edit it just like you would with any other video clip.

Making Two Clips into One Scene

Have you ever wondered if you have an evil twin somewhere in the world? With some simple videography tricks and Adobe Premiere Elements, you can easily make your evil twin a visual reality, as shown in Figure 17-2. No human cloning is necessary for this effect. You shoot the two scenes quickly, and then edit them together as a single scene in Premiere Elements.

To make this effect work, you first shoot one-half of the image, and then shoot the other half. This gives two clips that will be combined to make a single scene. One clip is placed in track Video 1, and the other clip — call it the *overlay clip* — is placed in track Video 2, as shown in Figure 17-2.

You then apply the Crop effect to the overlay clip so it only covers half the screen. Notice in Figure 17-2 that I have cropped 44.6% off the right side of my overlay clip. To apply the Crop effect, follow these steps:

1. **Click the Edit tab, and then click Effects.**

2. **Scroll down to the Transform category of video effects.**

3. **Click-and-drag the Crop effect from the Edit pane to an overlay clip in the Timeline.**

   An overlay clip should be in track Video 2 or higher.

4. **Click the overlay clip in the Timeline to select it.**

5. **Click Edit Effects at the bottom of the Edit pane.**

   Alternatively, right-click the overlay clip in the Timeline and choose Show Properties from the menu that appears.

6. **Expand the Crop effect options, as shown in Figure 17-2.**

   When you select the Crop effect, handles appear around the corners of the video image in the Monitor.

7. **Click-and-drag a corner of the video image to crop it.**

Click and drag handles to crop   Crop controls

Figure 17-2:
I used the
Crop effect
to remove
half of the
overlay clip.

Overlay clip   Underlaying clip

When you crop a video image in an overlay track, video images in underlying tracks show up in the cropped area. To make the "seeing double" effect successful, follow these simple rules:

- ✔ **Use a tripod.** A tripod is absolutely mandatory to make this effect work. You won't be able to hold the camera steady enough by hand, and a jiggling camera ruins the results.

- ✔ **Don't move the camera between shots.** The camera must remain absolutely still between each clip. If you have to reposition the camera, or if someone bumps it, reshoot both scenes. If your camcorder has a remote control, use it to start and stop recording so that even the slight touch of your finger doesn't move the camera.

- ✔ **Shoot the "before" and "after" scenes quickly.** If you're shooting outdoors, shadows and lighting can change quickly. Even subtle light changes will be apparent when you edit the two scenes together later. So stop reading and start shooting. Now!

- ✔ **Don't disturb the rest of the scene.** If your subject moves a chair or picks up an object between the "before" and "after" shots, the scenes will appear inconsistent when edited together.

Freeze-Framing Video

Have you ever watched those old "Road Runner" cartoons where Wile E. Coyote attempts to chase down the Road Runner? You probably remember a scene that appeared early in each cartoon — Road Runner would momentarily freeze, and its scientific name (*Acceleratii Incredibilus* or something along those lines) would appear on the screen.

You can add momentary freeze-frames to your video as well. To momentarily freeze a frame of video in the middle of a clip, and then make it play again, follow these steps:

1. **In the Timeline, move the CTI to the frame that you want to freeze.**

   Use the left- and right-arrow keys to move one frame at a time.

2. **Click the clip in the Timeline that you want to freeze to select it.**

3. **Choose Timeline⇨Split Clip.**

   The clip splits into two.

4. **Choose File⇨Export⇨Frame.**

5. **In the Export Frame dialog box that appears, give the exported frame a filename and click Save.**

   The exported frame now appears in your Organizer as a still image.

6. **On the Edit tab, click Project, and then click-and-drag the still image and drop it on the Timeline at the location of the CTI.**

   The still image is inserted between the two clips you created when you split the original clip in Step 3.

7. **Click the inserted still image in the Timeline to select it, and choose Clip⇨Time Stretch.**

8. **In the Time Stretch dialog box, enter the length of time that you want the frozen frame to appear next to Duration.**

   If you want the frame to freeze for three seconds, for example, enter 00;00;03;00.

9. **If an empty space appears in the Timeline after the still clip, right-click the empty space and choose Delete and Close Gap.**

Your Timeline will end up looking similar to the Timeline shown in Figure 17-3. When you play the Timeline, the frame appears to freeze momentarily.

Drag clip from here

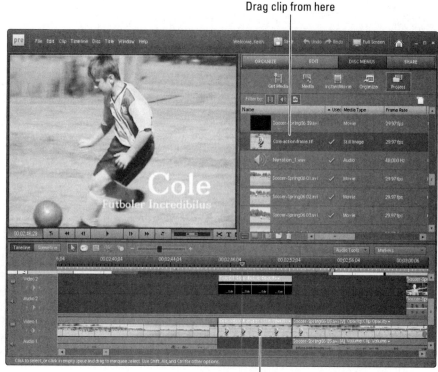

Figure 17-3:
Frames of
video can
be momen-
tarily frozen.

Drop still clip here

Recalling the Golden Age of Cinema

Motion pictures have been around for well over a century now. You can pay homage to the history of cinema by using some "old" (or at least old-*looking*) footage in your movie projects. Thankfully, creating old-looking footage doesn't require a trip to some dank film vault deep beneath a Hollywood studio. You can easily simulate old-fashioned film by following these tips:

- ✔ **Beware the anachronism!** Pay attention to your subjects and the scene. For example, cowboys of the Old West didn't carry cell phones at their hips, nor was the sky filled with condensation trails left by jet airplanes. Remove objects from the scene that don't fit the period you are trying to simulate, and make sure that the background doesn't depict modernity.

- ✔ **Remove color from the clip.** Perhaps the easiest way to convert a color image to grayscale is to use the Black & White filter in the Image Control category of Video Effects (click Effects on the Edit tab), although I prefer to use the Color Balance (HLS) effect. Adjust the saturation level to –100 to desaturate all colors in the clip. See Chapter 10 for more on adjusting video color.

  One advantage of using the Color Balance (HLS) effect is that you can use keyframes to change the effect in the middle of a clip.

  Grayscale is just a fancy way of saying black and white. Grayscale is a more technically accurate term because black-and-white video images are actually made using various shades of gray.

- ✔ **"Weather" the video image.** Film tends to deteriorate over time, so if you're trying to simulate old footage, you should simulate some of that deterioration. Use the Noise effect under Stylize to add some graininess to the video image. Video effects are described in Chapter 12.

- ✔ **Reduce audio quality and if possible use a mono setting.** Audio recordings made 75 years ago did not use 16-bit stereo sound. To reduce quality, reduce the sampling rate of the audio when you export your movie (see Chapters 14, 15, and 16 for more on movie export settings).

  Alternatively, you may want to go for the "silent movie" effect and not record any audio at all. Just use an appropriate musical soundtrack and insert title screens for dialogue.

- ✔ **Use the Old Film effect.** One of the NewBlue effects (see Chapter 12) that comes with Premiere Elements is the Old Film effect. If you don't feel like spending a lot of time manually aging your video images, simply click-and-drag this effect to your clips. It instantly adds 75 years to any video image.

Working with Mattes

TV screens are usually rectangular, and so most video images are rectangular, as well. But you can make a video image of virtually any shape you want by using *mattes.* Matte is simply a fancy name for a solid-colored screen or a screen with a monochrome shape. To use mattes, follow these steps:

1. **In a graphics program such as Photoshop Elements, create an image file with the shape you want to use for your matte.**

   I recommend creating a matte with just two contrasting colors (black and white provide the best contrast). Also, follow the guidelines I give in Chapter 5 for creating still images for use in movies. Save the image as a PSD (Photoshop Document) file.

2. **Choose File⇨Get Media From⇨PC Files and Folders, and import the matte image.**

   I describe how to import media into Premiere Elements in Chapter 5.

3. **Add the matte image to an overlay track in the Timeline, and click Yes when you are asked if you want to apply Videomerge to the clip.**

   Overlay tracks are tracks Video 2 or higher. In Figure 17-4, I have inserted a matte image that is shaped like a soccer ball.

Figure 17-4: This soccer ball matte has been added to track Video 2.

4. **Make sure the CTI in the Timeline is somewhere on the overlay clip so that it appears in the Monitor window, as shown in Figure 17-4.**

5. **Right-click the matte clip in the Timeline and choose Show Properties from the menu that appears.**

6. **In the effect controls that appear, click the arrow next to Videomerge to expand Videomerge settings.**

7. **Place a check mark next to Select Color.**

8. **Click the eyedropper icon under Select Color, and then click a portion of the matte that you want to make transparent.**

   The selected color becomes transparent, as shown in Figure 17-4.

9. **Click-and-drag the tolerance slider to fine-tune the matte's appearance.**

10. **If desired, place a check mark next to Invert Selection.**

11. **Choose Done to close the clip properties and save your changes.**

Adding a Lens Flare

Camera lenses, whether in still cameras or camcorders, are made of glass and are designed to collect light. Despite advanced lens coatings, those glass lenses can still reflect light when they're supposed to be collecting it. This phenomenon is especially common when the sun shines directly onto a camera's lens. Intense sunlight causes sharp reflections called lens flares.

Generally, lens flares are to be avoided. Higher-quality camcorders often incorporate large lens hoods to prevent lens flares. But sometimes a lens flare can be used for dramatic effect. Consider many recent movies that feature computer animation. Faux lens flares are often used to make the animated image seem more real. And in real video images that are washed out from too much sun, you can add manufactured lens flares to accentuate color and detail. Or you may want to add a lens flare to a properly lit desert scene simply to draw attention to the fact that the sun is blazing brightly overhead. To add a lens flare, follow these steps:

1. **In the Timeline, move the CTI to a frame where the sun appears or where you would otherwise like the sun to *appear* to appear.**

2. **Click the Edit tab, and then click Effects.**

3. **Click-and-drag the Lens Flare effect (in the Generate category) to a clip to which you want to add a lens flare.**

   A fake lens flare appears on your video image.

4. **Click Edit Effects on the Edit tab, and then click the arrow next to Lens Flare to open Lens Flare effect settings.**

5. **Click Lens Flare to select the effect.**

   A circle with cross hairs appears in the middle of the lens flare in the Monitor window, as shown in Figure 17-5.

6. **Click-and-drag the cross-hairs to reposition the lens flare.**

   Notice that as you move the center of the lens flare around the screen, the fake reflections move and adjust as well.

7. **Adjust the brightness of the flare, using the Flare Brightness slider.**

8. **Choose a lens type, using the Lens Type menu.**

   Each lens type gives a slightly different lens flare appearance. Experiment with each one, as well as with the Brightness slider and the flare center to achieve just the right look.

9. **Adjust the Blend With Original slider to reduce the flare's intensity.**

   This is a setting that calls for experimentation.

10. **Click Done when you are done fine-tuning your lens flare.**

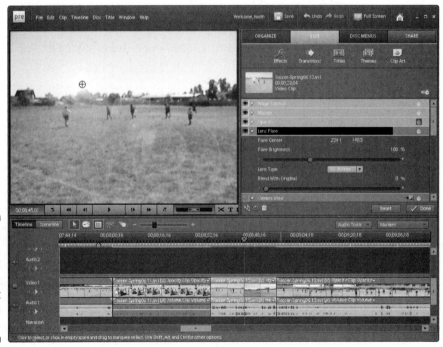

Figure 17-5:
Fine-tune lens flare settings in the Effect Controls window.

If the camera's view pans across a scene, the lens flare should appear to "move" with the lens. Use keyframes to change the position of the lens flare as the clip plays. I show how to use effect keyframes in Chapter 12.

Taking the Hum Out

As I point out in Chapter 8, audio is too often overlooked when editing video. One common editing problem is constant-frequency humming that sometimes occurs in audio recordings. The humming may be caused by interference from a fluorescent light or other electric device, or a flaw in the microphone or recording device.

Whatever the cause, if you have an audio recording with an annoying hum, Premiere Elements has a tool that may help you remove that hum. That tool is the Notch effect, which can be found in the list of Audio Effects on the Edit tab (click Effects on the Edit tab and choose Audio Effects from the category menu). The Notch effect removes all audio at or near a given frequency within the clip. Here's how to use it:

1. **Click and drag the Notch effect to the humming clip, and then click Edit Effects at the bottom of the Edit tab to open the Effect Controls.**

2. **Expand the Notch controls.**

3. **Adjust the Center slider to find the frequency causing the hum.**

   If the hum comes from a poorly shielded power cord, adjust the Center slider to 60 Hz if you live in an area that uses NTSC video, or 50 Hz if video equipment in your area uses PAL.

4. **Adjust the Q slider to broaden the frequency range of the sound that is removed.**

   Be careful not to broaden the range too much or the audio quality will diminish considerably.

A Zoom with a View

As I mention in Chapter 18, constantly zooming in and out with your camcorder's zoom lens is one of the most common mistakes made by amateur videographers. But sometimes zooming can have a desirable dramatic effect, especially when you want to show that the emphasis of the scene is suddenly shifting to a single point. Often, you realize that a shot or scene calls for a zoom effect only *after* you've shot your video and are using Premiere Elements to edit and fine-tune the project.

Adobe Premiere Elements can come to your rescue! Using the Camera View effect, you can quickly zoom in on a specific point in a video image. The Camera View effect is located in the Transform category of the Video Effects folder (click Effects on the Edit pane and scroll down to the Transform category). Here's what you do to zoom in:

1. **Click-and-drag the Camera View effect to a clip, and then click Edit Effects at the bottom of the Edit tab.**

2. **Expand the Camera View effect, and then adjust the Zoom slider.**

   The default zoom level on the slider is 10.

3. **To zoom in, drag the Zoom slider to the left.**

   Use keyframes (see Chapter 12 for more on controlling video effects using keyframes) to change the level of zoom as the clip plays.

You can zoom out on video images as well by using the Camera View effect, but keep in mind that as you zoom out, the edges of the video screen will become empty. Choose a fill color for the empty areas, using the Fill Color control. Black works best most of the time. And if you zoom in on a video image, the picture may start to look pixilated and blocky.

Chapter 18

Ten Videography Tips and Secrets

. . . .

In This Chapter

▶ Recording more interesting video shots

▶ Setting white balance

▶ Improving exposure and lighting

▶ Enhancing picture quality with filters and lens hoods

▶ Protecting your camera

. . . .

Have you ever watched a movie and wondered, "How did they do that?" Moviemakers have been perfecting their art and developing new techniques for over a century, and they've gotten pretty good at what they do. If you watch a "Making of . . ." documentary, you may get the impression that modern moviemaking is all about fancy computer animation effects and massive budgets, but even the biggest blockbuster projects still rely on many time-honored and proven techniques.

In this chapter I show you ten tips and secrets of videography that won't break the bank or require you to get a degree in computer animation. Here I show ten techniques to help you to shoot better video, record better audio, and more.

Keep Your Camera at the Ready

"I wish I had my camera!"

Have you ever said that? If so, then you already know the importance of keeping a camera with you at all times and having it ready to go. Some of history's most important video recordings were not part of formal video shoots; they were shot by people who just happened to be in the right place at the right time with a camera.

Fortunately, keeping a video camera handy has never been easier because modern camcorders — especially ones that use flash memory for storage — can be extremely small and lightweight. Video can also be recorded with other devices such as digital still cameras and cell phones.

Your camcorder isn't your only piece of video gear, although it is the most important. Here's a check list of items to have for almost any video shoot:

- ✔ Camcorder, owner's manual, and remote control (if your camcorder has one)
- ✔ Extra *charged* batteries and spare *blank* tapes, discs, or memory cards
- ✔ Lens cleaner and lens filters
- ✔ Tripod
- ✔ Black gaffer tape (available from photo/video shops)

I usually keep all these items in my camcorder bag so that if I have my camcorder, I have all my filters and spare batteries too. If you're going on a more formal video shoot, you may also want to bring:

- ✔ Lights, extension cords, reflectors, clamps, and backdrops
- ✔ AC adapter and/or battery charger for your camcorder
- ✔ Microphones and headphones
- ✔ Scene checklist

Balance Your Whites

Your fancy new camcorder features advanced image stabilization, high-def recording, crystal-clear audio, and is small enough to fit in your pocket. With all these advanced features, you would think it could at least record the color white correctly. Think again!

One thing modern camcorders still can't control is ambient light. Different light sources such as fluorescent lights, tungsten lights, or the sun greatly affect how whites and other colors appear in photos and video recordings. Colors that look warm and natural to your eye may appear gray and cold in your video.

To avoid unnatural color casts in your video, manually set the white balance on your camera. Some cheaper camcorders don't let you manually set white balance. Check the camera's documentation to see if and how to set white balance. If your camcorder doesn't allow you to manually set white balance, see the "Use Video Filters" section later in this chapter for information about color-correction filters.

If you can manually set white balance, follow these basic steps whenever you prepare to shoot in a new setting:

1. **Find a nonreflective solid white surface.**

   A letter-size sheet of white printer paper works great. Some people might tell you that you need a photo-specific white balance reference card. Such a card may indeed be a more perfect shade of white, but even in my professional video studio we use sheets of paper borrowed from the local office printer.

   Make sure that the white surface is actually white! Some white printer paper actually has a grayish tint, especially if it is recycled.

2. **Set up your lighting.**

   Whenever possible, you should white balance using exactly the same lighting that will be present when you shoot video. This avoids color and light inconsistency caused by different kinds of lighting.

3. **Hold the flat white surface several feet in front of your camera.**

4. **Zoom the camera in so that the white surface fills the entire video image.**

5. **Activate your camera's manual white balance setting.**

   Again, check the camera's documentation to see if white balance can be set, and if so, how to do it.

Expose the Highlights

As you shoot video, pay special attention to the highlights. I'm not talking about the most exciting parts of the video action — although you should pay attention to those too — I'm referring to the brightest areas of your video image.

Why pay attention to the highlights? If your video image is overexposed — that is, the camera is capturing too much light — the highlights will be blown-out white blotches, as shown in Figure 18-1. Color and details in blown-out highlights are lost, a problem that becomes especially apparent when viewing high-definition video on a HDTV.

Most camcorders set exposure automatically, but unfortunately, auto-exposure frequently leads to blown-out highlights. If your camcorder lets you manually adjust exposure, use that adjustment to turn down the exposure when you see blown-out highlights. It may seem like some parts of the video are under-exposed, but when it comes to high-def video it is usually better to be slightly underexposed rather than overexposed.

Figure 18-1:
Watch for
blown-out
highlights in
your video
images.

Some more-advanced camcorders offer an advanced exposure metering tool called a *zebra pattern.* The camcorder detects overexposed areas and shows a zebra-stripe pattern over those areas in the viewfinder or on the LCD screen. (Don't worry; the zebra stripes aren't actually recorded with your video.) If your camcorder can show zebra patterns, enable this handy feature and leave it on at all times.

Shade Your Lens

You may have noticed that pro-style video cameras usually have big hoods in front of the lens. The purpose of these hoods is to prevent glare or lens flares caused when a bright light source (such as the sun) reflects on the lens surface. A tiny speck of dust on the front of your lens can turn into a giant ugly spot on your video image if sunlight hits it just right.

Consumer camcorders usually don't have lens hoods, but making your own hood is easy. Obtain some flat black gaffer tape from your local photo and video specialty shop, and use a couple of strips of tape to construct a temporary shade around your lens on sunny days. Zoom your lens out to its widest angle, and then check the camera's viewscreen to make sure that your makeshift hood isn't visible in the corners of the video image.

For a more permanent solution, check with your camcorder's manufacturer to see if an accessory lens hood is available. If your camcorder has filter threads in a standard size such as 37mm, you may be able to buy aftermarket hoods that attach directly to the filter threads.

Is your camcorder's LCD screen hard to see on bright, sunny days? Construct a shade for the LCD screen by using strips of black gaffer tape. You can make a reusable shade with black-painted cardboard and gaffer tape, and then secure it to your LCD screen with rubber bands.

Use Video Filters

Say you're making a movie showing the fun people can have when they're stuck indoors on a rainy day. Such a movie wouldn't be complete without an establishing shot to show one of the subjects looking out a window at the dismal weather. Alas, when you try to shoot this scene, all you see is a big, nasty, glaring reflection on the window.

Reflections are among the many video problems you can resolve with a lens filter on your camcorder. Filters usually attach to the front of your camera lens, and change the nature of the light passing through it. Different kinds of filters have different effects. Common filter types include

- ✔ **Polarizing filter:** This type of filter sometimes features an adjustable ring and can be used to reduce or control reflections on windows, water, and other shiny surfaces. Polarizing filters are also useful for panoramic landscape shots. They eliminate haze so that those far-off mountains show up more clearly in your images.

- ✔ **Neutral-density (ND) filter:** This filter works kind of like sunglasses for your camcorder. It reduces the amount of light that passes through the lens, preventing overexposure in very bright conditions.

Because a ND filter reduces the amount of light going through the lens, the camcorder's aperture or iris must open wider. Wider aperture settings improve color saturation, and they reduce the picture's *depth-of-field,* which is the range of things in the image that are in focus. A bigger depth-of-field (caused by a smaller aperture) keeps more of your image in focus, but sometimes you may prefer a shallower depth-of-field to blur a distracting background.

- ✔ **Soft filter:** A soft filter softens details slightly in your image. This filter is often used to hide skin blemishes or wrinkles on actors who are more advanced in age.

- ✔ **Star filter:** Creates starlike patterns on extreme light sources to add a sense of magic to the video.

Many more kinds of filters are available. Check with the manufacturer of your camcorder to see whether the company also offers filters specially designed for your camera; check the camcorder's documentation to see what kinds of filters can work with your camcorder. Many camcorders accept standard 37mm or 58mm threaded filters, regardless of the manufacturer.

When you buy a new camcorder, always try to choose one with filter threads in front of the lens. Many cheaper camcorders don't have filter threads, and some have fake threads that can't actually be used for anything because they're tapered.

Avoid Auto-Focus Hunting

Auto focus has been a standard camcorder feature since the 1980s. Auto focus is a boon because it usually eliminates the need to manually focus your images, leaving you free to *focus* (get it?) your attention on other aspects of your video shoot.

But camcorders are machines, and machines don't always get things right. You've probably experienced the maddening problem of auto-focus hunting, where your subject goes in and out of focus unpredictably. Hunting is especially problematic in low-light shooting situations. Suppose, for example, you're shooting a school play. In the dark auditorium, many camcorders will hunt back-and-forth between the action on the stage and the backs of peoples' heads in the audience.

The only way to truly avoid auto-focus hunting is to turn off auto focus. Check your camcorder's documentation to see how to do it. If you're lucky, the camcorder has a focus ring around the lens to help you easily adjust focus manually. Otherwise you may have to resort to slider switches or arrow buttons on the camera's control panel. The easiest way to set focus manually is to let auto focus adjust to the desired subject. When the focus is set the way you want, disable auto focus.

Many camcorders give three focus options: Auto-Focus, Manual, and Infinity. On most consumer camcorders, the Infinity setting works for pretty much anything over 15 to 20 feet away.

Use (But Don't Abuse) the Zoom Lens

If every camcorder owner makes a single mistake, it's zoom-lens abuse. On most camcorders, the zoom feature is easy and fun to use, encouraging us to use it more than is prudent. Constantly zooming in and out is disorienting and creates a video image that just looks, well, amateur. Here are some general zoom-lens guidelines to follow on any video shoot:

- ✔ **If possible, avoid zooming in or out *while* you're recording.** Try to adjust zoom *before* you start recording.

- ✔ **If you must zoom while recording, try to zoom *only once* during the shot.** This will make the zoom look planned rather than chaotic.

- ✔ **Consider the merits of actually moving the camera closer to your subject rather than zooming in or out.**

- ✔ **Most cameras have variable zoom speeds.** Move the zoom slider a little, and it zooms slowly. Move the slider a bit more, and it zooms faster. Unfortunately, the zoom slider is usually tiny and hard to control. If you must zoom while recording, check your camcorder's settings to see if you can turn off variable zoom speed and set a slower speed. Slower zooms are more visually pleasing than fast zooms.

- ✔ **Practice using the zoom control.** Zooming slowly and smoothly is usually preferable, but it takes a practiced hand on the control.

If you have a difficult time using the zoom control smoothly, try taping or gluing a piece of foam to the zoom-slider button on your camcorder. The foam can help dampen your inputs on the control.

Hear Your Video

Ambient noise is the general din that we don't usually think much about because it surrounds us constantly. Ambient noise might come from chirping birds, an airplane flying overhead, chattering bystanders, passing cars, a blowing furnace, the little fans spinning inside your computer, and even the tiny motor turning the tape reels in your camcorder. Although it's easy to tune out these noises when you're immersed in them, they can be very loud and ugly when they are captured in your audio recordings.

If you're recording outdoors or in a public gathering place, you probably can't do much to eliminate the actual sources of ambient noise. But wherever you are recording, you can take basic steps to manage ambient noise:

- ✔ **Use a microphone.** I know, this is about the millionth time I've said it, but a microphone placed close to your subject can go a long way toward ensuring that the sound you actually *want* to record is not totally over-whelmed by ambient noise.

- ✔ **Wear headphones.** Many camcorders have headphone jacks. If you plug in a set of headphones, you can listen to the audio that is actually being recorded, and possibly detect potential annoyances at the beginning of shooting — before they become actual problems.

- ✔ **Record and preview some audio.** Record a little bit of audio and then play it back. How does it sound? This preemptive strategy helps you identify ambient noise or other audio problems.

- ✔ **Shield the camcorder's mic from wind.** A gentle breeze may seem almost silent to your ear, but the camcorder's microphone may pick it up as a loud roar that overwhelms all other sound. If nothing else, you can position your hand to block wind from blowing directly across the screen on the front of your camcorder's mic.

- ✔ **Minimize sound reflection.** Audio waves reflect off hard surfaces, which can cause echoing . . . echoing . . . in a recording . . . in a recording. Hang blankets on walls and other hard surfaces to reduce sound reflection.

- ✔ **Turn off fans, heaters, and air conditioners.** Air rushing through vents creates a surprising amount of unwanted ambient noise. If possible, tem-porarily turn off your furnace, air conditioner, or anything else with fans (including computers and game consoles) while you record. Listen for other noise sources, too, such as lawn mowers and leaf blowers.

- ✔ **Turn off cell phones.** You know how annoying it is when someone's cell phone rings while you're trying to *watch* a movie; just imagine how bothersome it will be when you're *making* a movie! Make sure that you and everyone else on the video shoot turns those things off. And I do mean *off,* not just silenced. Some cell phones emit electromagnetic inter-ference when they receive data or text messages, and that interference may be picked up as loud buzzing on audio recordings.

- ✔ **Warn everyone else to be quiet.** If other people are in the building or general area, ask them to be quiet while you are recording audio. Noises from the next room may be muffled, but they still contribute to ambi-ent noise. And of course, resist the urge to chat with off-camera people while you record; even your faint whispering will be recorded.

Deal with the Elements

You may, at times, deal with extremes of temperature or other weather conditions while shooting video. No, this section isn't about making sure the people in your movies wear jackets when it's cold (although it's always wise to bundle up). I'm more concerned about the health of your camcorder right now, and several environmental factors can affect it:

- ✔ **Condensation:** If you quickly move your camera from a very cold environment to a very warm environment (or vice versa), condensation can form on or even inside the lens. Avoid subjecting your camcorder to rapid, extreme temperature changes.

- ✔ **Heat:** Don't leave your camcorder or tapes in a roasting car when it's 105 degrees out. Consider storing tapes in a cooler (but *not* the one holding your lunch). Your videotape cooler shouldn't contain any food or liquids. Simply placing the tapes in an empty cooler helps insulate them from temperature extremes.

- ✔ **Water:** A few drops of rain can quickly destroy the sensitive electronic circuits inside your camcorder. If you believe that water may be a problem, cover your camcorder with a plastic bag, or shoot your video at another time, if possible.

- ✔ **Wind:** Even a gentle breeze blowing across the screen on your camcorder's microphone can cause a loud roaring on the audio recording. Try to shield your microphone from wind unless you know that you'll be replacing the audio later during the editing process.

Another environmental hazard in many video shoots is the sun — that big, bright ball of nuclear fusion that crosses the sky every day. The sun makes plants grow, provides solar energy, and helps humans generate Vitamin D. But like all good things, the sun is best enjoyed in moderation. Too much sunlight causes skin cancer, fades the paint on your car, and overexposes the subjects in your video. Earlier in this chapter, I describe how to use lens hoods and video filters to deal with some sun-related problems. Other tips for shooting in bright sunlight include:

- ✔ **If possible, position your subject in a shaded area.** Shade allows you to take advantage of the abundant natural light without overexposure. It also helps your subjects avoid squinting.

- ✔ **Avoid backlit situations.** Even if your subject is in shade, you can have problems if you shoot video at such an angle that the background is very bright. This is the recipe for creating a severely backlit situation;

your subject will appear as a black shadow against a brightly glowing background. Shoot subjects against a more neutral or dark background whenever possible.

✔ **Wear sunscreen.** Your video image isn't the only thing you should protect from the sun!

Shoot Multiple Angles

If you have access to multiple cameras, enlist some helpers to shoot video of the same event from multiple angles. At a school play, for example, it might be nice to have footage of the play, as well as some shots showing audience reactions to key scenes. Likewise, when you're shooting an activity such as bicycling or snowboarding, it would be cool to show first- and third-person perspectives of the same scene. Later, Premiere Elements makes it easy to combine multiple shots into one exciting movie.

It is possible to fake multiangle video shoots by shooting multiple occurrences of the same activity and then editing them together later. But if you have more than one camera, take advantage of them! And this doesn't mean that you have to spend thousands of dollars on two brand-new high-def camcorders. Instead:

✔ **Keep that old camcorder.** After you buy a new HD camcorder, it's tempting to put your old camcorder on Craigslist or eBay. But you'll find that it's probably not worth very much money, so why not just keep it and let your kids or friends use it? The alternate views you get will probably be far more valuable than the camera itself.

✔ **Invest in a helmet cam.** In Chapter 19, I describe a new generation of ultra-portable video cameras that are available. They are often called helmet or bullet cams, and some can be purchased for as little as $100.

✔ **Use a still camera or cell phone.** Yes, still cameras and cell phones usually record pretty low-quality video, but they're small, they can provide some interesting video angles, and you probably already own one.

Chapter 19

Ten Essential Extras for Moviemaking

1 don't know about you, but I consider myself a gadget hound. As such, videography is a great hobby to pursue because there are definitely lots of video-related gadgets to play with — and new technologies are being developed every day. There are fancy camcorders and accessories, cool multimedia programs, and even some nifty add-ons for your computer. But I don't want to kid you — digital photography, editing, and multimedia technologies are among the more expensive technologies out there, so you have picked a rewarding (but expensive) hobby to pursue.

If you have money burning a hole in your pocket and you want to find out what kind of gear you need to be a more serious video enthusiast, this chapter is for you. In this chapter I show you hardware and software that help you create, edit, and share video more effectively — and more expensively.

Adobe Premiere Pro

I know what you're thinking. This is a book about Adobe Premiere Elements, and I'm already trying to up-sell you into a more expensive program. Not really; Adobe Premiere Elements is a great program, especially considering its very low price. But at some point you may decide that you need even more capabilities than those offered by Premiere Elements. And if you decide to turn your videography hobby into a profession, you may find that you need more-advanced editing features and broader format compatibility than what Adobe Premiere Elements offers.

Adobe Premiere Pro is your next logical step up, for two important reasons. First, because Premiere Elements is based on Premiere Pro you won't have a steep learning curve if you upgrade to Premiere Pro. If you know how to use Premiere Elements, you can get right to work in Premiere Pro. Also, Adobe usually offers upgrade discounts, so as a registered Premiere Elements user you can probably get a better price on Premiere Pro than you could if you switch to a competing program like Apple Final Cut Pro or Avid Xpress (both of which are also great programs, by the way).

What does Premiere Pro offer over the basic Premiere Elements? Here are a few key features:

- **Multiple Timelines:** The Premiere Pro Timeline allows you to create and use multiple sequences. Each sequence is like a separate timeline. You can use these multiple timelines to create alternate versions of a project, or use them to manage subsections of large projects. Sequences can be linked together in a process called *nesting.*

- **Multiple Camera Editing:** If your project calls for multiple camera angles of a single scene, Premiere Pro makes it easy to import, synchronize, and edit video from multiple camera sources.

- **Advanced Color Corrector:** Premiere Pro incorporates an advanced, professional-grade color correction tool that gives you precision control over the color and light in your video images. Also included are broadcast-style video scopes such as a waveform monitor, vectorscope, and YCbCr parade. These scopes help you more precisely measure the color and light in your video images.

- **Audio Mixer:** The more you work with video, the more you realize the importance of great audio. Premiere Pro incorporates an advanced audio mixer to give you greater control over your audio. Premiere Pro supports 5.1 channel surround sound audio tracks, and you can easily pan 5.1 audio by using the Premiere Pro audio mixer.

- **Batch Capture:** Video capture can be a time-consuming process, but in Premiere Pro you can create *batch lists,* which automate much of this process.

- **Broad Format Support:** Premiere Elements is designed to work with the most common types of digital video, but Premiere Pro can handle additional formats, such as analog video, 24p, and some professionally oriented formats. You also have more precise control over your output, so you can tweak your exported movies to match requirements dictated by online and broadcast media solutions.

✔ **Integration with After Effects, Soundbooth, and Encore:** Premiere Pro works seamlessly with other professional-grade video products from Adobe, including Adobe After Effects, Soundbooth, and Encore. After Effects is the industry standard for advanced visual-effects editing, while Soundbooth gives you pro-caliber audio mixing and editing capabilities. Encore is a professional-grade DVD authoring program that gives you far more creative control over menus and other DVD features than what is found in Premiere Elements.

Adobe Premiere Pro offers other advantages over Premiere Elements as well, including even more effects and transitions, and additional output options. If you decide to move up to Premiere Pro, make sure that you also move up to *Adobe Premiere Pro For Dummies*, by Yours Truly (Wiley Publishing, Inc.).

Audio Recorders

I know, I know, your camcorder records audio along with video, and it's already perfectly synchronized. So what's the point of a dedicated audio recorder? Well, you may need the capabilities of an audio recorder in many situations. Take, for example, these three:

✔ You may want to record a subject who is across the room — in which case, have the subject hold a recorder (or conceal it so it's off-camera), and attach an inconspicuous lavalier microphone. (See the section on microphones later in this chapter.)

✔ You may want to record only a special sound, on location, and add it to the soundtrack later. For example, you might show crashing waves in the distant background, but use the close-up sound of those waves for dramatic effect.

✔ You can record narration for a video project, tweak it till it suits you, and then add it to the soundtrack of your movie.

Recording decent audio used to mean spending hundreds or even thousands of dollars for a DAT (digital audio tape) recorder. However, these days I think the best compromise for any moviemaker on a budget is to use an MP3 player with an internal or external microphone. The internal microphones in most MP3 players are pretty pathetic, but if you use a good external microphone, you can achieve CD-quality results. Belkin, Griffin, Macally, and XtremeMac all make iPod-compatible stereo microphones.

Another option is a MiniDisc player/recorder that records CD-quality audio in WAV format. Pop the MiniDisc into your computer's tray-loading CD-ROM drive (MiniDiscs don't work in slot-loading drives) and you can easily import it into a Premiere Elements project. Countless MiniDisc recorders are available for less than $200 from companies that include Aiwa, Sharp, and Sony.

You also need a slate

If you use a secondary audio recorder during a video shoot, one of the biggest challenges you may face is synchronizing your separate audio and video recordings. Professionals ensure synchronization of audio and video by using a *slate* — that black-and-white board that you often see production people snapping shut on camera just before the director yells, "Action!"

The slate is not just a kitschy movie prop. The snapping of the slate makes a noise that can be picked up by all audio recorders on-scene.

When you are editing audio tracks later, this noise will show up as a visible spike on the audio waveform. Because the slate is snapped in front of the camera, you can later match the waveform spike on the audio track with the visual picture of the slate snapping closed on the video track. If you're recording audio with external recorders, consider making your own slate to ease audio-video synchronization. You can easily make a slate, or you can buy one for less than $10 from a video equipment supplier such as www.bhphotovideo.com.

If you frequently need to record studio-quality audio, I recommend a professional digital recorder that uses hard drives or flash memory to record audio. Marantz, Roland, Sony, and many others offer professional audio recording devices for under $1,000.

Microphones

Virtually all digital camcorders have built-in microphones with 48-bit stereo sound-recording capabilities, but you'll soon find that the quality of the audio you record is still limited primarily by the quality of the microphone you use. Therefore, if you care even a little about making great movies, you *need* better microphones than the one built into your camcorder.

Your camcorder should have connectors for external microphones, and your camcorder's manufacturer may offer accessory microphones for your specific camera. Accessory cameras may mount on your camcorder's accessory shoe, connect to a microphone port, or offer wireless connectivity.

One type of special microphone you may want to use is a *lavalier* microphone — a tiny unit that usually clips to a subject's clothing to pick up his or her voice. You often see lavalier mics clipped to the lapels of TV newscasters. Some lavalier units are designed to fit inside clothing or costumes, although practice and special shielding may be required to eliminate rubbing noises. You may also need to coach your subjects to sit still so that the lavalier mics can pick up their voices more effectively.

You might also use a condenser microphone to record audio. Some *prosumer* (or *professional-consumer*) camcorders come with large, boom-style condenser mics built in. Although these are nice, if you want to record the voice of a subject speaking on camera, such mics may still be inferior to a handheld or lavalier mic.

Microphones are generally defined by the directional pattern in which they pick up sound. The three basic categories are *cardioid* (which has a heart-shaped pattern), *omnidirectional* (which picks up sound from all directions), and *bidirectional* (which picks up sound from the sides).

If you're in the market for a new mic, here's where you should look:

✔ A good place to look for high-quality microphones is a musicians' supply store. Just make sure that the connectors and frequency range are compatible with your camcorder or other recording device (check the documentation).

✔ You may also want to check with your camcorder's manufacturer; it may offer accessory microphones specially designed to work with your camcorder.

✔ The Internet is always a good resource as well. One especially good resource is www.shure.com, the Web site of Shure Incorporated. Shure sells microphones and other audio products, and the Web site is an excellent resource for general information about choosing and using microphones.

Video Converters

You have a hot computer for video editing, and you want to capture analog video. What are you going to do? You have many, many solutions, of course. You could install an analog video capture card, but a good one is expensive and installing it means tearing apart your computer. Plus, Premiere Elements can't capture video using an analog capture card, meaning you'll have to use different software with your analog video capture card.

A simpler solution may be to use an external *video converter* — usually a box that connects to your computer's FireWire or USB 2.0 port. The box includes analog inputs so you can connect an analog VCR or camcorder to the box. The unit itself converts signals from analog media into DV-format video, which is then captured into your computer — where you can easily edit it using Premiere Elements.

If you have worked with analog video a lot, you're probably aware that each time you make a copy of the video some quality is lost. This is called *generational loss* (see Chapter 3 for more on this subject). Video converters like the ones described here don't present any more of a generational-loss problem than a standard video capture card: After the signal is converted from analog to digital, generational loss is no longer a problem until you output the video back to an analog tape again.

Most converter boxes can also be useful for exporting video to an analog source. You simply export the DV-format video from Premiere Elements, and the converter box converts it into an analog signal that you can record on your analog tape deck. Among other advantages, this method of export saves a lot of wear and tear on the tape-drive mechanisms in your expensive digital camcorder. Features to look for in a video converter include

- Analog output
- Broadcast standard support (NTSC or PAL)
- Color-bar output
- Multiple FireWire and analog inputs/outputs

Video converters range in price anywhere from $20 to $300 or more. Visit your local consumer electronics store to see what's available. I recommend products such as the ADS Movie Capture Xpress (about $50), Pinnacle Studio MovieBox (about $125), or the Canopus ADVC-55 (about $200).

Multimedia Controllers

Manipulating some of the playback and editing controls in Premiere Elements with a mouse isn't always easy. Sure, there are keyboard shortcuts for most actions, and you may find yourself using those keyboard shortcuts quite a bit. In particular, I find that controlling playback with the J, K, and L keys is a lot easier than using the mouse; and using the arrow keys to frame forward or back is vastly superior to clicking the Next Frame and Previous Frame buttons in the Monitor window.

Useful though the keyboard may be, an even better way is to control Premiere Elements with an external multimedia controller, such as the ShuttleXpress or ShuttlePRO v. 2 from Contour Design. The ShuttlePro, shown in Figure 19-1, costs about $100 and features 13 buttons and a 2-part dial control in an ergonomically designed housing. The overall design of the ShuttlePro is based on professional video-editing controllers. The dials can be used to shuttle forward and back in your video, and the various buttons control various other program features. The unit plugs into a USB port, which can be found on virtually any modern computer. If you do a lot of video editing, you can save a lot of time and effort by using a multimedia controller. Find out more about multimedia controllers online at

www.contourdesign.com

A less expensive version of this controller, the ShuttleXpress, is also available from Contour Design. The ShuttleXpress is about half the price of the ShuttlePro and also works great.

Figure 19-1:
Ergonomic multimedia controllers make editing in Premiere Elements fun and easy.

Lights and Accessories

One of the biggest obstacles you encounter as you try to shoot better video is light. You need to shed enough light on your subjects so that they're clearly visible, but you don't want so much light that highlights get blown out. Modern camcorders have pretty good light sensitivity, but if you pay attention to the pros, you'll notice that they usually set up additional lighting for their video shoots. (Check out Chapters 3 and 18 for video lighting tips.)

Professional light systems for photo and video work are ideal, but they're also breathtakingly expensive. If your budget is tight, here are some more affordable lighting options:

✔ Visit your local hardware store and buy some low-cost halogen shop lights. These throw a lot of light and usually come with adjustable stands or clips so they can be easily mounted to stationary objects.

✔ To diffuse or change the color of your light, place transparent or translucent plastic sheets in front of your lights. Transparent sheets are called *gels,* and translucent sheets are called *scrims.* They can be purchased cheaply at better photo and video supply stores. Alternatively, use colored document protectors from your local office supply store. Use wooden clothespins to clip gels and scrims in place.

Check your gels and scrims frequently to make sure that they aren't getting overheated by the lights. And most important, *never* leave your scene lighting turned on and unattended. Lights generate a lot of heat and can become a fire hazard.

✔ Find out if your camcorder manufacturer offers an accessory light that mounts directly on your camera. If the camera-mounted light is so bright that your subjects squint and their faces turn to white glares, soften the light with a diffusing scrim.

✔ For more-subtle lighting effects, bounce light off white or foil-covered poster board. Umbrella-style light reflectors can be purchased from photo supply stores for under $20.

Tripods and Other Stabilization Devices

The need for image stabilization will probably become apparent the first time you watch your footage on a large TV screen. No matter how carefully you try to hold the camera, some movement is going to show up on the image. Of course, at times, a handheld shoot makes the most sense, but many other times, a totally stable image is best. To get that stability, you need a tripod.

Tripods are generally available for as low as $20 at your local department store. Alas, as with so many other things in life, when you buy a tripod you get what you pay for. High-quality video tripods incorporate several important features:

✔ **Stout, braced legs:** Strong legs give the tripod its stability, especially during panning shots. Braces at the base or middle of the tripod's legs enhance stability. Weaker tripods introduce subtle vibrations into the video image that perceptibly degrade your image quality.

✔ **High-tech materials:** You'll soon get tired of lugging a 15- to 20-pound tripod around with your camera gear. Higher-quality tripods usually use high-tech materials (including titanium, aircraft-quality aluminum, and carbon fiber) that are both strong and lightweight, making the gear less cumbersome to transport and use.

✔ **Bubble levels:** Built-in bubble levels help you ensure that your camera is level, even if the ground underneath the tripod isn't.

✔ **Fluid heads:** High-quality tripods have fluid heads to ensure that pans will be smooth and jerk-free.

✔ **Counterweights:** The best tripods have adjustable counterweights so the head can be balanced for your camera and lens (telephoto lenses, for example, can make the camera a bit front-heavy). Counterweights allow smooth use of the fluid head while still giving you the option of letting go of the camera without having it tilt out of position.

For a tripod with all these features, you can expect to spend a couple of hundred dollars (if not *many* hundreds of dollars). If that kind of money isn't in your tripod budget right now, try to get a tripod that incorporates as many of these features as possible. Budget at least $75 to $150 for an entry-level tripod that offers adequate vibration damping and a basic fluid head.

Tripods aren't the only stabilization devices available. You may also want to keep a *monopod* handy for certain occasions. As the name suggests, a monopod has only one leg (just as tripods have three legs, octopods have eight, and . . . never mind). Although by definition (and by design) a monopod inevitably allows some camera movement — you have to keep the camera balanced on the monopod — you can still get more stability than you'd have if you simply hold the camera without any stabilization device. Some monopods double as walking sticks.

For moving shots, you may want to try a mobile stabilizer such as a Steadicam (www.steadicam.com). Devices like the Steadicam use a system of weights and harnesses to keep the camera remarkably stable even as the operator moves around a scene.

Mass Storage

In 1996, I spent $200 on a 1.6GB drive. It seemed massive at the time, but that drive would only hold about six or seven minutes of digital video if I were still using it. Today, $200 can buy 1,000 times as much storage space! And you'll need it, because digital video gobbles hard drive space in a hurry.

As I mention in Chapter 2, you should use your computer's internal hard drives for video editing. But for storage of completed projects, I recommend an external drive that connects to your computer's FireWire or USB 2.0 port. Many are now available with capacities at or above 1TB (*terabyte*). One terabyte will hold about 75 hours of full-quality digital video. External hard drives improve your life in a couple of ways:

- ✔ By offloading large video files to an external drive for storage, you free up space on your internal drives. Internal drives perform better when they have lots of free space.

- ✔ Big video files can be easily transferred from one computer to another. Simply unplug the external drive from one computer and plug it into another!

Hard drives are not reliable long-term storage devices. I recommend that you back up your video on multiple DVDs. If your camcorder uses MiniDV tapes, don't reuse the tapes; instead, archive them to preserve your original taped source footage.

Helmet Cams

Would you like to give your audience a first-person perspective of the action? You can capture some interesting shots with a mini-camera small enough to be mounted on a helmet, a remote-control car, or any other moving object. The term "helmet cam" comes from videographers who mount these tiny cameras to their helmets and then go for a heart-pumping ride on a motorcycle, bicycle, snowboard, shopping cart, or any other form of extreme-sports conveyance.

Helmet cams have been available for a while, but most older designs used analog video connections that had to be connected to a camcorder for recording. Unfortunately, many digital camcorders no longer have analog inputs, so the older style helmet cams might not work for you.

Instead, look for a self-contained camera that records VGA-quality or better video onto internal flash memory. Such cameras are available for under $200 from companies such as GoPro and Oregon Scientific. The video quality won't be high-def, but if you make the action exciting enough your audience won't care!

If you want better video quality you may need to step up to a more expensive wired-cam that connects to a camcorder. Just make sure that the camera you want is compatible with your specific camcorder. Helmet cam manufacturers usually provide camcorder compatibility lists on their Web sites.

Web Space

The Internet seems like a natural place to share your movies with others, but video files are often very big, and that means problems if you're trying to find an online home for your movies. Video sharing sites like YouTube are often the best solution, but if you want to avoid all the advertising banners and random links to other peoples' videos, you may want to get Web space of your own.

Many low-cost Web hosting options are now available. For example, as of this writing, GoDaddy.com (www.godaddy.com) offers a Web hosting plan which provides 150GB of Web server space and 1,500GB of monthly data transfer for under $7 per month. This type of account offers enough space and bandwidth to support typical online movie hosting for personal use. The downside is that with many Web hosting services you have to know how to create, upload, and maintain Web pages.

When looking for online Web space, consider the following features:

✔ **Storage space:** Get a lot more space than you think you'll need. 10GB may sound like a lot, but if you get serious about online video sharing you can gobble that space up surprisingly fast.

✔ **Bandwidth:** Usually listed as "monthly data transfer," the bandwidth is just as important as the total space. If you put a 50MB movie online and it is downloaded by ten people, those downloads will use up 500MB of bandwidth. Make sure that you have more than enough monthly bandwidth, and read the fine print to find out whether and how you will be charged for exceeding your monthly bandwidth allotment (believe me — you will be charged). While you're reading that fine print, see if there are daily bandwidth limits as well as monthly limits.

✔ **Cost:** Some Web sites offer free storage space, but these so-called "free" sites also usually also require visitors to view annoying ads and pop-up windows. Pay sites usually don't have ads or pop-ups, because you have to, um, pay for the site. Review the plan details carefully to make sure that your pay plan doesn't also subject users to pop-up windows and ads. If the site charges setup fees or lots of other obscure service fees, consider looking elsewhere because lots of choices are available.

- ✓ **Reliability:** Is the site reliable? Will you be stuck with hidden charges? Will the site fold in a few days or weeks? Talk to friends about Web hosting services they use, and check Web sites such as www.tophosts. com or www.findmyhosting.com for consumer reviews and feature-by-feature comparisons of various Web hosting services.

- ✓ **Extras:** Does the service include extra e-mail addresses or affordable domain name registration? Can you upload movie files using a simple Web browser page, or will you have to figure out how to use FTP software and other Internet technologies?

Glossary

analog: Technology that records data as waves with infinitely varying values. Analog recordings are usually electromechanical, so they often suffer from generational loss. *See also* digital, generational loss.

aperture: The size of the opening behind a camera lens. Like the iris in a human eye, a large aperture lets in more light and a small aperture lets in less light. The aperture's size is expressed as an F-number, with lower numbers like f1.8 indicating a large aperture opening and higher aperture numbers like f16 indicating a small aperture opening. *See also* depth of field.

aspect ratio: The shape of a video image as determined by its width compared to height. Older TV screens had an aspect ratio of 4:3, meaning that the screen is four units wide and three units high. Most HDTVs use a "widescreen" aspect ratio of 16:9. Image pixels can also have various aspect ratios. *See also* HDTV, pixel.

ATSC (Advanced Television Systems Committee): The digital broadcast-video standard used in North America. *See also* DVB, NTSC, PAL, SECAM.

AVCHD (Advanced Video Codec High Definition): The recording format of high definition camcorders that record video onto hard drives, flash memory, or DVDs. *See also* DV, HDV, MiniDV.

bars and tone: A video image that serves the function of the "test pattern" used in TV broadcasting: Standardized color bars and a 1-kHz tone are usually placed at the beginning of movie projects. The test pattern helps broadcast engineers calibrate video equipment. The format for color bars is standardized by the SMPTE. Adobe Premiere Elements can generate bars and tone. *See also* SMPTE.

bit depth: A unit of measurement for color and sound quality. The amount of data that a single piece of information can hold depends upon how many bits are available. Bit depth usually measures color or sound quality. A larger bit-depth number means a greater range of color or sound.

Blu-Ray: A high-definition optical storage disc that is the same size and shape as a standard DVD. Blu-Ray won the high-def format war to become the de facto standard for high-definition movie distribution. *See also* DVD, HD DVD.

capture: The process of recording digital video or other media from a camcorder or VCR tape onto a computer's hard drive.

CCD (charged-coupled device): The unit in many camcorders that interprets light photons and converts the information into an electronic video signal. CCDs are also used by digital still cameras. *See also* CMOS.

chrominance: A fancy word for color. *See also* luminance.

clip: One of various segments making up the scenes of a video project. You edit individual clips into the Premiere Elements Timeline to form complete scenes and a complete story line. *See also* timeline.

CMOS (complementary metal-oxide semiconductor): The unit in some newer camcorders that interprets light photons and converts the information into an electronic video signal. CMOS sensors are also used by some digital still cameras. *See also* CCD.

coaxial: Cables used to carry a cable TV signal. Coaxial connectors are round and have a single thin pin in the middle of the connector. Coaxial cables carry both sound and video. Although most TVs and VCRs have coaxial connectors, digital camcorders usually do not. Coaxial cables usually provide inferior video quality when compared to component, composite, HDMI, and S-Video cables. *See also* component video, composite video, HDMI, S-Video.

codec: A scheme used to compress, and later decompress, video and audio information so that it can be passed more efficiently over computer cables and Internet connections to hard drives and other components.

color gamut: The total range of colors a given system can create (by combining several basic colors) to display a video image. The total number of individual colors that are available is finite. If a color cannot be displayed correctly, it is considered *out of gamut.*

color space: The method used to generate color in a video display. *See also* color gamut, RGB, YUV.

component video: A high-quality connection for analog and digital video. Component video splits the video signal over three separate cables, color-coded red, green, and blue. Component video provides superior video quality to coaxial, composite, and S-Video connections, but is inferior to HDMI. Component video can carry high-definition video signals. *See also* analog, coaxial, composite video, HDMI, S-Video.

composite video: A connection for analog video, typically using a single video connector cable (color-coded yellow). The connector type is sometimes called an *RCA connector,* and is often paired with audio cables that have red and white connectors. Composite video is inferior to S-Video, HDMI, and component video because they tend to allow more signal noise and image artifacts. *See also* analog, coaxial, component video, HDMI, S-Video.

DAT (digital audio tape): A digital tape format often used in audio recorders by professional video producers.

data rate: The amount of data that can pass over a connection in a second. The data rate of DV-format video is 3.6MB (megabytes) per second. High-definition video data rates can vary from 2.4MB to 3.6MB per second.

depth of field: The range of a video image that is in focus. With a broad depth of field, much of the video image is in focus. A shallow depth of field means the subject is in focus and the background is blurry. Smaller lens apertures give broader depth of field. *See also* aperture, shutter speed.

device control: A technology that allows a computer to control the playback functions on a digital camcorder (such as play, stop, and rewind). For example, clicking Rewind in the program window on the computer causes the camcorder tape to actually rewind.

digital: A method of recording sound and light as data made up of discrete, binary values (expressed as ones and zeros). *See also* analog.

Digital8: A standard definition digital camcorder format that uses Hi-8 tapes. *See also* digital, DV, MicroMV, MiniDV.

driver: Pre-1980, the person in control of a car or horse-drawn carriage. Post-1980, a piece of software that allows a computer to use a piece of hardware, such as a video card or a printer.

drop-frame timecode: A type of timecode specified by the NTSC video standard, usually with a frame rate of 29.97 fps (frames per second). To maintain continuity, two frames are dropped at the beginning of each minute, except for every tenth minute. *See also* timecode.

DV (Digital Video): A standard format and codec for digital video. Digital camcorders that include a FireWire interface usually record DV-format video. *See also* codec, FireWire, HDV.

DVB (Digital Video Broadcasting): The digital broadcast-video standard used in most of the world except North America. *See also* ATSC, NTSC, PAL, SECAM.

DVCAM: A professional-grade version of the MiniDV digital-tape format developed by Sony. DVCAM camcorders are usually pretty expensive. *See also* digital, DVCPro, MiniDV.

DVCPro: A professional-grade version of the MiniDV digital-tape format developed by Panasonic. Like DVCAM camcorders, DVCPro camcorders are usually expensive. *See also* digital, DVCAM, MiniDV.

DVD (Digital Versatile Disc): A category of optical disc that allows capacities from 4.7GB (gigabytes) up to 17GB. Virtually all modern computers can record single-layer (4.7GB) DVDs, and many can also record dual-layer (8.5GB) DVDs.

field: One of two sets of scan lines in an interlaced video frame. Each field contains every other horizontal resolution line. Immediately after one field is drawn on the screen, the other is drawn in a separate pass, resulting in a complete image. *See also* frame, interlacing.

FireWire: Also known by its official designation IEEE-1394, or by other names such as i.Link, FireWire is a high-speed computer peripheral interface standard developed by Apple Computer. FireWire is often used to connect digital camcorders, external hard drives, and other devices to a computer. FireWire has contributed greatly to the affordability of modern video editing.

frame: A single still image in a sequence of many that make up a moving picture. *See also* frame rate.

frame rate: The speed at which the frames in a moving picture change, measured in frames per second (fps). Video images usually display 25 to 30 fps, providing the illusion of movement to the human eye. Slower frame rates save storage space, but can produce jerky motion; faster frame rates produce smoother motion but use up more storage space.

gamut: *See* color gamut.

gel: A translucent or colored sheet that is placed in front of a light to diffuse the light or otherwise change its appearance. *See also* scrim.

generational loss: A decrease in the quality of an analog recording with every generation (copy) of the recording that is made. Each copy (especially if it's a copy of a copy) represents a later, lower-quality *generation* of the original. *See also* analog.

grayscale: The proper name of a black-and-white picture or video image. Black-and-white images are actually made up of varying shades of gray.

HD DVD (High Definition DVD): A high-definition optical storage disc that was a competing format to Blu-Ray, but Blu-Ray eventually won industry support. *See also* Blu-Ray, DVD.

HDMI (High Definition Multimedia Interface): A digital interface technology used by many high-definition TVs, disc players, and cameras. HDMI provides the best quality connection between high-definition devices. *See also* coaxial, component video, composite video, FireWire, S-Video.

HDTV (High Definition Television): A set of broadcast-video standards that incorporates resolutions and frame rates higher than those used for traditional analog video. HDTV usually offers 720 or 1,080 horizontal lines of resolution. *See also* NTSC, PAL, SECAM.

HDV (High Definition Video): The recording format of high-definition camcorders that record video onto tapes. Most HDV camcorders use MiniDV tapes. *See also* AVCHD, DV, MiniDV.

IEEE-1394: *See* FireWire.

i.Link: *See* FireWire.

interlacing: The production of an image by alternating sets of scan lines on-screen. Most video images are actually composed of two separate fields, drawn on consecutive passes. Each field contains every other horizontal resolution line of a video image. Each field is drawn so quickly that the human eye perceives a complete image. *See also* field, progressive scan.

jog: *See* scrub.

lavalier: A tiny microphone designed to clip to a subject's clothing. Lavalier mics are often clipped to the lapels of TV newscasters.

luminance: A fancy word for brightness in video images. *See also* chrominance.

MicroMV: A short-lived digital camcorder tape format developed by Sony for ultra-compact camcorders. *See also* digital, Digital8, DV, MiniDV.

MiniDV: The most common tape format used by tape-based standard and high-definition digital camcorders. *See also* digital, Digital8, DV, MicroMV.

moiré pattern: A wavy or shimmering artifact that appears in video images when tight parallel lines appear in the image. This problem often occurs when a subject wears a pinstriped suit or coarse corduroy.

NLE (nonlinear editor): A computer program that can edit video, audio, or other multimedia without confining the user to an unchangeable sequence of frames from beginning to end. NLEs let you edit the work in any order you choose. Adobe Premiere Elements is one example of a video NLE program.

NTSC (National Television Standards Committee): The analog broadcast-video standard used in North America, Japan, the Philippines, and elsewhere. *See also* ATSC, DVB, PAL, SECAM.

overscan: What happens when a TV cuts off portions of the video image at the edges of the screen. Most standard TVs overscan to some extent.

PAL (Phase Alternating Line): An analog broadcast-video standard used in Europe, Australia, Southeast Asia, South America, and elsewhere. *See also* ATSC, DVB, NTSC, SECAM.

pixel: The smallest element of a video image, abbreviated from *picture element*. Still images are usually made up of grids containing thousands, even millions, of pixels. A screen or image size that has a resolution of 640 x 480 is 640 pixels wide by 480 pixels high.

progressive scan: A scan display that draws all the horizontal resolution lines in a single pass. Most computer monitors use progressive scan displays. *See also* interlacing.

render: To produce a playable version of an altered video image. When you apply an effect or other change to a video image, Premiere Elements figures out how each frame should look after the change. The rendering process applies these changes. Usually, the rendering process generates a preview file that is stored on the hard drive. *See also* transition.

RGB (red-green-blue): The color space (method of creating on-screen colors) used by computer monitors; all the available colors result from combining red, green, and blue pixels. *See also* color space, YUV.

sampling rate: The number of samples obtained per second during a digital audio recording. When audio is recorded digitally, the sound is sampled thousands of times per second. 48-kHz audio has 48,000 samples per second.

scrim: A semitransparent or opaque screen that is placed in front of studio lights to dim or diffuse the light. *See also* gel.

scrub: To move back and forth through a video project, one frame at a time. Some video-editing programs have a scrub bar located underneath the video preview window (also called the *jog control*). *See also* shuttle.

SECAM (Sequential Couleur Avec Memoire): An analog broadcast-video standard used in France, Russia, Eastern Europe, Central Asia, and elsewhere. *See also* ATSC, DVB, NTSC, PAL.

shutter speed: The length of time (expressed in fractions of a second) that the camera's image sensor is exposed to light. A shutter speed of 100 means that light is gathered for 1/100th of a second. *See also* aperture.

shuttle: To roll video images slowly forward or back, often to check a detail of motion. Professional video decks and cameras often have shuttle controls. Some video-editing programs also have shuttle controls. *See also* scrub.

slate: The black-and-white hinged board that moviemakers snap closed in front of the camera just before action commences. The snapping noise helps synchronize video and audio recordings made by separate machines.

SMPTE (Society for Motion Picture and Television Engineers): The organization that develops standards for professional broadcasting equipment and formats. Among other things, the SMPTE defines standards for bars and tone, counting leaders, and timecode.

standard definition: Non-high-definition digital video. Standard-definition digital video usually has 480 horizontal lines of resolution. *See also* HDTV.

S-VHS: A higher-quality version of the VHS videotape format.

S-Video: A high-quality connection technology for analog video. S-Video connectors separate the color and brightness signals, resulting in less signal noise and fewer artifacts. Some digital camcorders include S-Video connectors for analog output. Analog capture cards and S-VHS VCRs usually have S-Video connectors as well. *See also* analog, capture, coaxial, composite video, component video, HDMI, S-VHS.

timecode: The standard system for identifying individual frames in a movie or video project. Timecode is expressed as `hours:minutes:seconds:frames` (as in `01:20:31:02`) or 1 hour, 20 minutes, 31 seconds, and 3 frames. This format has been standardized by the SMPTE. Non-drop-frame timecode uses colons between the numbers; drop-frame timecode uses semicolons. *See also* drop-frame timecode, SMPTE, timecode break.

timecode break: An inconsistency in the timecode on a camcorder tape. *See also* timecode.

timeline: The working space in most video-editing programs, including Adobe Premiere Elements. Clips are arranged along a line that represents the duration of the movie project. The left side of the timeline represents the beginning of the movie, and the right side represents the ending. The timeline may include multiple video tracks, multiple audio tracks, transitions, effects, titles, and other features. *See also* clip.

title: Text that appears on-screen to display the name of the movie or give credit to the movie crew. A *subtitle* is a special type of title, often used to show translations of dialogue spoken in foreign languages.

transition: The method by which one clip ends and another begins in a movie project. A common type of transition is when one clip gradually fades out as the next clip fades in. *See also* clip, render.

USB (Universal Serial Bus): A computer-port technology that makes it easy to connect a mouse, printer, or other computer peripheral. Some digital camcorders have USB ports. Connected to a computer's USB port, these cameras can often be used as Web cams. Most computers built after Spring 2002 use a faster version of USB called USB 2.0. Adobe Premiere Elements *cannot* capture video from a tape-based camcorder that is connected to a USB port, but it can use USB to download video from most tapeless camcorders.

video card: This term can refer to either of two different kinds of devices inside a computer: The device that generates a video signal for the computer's monitor; or the card that captures video from VCRs and camcorders onto the computer's hard drive. Some hardware manufacturers refer to FireWire cards as video cards because FireWire cards are most often used to capture video from digital camcorders. *See also* capture, FireWire.

waveform: A visual representation of an audio signal. Viewing a waveform on a computer screen allows precise synchronization of sound and video.

YCbCr: An alternative acronym for the YUV color space. *See also* YUV.

YUV: The acronym for the color space used by most TVs and digital camcorders. For some obscure reason, YUV stands for *luminance-chrominance*. *See also* chrominance, color space, luminance, RGB.

zebra pattern: An overexposure warning feature found in some high-end camcorders. A striped pattern appears in the viewfinder over image areas that will be overexposed unless the camcorder is adjusted to compensate.

Index